Dear NFT User:

Once upon a time, there were unicorns and trolls, dog breeds were dog breeds, and guidebooks were widely agreed to be useful tools of navigation and exploration. But now that even your curmudgeonly old Uncle Max has an Android and Street View and a tiny Bluetooth delivering user ratings directly into his amygdala, why spend a hard-earned Hamilton to take home this old-fashioned pack of paper?

You hold in your hands the anti-Yelp: a thoughtfully assembled, well-edited collection of maps, listings, and descriptions designed to help you find the best of Brooklyn and not waste a nanosecond of your time on anything else. The notable. The bizarre. That indispensable boutique. That life-saving pharmacy. That cozy yet criminally overlooked bar. Bagels. Basically, the neighborhood staples…and neighborhood Staples!

That's right, friends—for the price of a couple cocktails at Brooklyn's venerable Brooklyn Inn—or a little less than what you'd spend for three helpings of tacos from Sunset Park's Tacos Matamoros…or for just about what you'd spend for a dozen or so pupusas at the Red Hook Ballfields—you'll have not one, not two, not three but four—yes, four—detailed maps for every neighborhood that we cover—a fully updated catalog of local restaurants, bars, shops, and landmarks, plus extended coverage of parks, beaches, sports arenas, and museums. If you're nonplussed by the giant super expensive glossy foldout map in the back, think about this: Do you really want to try puzzling out how to get from Greenpoint to Crown Heights on a two-inch cell phone screen?

And new for this edition is a reconsidered, thoroughly revamped, and utterly revolutionary (for us, anyway) format that frees all those artful NFT blurbs from their former desolate perch in the forgotten back section of the guide. Now you will never, ever, ever have to frantically flip back and forth to know what NFT thinks about, say, Tom's Diner in Prospect Heights ("Old-school mom-and-pop diner since 1936. A cholesterol love affair."). Substantial neighborhood overviews now call out all the NFT Landmarks, and our incomparable team of crack writers and researchers have pounded the pavement and lent their invaluable, immeasurable body of knowledge to afford you, the reader, an expert's sense of the overall feel of the sixteen neighborhoods in this guide. It's a big step forward for us, and we're so damn excited for you to reap the full benefits of our labor.

Face it: you need us. Wrap your furry paws around this superior guide of all things Brooklyn and get ready to scout the tastiest dim sum, the artiest art, the rowdiest pubs, the prettiest parks, the quirkiest 24-hour bowling alleys, and all the rest of the borough's hidden treasures. When you come across something we missed, send us a note at www.notfortourists.com. The only thing we like more than your incalculable admiration is snappy and pointed, yet pertinent, critique.

See you at the new Freddy's Bar!

Jane, Rob, Craig, et al.

Queens

New
Jersey

Manhattan

1

2

3

4

5

6

7

8

9

10

Upper
New York
Bay

Prospect
Park

PAGE 142

11

12

13

14

15

16

Lower
New York
Bay

Coney Island

PAGE 136

Map 1

Longtime residents of this neighborhood are glad Greenpoint's no longer considered "the next big thing." Due to its glut of converted factory spaces and rows upon rows of picturesque streets, the label was inevitable once Williamsburg's 15 minutes were up. With the large number of Polish immigrants and businesses in the neighborhood, you can close your eyes, inhale the scents from nearby bakeries, and feel like you're in Europe. But then a hipster walks by, and you're immediately reminded that you're merely in the cool epicenter of the universe. Careful though, don't show how wowed you are. You'll look like an outsider.

Greenpoint sits on the nexus of the Newtown Creek and the East River as the northernmost neighborhood of Brooklyn, which is the tip of Long Island. The Newtown Creek and its dubious **Nature Walk** have smelly reputations that literally precede it. The reason: the **Newtown Creek Sewage Treatment Plant** that sits on the site of the largest underground oil spill. Gross. As a longtime vital part of shipping and manufacturing for the entire New York area, Greenpoint had workers in these industries as its first residents. The **Greenpoint Historical District** was originally housing that was created for these factory workers. While there has been a noticeable increase in higher end restaurants, bars, and boutiques, Greenpoint still retains its working-class affordability and there are bargains aplenty, especially when measured against Manhattan prices.

Most of the action in Greenpoint is centered on four main streets: Manhattan Avenue, Nassau Avenue, Greenpoint Avenue, and Franklin Street. Manhattan Avenue serves as the main artery of the neighborhood. Virtually anything you can think of can be found along the avenue. Buses and the G subway line run along it. At the southern end, hipsters converge at **Enid's** while farther north, blue collar immigrants attend mass at **Saint Anthony of Padua Church**. Turning down Greenpoint Avenue from Manhattan Avenue towards the water will take you past great bars like the **Black Rabbit** and the **Pencil Factory**. Franklin Street intersects Greenpoint Avenue and is a relaxing antidote to the grimy bustle of Manhattan Avenue. Head north on Franklin to grab a bite at **Brooklyn Label** or a glass of wine at **Dandelion Wine**. Or head south and shop at **Alter 140** or **Word**, the area's only English language independent bookstore. Don't forget to visit Greenpoint east of McGuinness Boulevard. You can find cheap bars (like **Palace Cafe**), liquor stores, and restaurants (like **Relax**) that the locals frequent as this part of Greenpoint has less cachet than the Manhattan Avenue drag.

One exciting aspect of Greenpoint (though not for locals with cars) is the frequent number of movie and television productions being filmed here at any given time. Again, because of its proximity to Manhattan and Long Island City (where a number of studios are based), Greenpoint serves as an ideal location for a production that is looking for a green, industrial, or cozy neighborhood setting. Finding these locations can be a fun endeavor. Flight of the Conchords shot their French song video in McGolrick Park. 30 Rock once filmed in front of a dollar store on Manhattan Avenue. Recent productions have included The Bounty Hunter, Date Night, and Boardwalk Empire. If you keep your ears open at a bar, you may even hear someone who worked on a shoot giving the lowdown on which star is a bitch or which guy played the diva and spent the entire shoot moaning about a recent breakup. Ah, New York.

Barflies of every stripe can find something to suit their tastes, from sports bars (**Red Star**) to cocktail lounges (**Manhattan Inn**) to dives (**Van Gogh's Radio Lounge**). Look for ridiculously cheap happy hour deals. NFT staffers can be found at the **Palace Cafe**.

 Bars

- **Alligator Lounge II** •
  113 Franklin St [Greenpoint Ave]
  718-383-6000
  Like its reptilian brothers: decent beers and free pizza!
- **Black Rabbit** • 91 Greenpoint Ave [Franklin St]
  718-349-1595
  Fantastic fireplace, delicious mini-burgers. Trivia night is packed.
- **Blackout** • 916 Manhattan Ave [Kent St]
  718-383-0254
  Heavily veneered wood, tin ceilings, candlelit tables... and heavy-hitting DJs.
- **Coco 66** • 66 Greenpoint Ave [Franklin St]
  718-389-7392
  Like an LA bar. Dark, druggy, and full of people talking about themselves.
- **The Diamond** • 43 Franklin St [Calyer St]
  718-383-5030
  Wine, massive beer selection, and shuffleboard.
- **Enid's** • 560 Manhattan Ave [Driggs Ave]
  718-349-3859
  Greenpoint's finest hipster stand-by.
- **Europa** • 98 Meserole Ave [Manhattan Ave]
  718-383-5723
  Strobe light extravaganza.
- **The Habitat** • 988 Manhattan Ave [Huron St]
  718-383-5615
  Featuring waffle fries and "zero attitude."
- **The Manhattan Inn** •
  632 Manhattan Ave [Nassau Ave]
  718-383-0885
  Dark bar, pricey but delicious food, piano man in back.
- **The Mark Bar** • 1025 Manhattan Ave [Green St]
  718-349-2340
  XXXtreme Bingo Wednesdays, free bagel Sundays, and lots of beer always.
- **Matchless** • 557 Manhattan Ave [Driggs Ave]
  718-383-5333
  Weekly music showcases, heavy metal karaoke, and foosball.
- **Palace Café** • 206 Nassau Ave [Russell St]
  718-383-9848
  Heavy jukebox and stiff drinks. Metal lives!
- **Pencil Factory** •
  142 Franklin St [Greenpoint Ave]
  718-609-5858
  Great beer; great vibe. Perfectly understated.

- **Pit Stop Bar** •
  152 Meserole Ave [McGuinness Blvd]
  718-383-0981
  Buy a couple scratch-offs and experience blue-collar Brooklyn.
- **Red Star** • 37 Greenpoint Ave [West St]
  718-349-0149
  A real sports bar. 2 floors and terrific wings.
- **Shayz Lounge** • 130 Franklin St [Milton St]
  718-389-3888
  Irish pub in a sea of Polish.
- **TBD Bar** • 224 Franklin St [Green St]
  718-349- 6727
  Backyard "beer garden" is tops on nice days.
- **Tommy's Tavern** •
  1041 Manhattan Ave [Freeman St]
  718-383-9699
  Super-dive with live music on weekends.
- **Van Gogh's Radio Lounge** •
  147 Franklin St [Java St]
  718-701-4004
  Darts, jukebox, and leering looks on ladies' night.
- **Warsaw** • 261 Driggs Ave [Eckford St]
  718-387-0505
  Brooklyn's best concert venue.

Billiards

- **Risque** • 213 McGuiness Blvd [Calyer St]
  718-349-1445
  Cheap beer mixes well with billiards and ping pong.

Map 1 • Greenpoint

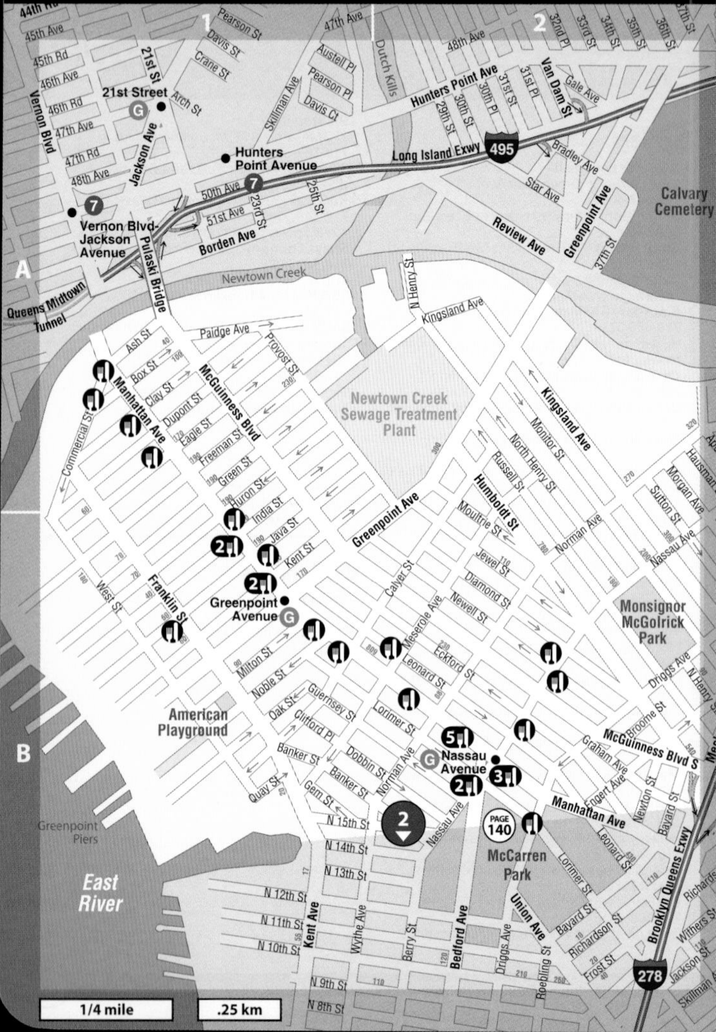

A Greenpoint visit must include a meal at any of the area's cheap and hearty Polish restaurants, like **Christina's**. Or visit disparate places like Thailand (**Ott**) or Turkey (**Kestane Kebab**). Afterwards, get a donut at neighborhood institution **Peter Pan**. On weekends, **Lamb & Jaffy** is the place for brunch.

Restaurants

- **Acapulco** • 1116 Manhattan Ave [Clay St]
  718-349-8429 • $
  Authentic Mexican includes homemade chips
  and telenovelas at full volume.
- **Ashbox** • 1154 Manhattan Ave [Ash St]
  718-389-3222 • $
  Japanese-influenced cafe fare at the mouth of
  Newton Creek.
- **Brooklyn Ice Cream Factory** •
  97 Commercial St [Box St]
  718-349-2506 • $
  As yummy as the DUMBO shop, without the lines.
- **Brooklyn Label** • 180 Franklin St [Java St]
  718-389-2806 • $
  Scrumptious sandwiches in the stately Astral
  building.
- **Christina's** • 853 Manhattan Ave [Noble St]
  718-383-4382 • $
  Traditional Polish food, cheap breakfasts!
- **Divine Follie Café** • 929 Manhattan Ave [Kent]
  718-389-6770 • $$
  Large selection of meats, pastas, and pizza.
- **Eat** • 124 Meserole Ave [Leonard St]
  718-389-8083 • $
  Rotating menu created of regional purveyors'
  goods; Oregon vibe via NYC.
- **Enid's** • 560 Manhattan Ave [Driggs Ave]
  718-349-3859 • $$
  Popular brunch on weekends; also dinner
  weeknights.
- **Erb** • 681 Manhattan Ave [Norman Ave]
  718-349-8215 • $$
  Terrific Thai; try the curry noodles.
- **Five Leaves** • 18 Bedford Ave [Nassau Ave]
  718-383-5345 • $$$
  Heath Ledger's post-mortem restaurant is
  cooler than you.
- **Fresca Tortilla** • 620 Manhattan Ave [Nassau]
  718-389-8818 • $$
  Cheap Mexican take-out.
- **God Bless Deli** • 818 Manhattan Ave [Calyer]
  718-349-0605 • $
  The only 24-hour joint in the 'hood. Cheap
  sandwiches and burgers.
- **Kam Loon** • 975 Manhattan Ave [India St]
  718-383-6008 • $
  Chinese take-out and buffet.
- **Kestane Kebab** • 110 Nassau Ave [Eckford St]
  718-349-8601 • $
  Refuel your party tank around the clock for cheap.

- **Kyoto Sushi** • 161 Nassau Ave [Diamond St]
  718-383-8882 • $$
  Best sushi in Greenpoint; dine in for the sake
  and after-dinner Dum Dums.
- **La Brique** • 645 Manhattan Ave [Bedford Ave]
  718-383-1690 • $
  Restaurant schizophrenia is tasty when it's this
  inexpensive.
- **La Taverna** • 946 Manhattan Ave [Java St]
  718-383-0732 • $$
  Hearty Italian for cheap? Si, per favore!
- **Lamb & Jaffy** • 1073 Manhattan Ave [Eagle St]
  718-389-3638 • $$$
  Classy date spot.
- **Lokal** • 905 Lorimer St [Nassau Ave]
  718-384-6777 • $
  Vaguely Mediterranean on McCarren.
- **Lomzynianka** • 646 Manhattan Ave [Nassau]
  718-389-9439 • $
  Get your kitschy Polish fix dirt cheap.
- **Manhattan 3 Decker** •
  695 Manhattan Ave [Norman Ave]
  718-389-6664 • $$
  Greek and American fare.
- **Ott** • 970 Manhattan Ave [India St]
  718-609-2416 • $$
  Another excellent Thai choice on Manhattan.
- **Peter Pan Doughnuts** • 727 Manhattan Ave
  [Norman Ave]
  718-389-3676 • $
  Polish girls in smocks serving tasty donuts.
- **Pio Pio Riko** • 996 Manhattan Ave [Huron St]
  718-349-5925 • $
  Peruvian. It's all about the rotisserie chicken,
  but the ceviche mixto is also good.
- **Relax** • 68 Newell St [Nassau Ave]
  718-389-1665 • $
  Polish diner w/ good prices and excellent
  soups—a neighborhood favorite.
- **Sapporo Haru** • 622 Manhattan Ave [Nassau]
  718-389-9697 • $$
  Fresh sushi, friendly service.
- **Schmook's Pizza** • 86 Nassau Ave [Manhattan]
  718-389-0501 • $
  "It's a Pizza Place!"
- **Thai Café** • 925 Manhattan Ave [Kent St]
  718-383-3562 • $
  Vast menu, veg options, eat in or take out.
- **Valdiano** • 659 Manhattan Ave [Bedford Ave]
  718-383-1707 • $$
  Southern Italian.

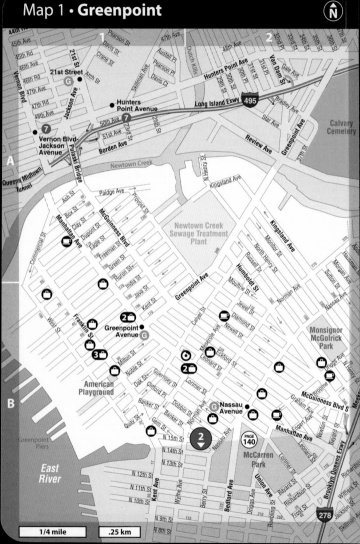

Bagels, Coffee, & Shopping

Map 1

Polish people know sausage. Hit the links at **Steve's Meat Market**. Fashion-wise, vintage can be found at **Old Hollywood** while refurbished is in style at **Alter 140** (menswear is across the street at **Alter 109**). Music hounds should get their ears to **Permanent Records** and get their vinyl on.

Bagels

- **Baker's Dozen** • 788 Manhattan Ave [Meserole]
  718-349-2222
  Home of the whole wheat everything bagel & most confusing line in the 'Point.

Coffee

- **Café Grumpy** • 193 Meserole Ave [Diamond]
  718-349-7623
  The finest coffee house in Brooklyn now has its own roastery.
- **Champion Coffee** • 1108 Manhattan Ave [Clay]
  718-383-5195
  Best espresso north of Greenpoint Ave.
- **Lucky Shot** • 145 Driggs Ave [Russell St]
  347-599-2351
  Finally, good espresso on McGolrick Park.
- **Uro Café** • 277 Driggs Ave [Leonard]
  718-599-1230
  Best espresso south of Greenpoint Ave.

Shopping

- **Alter** • 109 Franklin St [Greenpoint Ave]
  718-349-0203
  Nice selection of vintage and hard-to-find labels.
- **Angel Street Thrift Shop** • 67 Guernsey St [Norman Ave]
  212-229-0546
  Chelsea outpost thrift shop. Cleaner and quieter than Beacon's.
- **Brouwerij Lane** • 78 Greenpoint Ave [Franklin]
  347-529-6133
  For beer junkies. Global bottles or pour your own growler.
- **Cracovia Liquors** • 150 Nassau Ave [Newell St]
  718-383-2010
  Easiest place to spot a bum in Greenpoint. Open late.
- **Dalaga** • 150 Franklin St [Greenpoint Ave]
  718-389-4049
  Cute boutique with clothes and accessories from young designers.
- **Dandelion Wine** • 153 Franklin St [Java St]
  347-689-4563
  Knowledgeable staff and frequent wine tastings—double win!

- **The Garden** • 921 Manhattan Ave [Kent St]
  718-389-6448
  Awe-inspiring natural foods selection.
- **Hayden-Harnett** • 211 Franklin St [Freeman]
  718-349-2247
  Trekking to this leather handbag mecca is so worth it.
- **Kill Devil Hill** • 170 Franklin St [Java St]
  347-534-3088
  Interior decorating with skeletal remains.
- **Maria's Deli** • 136 Meserole Ave [Eckford St]
  718-383-9063
  One of many Polish bodegas. Pickle soup & mayonnaise salads!
- **Old Hollywood** •
  110 Meserole Ave [Manhattan Ave]
  718-389-0837
  From the folks who brought you the retro gentrification of North Brooklyn.
- **Open Air Modern** •
  606 Manhattan Ave [Nassau Ave]
  718-383-6465
  Old and rare books and furniture.
- **Permanent Records** • 181 Franklin St [Huron]
  718-383-4083
  Stellar selection of new and used vinyl, friendly service.
- **Photoplay** • 928 Manhattan Ave [Kent St]
  718-383-7782
  JP's favorite Greenpoint video store.
- **Pop's Popular Clothing** •
  7 Franklin St [Meserole Ave]
  718-349-7677
  Work clothes & boots for blue-collar authenticity.
- **Steve's Meat Market** • 104 Nassau Ave [Leonard]
  718-383-1780
  Sausages double smoked for her pleasure.
- **The Thing** • 1001 Manhattan Ave [Huron St]
  718-349-8234
  Unusual second-hand store offers thousands of used LPs.
- **Wedel** • 772 Manhattan Ave [Meserole Ave]
  718-349-3933
  Old School chocolate shop, straight out of Poland.
- **Word** • 126 Franklin St [Milton St]
  718-383-0096
  Literary fiction, non-fiction, and kids' books.

Map 2 • **Williamsburg**

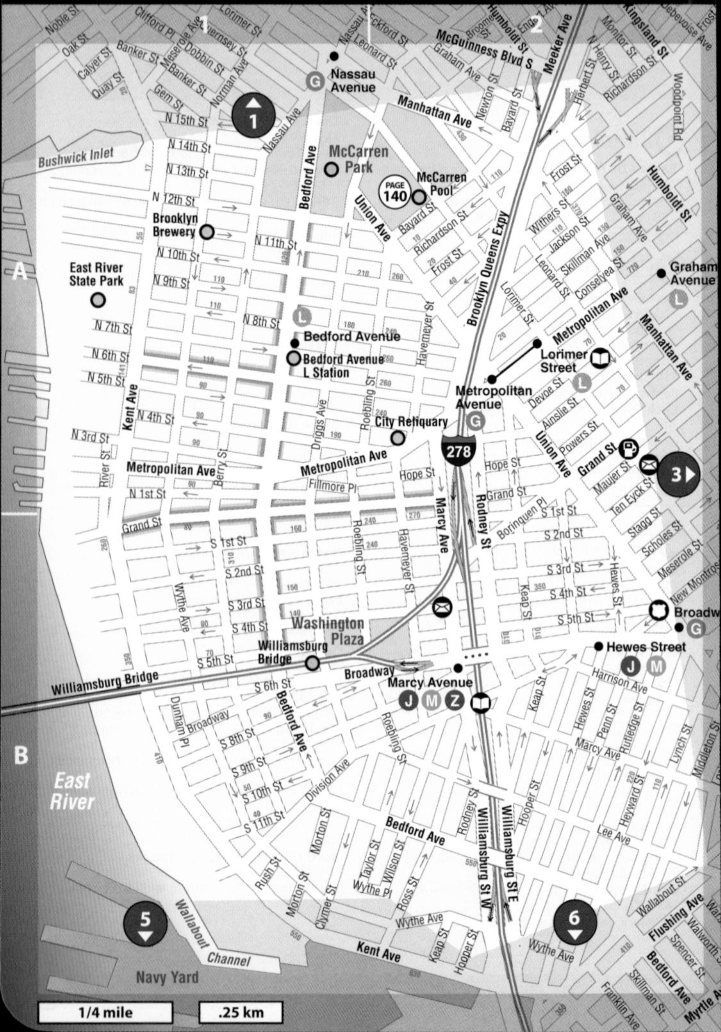

(N)

Clifford Pl
Lorimer St
Nassau Ave
Guernsey St
Eckford St
Leonard St
McGuinness Blvd S
Graham Ave
Newton St
Humboldt St
Meeker Ave
Kingsland Ave
Lombardy St
Monitor St
Newel St
Herbert St
Richardson St
Woodpoint Rd

Oak St
Calyer St
Noble St
Banker St
Dobbin St
Nassau Ave
Manhattan Ave
Frost St

(G) **Nassau Avenue**

Quay St
Bem St
Banker St
Norman Ave
N 15th St
Bedford Ave
Union Ave
Manhattan Ave
Withers St
Jackson St
Skillman Ave
Conselyea St
Frost St
Graham Ave
Humboldt St

Bushwick Inlet
N 14th St
N 13th St
N 12th St
McCarren Park
PAGE 140
McCarren Pool
Leonard St
Skillman Ave
Conselyea St
Metropolitan Ave

(1)

Bayard St
Richardson St

Brooklyn Brewery
N 11th St
N 10th St

(A)

East River State Park
N 9th St
N 8th St
N 7th St
N 6th St
N 5th St
Kent Ave
Roebling St
Driggs Ave
Havemeyer St
Bedford Avenue
(L) **Bedford Avenue L Station**
Lorimer St
Brooklyn Queens Expwy
Metropolitan Avenue
Frost St
Lorimer Street (L)
Devoe St
Metropolitan Avenue
Ainslie St
Powers St
Grand St (L)
Union Ave

N 4th St
Berry St
(L) **City Refinery**
(G) **Metropolitan Avenue**
278
Maujer St
Tan Eyck St
Stagg St
Scholes St
(3)

Metropolitan Ave
N 3rd St
Metropolitan Ave
Hope St
Hope St
S 1st St
Grand St
Meserole St
New Montro

Metropolitan Ave
N 1st St
Fillmore Pl
Grand St
Marcy Ave
Rodney St
Borinquen Pl
S 1st St
S 2nd St
S 3rd St
S 4th St
S 5th St
Keap St
Hewes St
Keap St
(B) **Broadwa**
(G)

Grand St
S 1st St
S 2nd St
Roebling St
Havemeyer St
Hewes Street
(J) (M)

S 3rd St
S 4th St
Washington Plaza
Williamsburg Bridge
Harrison Ave

(B)

East River

Williamsburg Bridge
S 5th St
S 6th St
Bedford Ave
Broadway
Broadway
Marcy Avenue
(J) (M) (Z)
Kent Ave
Penn St
Rutledge St
Marcy Ave

Dunham Pl
S 7th St
S 8th St
Division Ave
Lee Ave
Heyward St

Broadway
S 9th St
S 10th St
S 11th St
Marton St
Rush St
Clymer St
Taylor St
Wilson St
Bedford Ave
Ross St
Wythe Pl
Wythe Ave
Hooper St
Williamsburg St W
Hewes St
Lynch St

Middleton St
Walton St
Flushing Ave
Myrtle
Graham Avenue
Bedford Ave

(5)

(6)

Wallabout St
Wallabout Channel
Navy Yard
Kent Ave
Wythe Ave
Skillman Ave
Franklin Ave

| 1/4 mile | .25 km |

It's true, Williamsburg is the white hot center of New York's hipster scene. The stretch of blocks from the river to the BQE are rarely lacking in skinny pants or ironic record collections; you can usually buy both at the sidewalk sales along Bedford Avenue. But the art school crowd isn't out here all alone: luxury condo buyers—and their strollers—are quickly filing in, while the deeply rooted Italian and Polish locals still shape the neighborhood's contours (and still sell the best pastries). For now, there's something in the area for everyone—signless speakeasies for the too-cool kids, locally designed baby gear for new parents, and bowling alleys (**The Gutter**, **Brooklyn Bowl**) for the rest of us.

Williamsburg is a neighborhood partially frozen in transition. The boom brought in a new set of glass-and-steel high rises, but the 2009 bust stopped much of the development in its tracks. Around the construction sites, hundred year-old brick storefronts and residences still dot the tree-lined streets, and hints of the area's grittier past can be found poking up along the way. To find out more about pre-gentrified Williamsburg, start at **City Reliquary**, a clever little museum filled with New York City artifacts and historical tidbits. Better yet, pick up that requisite copy of *A Tree Grows in Brooklyn* at **Spoonbill & Sugartown**, and learn about the neighborhood's tenement days.

As it's currently one of the most influential zip codes in the indie rock world, Williamsburg draws in young musicians and their blog-writing fans like a vortex. For anyone who loves new sounds and intimate venues, the 'Burg is the jackpot: there's rarely a night around here without at least one decent show. The legendary **Knitting Factory**—recently relocated from TriBeCa—joins the **Music Hall of Williamsburg** in hosting slightly better-known acts; those who prefer their bands firmly below the radar will feel at home at **Zebulon**, **Pete's Candy Store**, **Trash**, and **Bruar Falls**.

During the summer, live music also emanates from the **East River State Park**, the new home of an open-air concert series that once belonged to the **McCarren Pool** (now under renovation to become a working pool once more). Even after the stage is gone, however, this stretch of green is worth a weekly trip; the picnic tables at the river's edge are one of the best spots in Brooklyn to gawk at that gorgeous skyline. For a more structured outdoor space, head to **McCarren Park**, 35 acres of ball fields, dog runs, and gardens where residents of every stripe convene when the sun is out.

While Williamsburg has long had restaurants worth a trip over the bridge, it's now a destination for home cooks, especially those who seek a greater connection with their food. **Marlow & Daughters** dispenses locally sourced, top quality (okay, expensive) meats and detailed preparation advice; **Bedford Cheese Shop** and **UVA Wines** are similarly staffed with geeks who really know their goods. For amateur chefs with more ambition than kitchen space, **The Brooklyn Kitchen Labs** offers classes on everything from pickling to pig butchering.

Map 2 • **Williamsb**

Watch where you step, you might join a band: these venue-heavy blocks (**Music Hall**, **Public Assembly**, **Pete's Candy Store**, **Glasslands Gallery**) are so flush with performers even **Brooklyn Bowl** has a stage. After the show, head to **Spuyten Duyvil** for rare beers, **Hotel Delmano** for spiffy cocktails, or **Barcade** for retro-game goodness.

🍸 Bars

- **Barcade** • 388 Union Ave [Ainslie St]
  718-302-6464
  Paradise for '80s console champions and craft-beer guzzlers.
- **Bembe** • 81 S 6th St [Berry St]
  718-387-5389
  Hookahville.
- **Berry Park** • 4 Berry St [N 14th St]
  718-782-2829
  Williamsburg's best rooftop: great beer and plenty of skyline.
- **Bruar Falls** • 245 Grand St [Roebling St]
  347-529-6610
  Cake Shop's Brooklyn outpost.
- **Clem's** • 264 Grand St [Roebling St]
  718-387-9617
  Classic narrow bar + drink specials = a neighborhood staple.
- **Daddy's** • 437 Graham Ave [Frost St]
  718-609-6388
  Friendly hipster hideaway.
- **East River Bar** • 97 S 6th St [Berry St]
  718-302-0511
  Fun interior, patio, and live music.
- **Glasslands Gallery** • 289 Kent Ave [S 2nd St]
  718-599-1450
  Community experimental music and art venue.
- **Greenpoint Tavern** • 188 Bedford Ave [N 7th]
  718-384-9539
  Cheap beer in Styrofoam cups.
- **Hotel Delmano** • 82 Berry St [N 9th St]
  718-387-1945
  Classic cocktails. Great date spot.
- **Huckleberry Bar** • 588 Grand St [Lorimer St]
  718-218-8555
  Solid cocktails, nice garden out back.
- **Iona** • 180 Grand St [Bedford Ave]
  718-384-5008
  Plenty of choices on tap.
- **Knitting Factory Brooklyn** •
  361 Metropolitan Ave [Havemeyer St]
  347-529-6696
  Fifth-carbon of its former greatness.
- **Larry Lawrence** • 295 Grand St [Havemeyer]
  718-218-7866
  Laid-back bar with a lovely loft for smokers.
- **The Levee** • 212 Berry St [Metropolitan Ave]
  718-218-8787
  Formerly Cokies, now a laid-back vibe with free cheese balls.

- **Music Hall of Williamsburg** • 66 N 6th St [Kent]
  212-260-4700
  Formerly Northsix, now Brooklyn's Bowery Ballroom.
- **Nita Nita** • 146 Wythe Ave [N 8th St]
  718-388-5328
  Friendly, low-key spot with better-than-average bar snacks.
- **Pete's Candy Store** • 709 Lorimer St [Richardson]
  718-302-3770
  Live music, trivia nights, awesome back room, and Scrabble.
- **Public Assembly** • 70 N 6th St [Wythe Ave]
  718-782-5188
  Reflecting pool, candles, and attractive people.
- **Radegast Hall** • 113 N 3rd St [Berry St]
  718-963-3973
  German beer hall with retractable roof. Only in Williamsburg.
- **Spuyten Duyvil** •
  359 Metropolitan Ave [Havemeyer St]
  718-963-4140
  Join the Belgian beer cult.
- **Turkey's Nest** • 94 Bedford Ave [N 12th St]
  718-384-9774
  Best dive in Williamsburg.
- **Union Pool** • 484 Union Ave [Rodney St]
  718-609-0484
  Good starting point—or finishing point.
- **Zebulon** • 258 Wythe Ave [N 3rd St]
  718-218-6934
  World-fusion and jazz music with Mediterranean bar food.

🎳 Bowling

- **Brooklyn Bowl** • 61 Wythe Ave [N 12th St]
  718-963-3369
  Bowl (16 lanes), eat (Blue Ribbon!), and rock out (music venue too).
- **The Gutter** • 200 N 14th St [Wythe Ave]
  718-387-3585
  Vintage-style bowling alley with great brews on tap—what could be better?

😃 Movie Theaters

- **Indie Screen** •
  285 Kent Ave [S 2nd St]
  347-512-6422
  Dinner and an art house movie under one roof.

Map 2 • Williamsburg

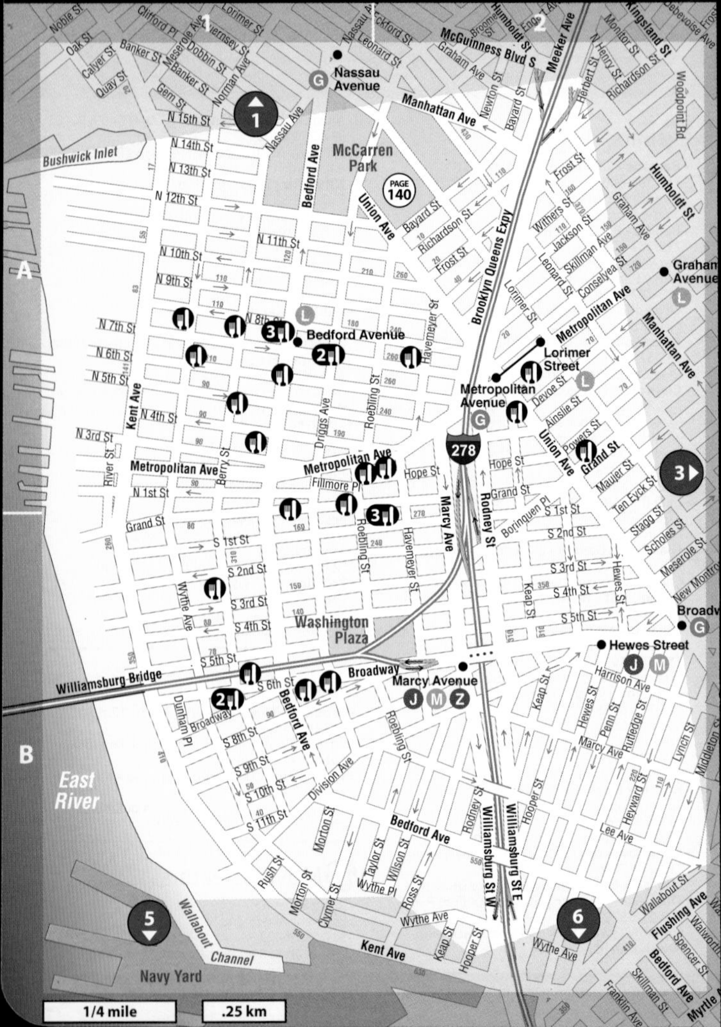

Oasis has perfect falafel and nothing soaks up booze like a Vinnie's slice, but the real gems are the dressed-up American spots (Walter Foods, Dressler, Rye). Diner and Egg elevate breakfast to an art; Fette Sau and Peter Luger do such joyous things to meat that all carnivores must pay their respects.

Restaurants

- **Acqua Santa** • 556 Driggs Ave [N 7th St]
  718-384-9695 • $$
  Bistro Italian—amazing patio.
- **Baci & Abbracci** • 204 Grand St [Driggs Ave]
  718-599-6599 • $$
  Old-world Italian in a modern setting.
- **Bakeri** • 150 Wythe Ave [N 8th St]
  718-388-8037 • $$
  Adorably Amish decor and hipster vibe.
  Excellent baked goods.
- **Banh Mi** • 172 Bedford Ave [N 7th St]
  718-384-0028 • $
  Tasty, fresh-baked banh mi, five bucks a pop.
- **Blackbird Parlour** • 197 Bedford Ave [N 6th St]
  718-599-2707 • $
  Cozy European style café with tasty sandwiches.
- **Bozu** • 296 Grand St [Havemeyer St]
  718-384-7770 • $$
  Amazing Japanese tapas and sushi bombs.
- **The Brooklyn Star** • 33 Havemeyer St [N 8th]
  718-599-9899 • $$
  Lovingly-presented southern classics from a
  Momofuku veteran.
- **Diner** • 85 Broadway [Berry St]
  718-486-3077 • $$
  Amazing simple food like you've never
  tasted—never disappoints.
- **Dressler** • 149 Broadway [Bedford Ave]
  718-384-6343 • $$$$
  So darn classy, you'll feel like you're in Park Slope.
- **DuMont** • 432 Union Ave [Devoe St]
  718-486-7717 • $$
  Continually changing market-fresh menu and
  yummy desserts.
- **Egg** • 135 N 5th St [Bedford Ave]
  718-302-5151 • $$
  Organic breakfast and free range burgers.
- **Fatty 'Cue** • 91 S 6th St [Berry St]
  718-599-3090 • $$$$
  Asian-inspired barbecue by the Fatty Crew.
- **Fette Sau** • 354 Metropolitan St [Roebling St]
  718-963-3404 • $$
  Enjoy pounds of meat and casks of beer in a
  former auto-body repair shop.
- **Fiore** • 284 Grand St [Roebling St]
  718-782-8222 • $$
  Rustic, delicious Italian at best-bargain-in-
  Williamsburg prices.

- **Juliette** • 135 N 5th St [Bedford Ave]
  718-388-9222 • $$
  Northside bistro with rooftop deck.
- **La Superior** • 295 Berry St [S 2nd St]
  718-388-5988 • $$
  Authentic Mexican street food.
- **Le Barricou** • 533 Grand St [Union Ave]
  718-782-7372 • $$
  Everyone's all about the bouillabaisse.
- **Marlow & Sons** • 81 Broadway [Berry St]
  718-384-1441 • $$$
  Oysters and beer, old timey-like—go for Happy
  Hour.
- **Northside Bakery** • 149 N 8th St [Bedford Ave]
  718-782-2700 • $
  Best Polish bakery this side of Greenpoint/
  Williamsburg. Perfect chocolate croissants.
- **Oasis** • 161 N 7th St [Bedford Ave]
  718-218-7607 • $
  Cheap Middle Eastern delights right by the L,
  and open late.
- **Peter Luger Steak House** •
  178 Broadway [Driggs Ave]
  718-387-7400 • $$$$$
  Best steak, potatoes, and spinach in this solar
  system.
- **Roebling Tea Room** •
  143 Roebling St [Metropolitan Ave]
  718-963-0760 • $$$
  Fancy tea eatery.
- **Rye** • 247 S 1st St [Roebling St]
  718-218-8047 • $$$
  Lush, lovely speakeasy (no sign!) that serves a
  mean meatloaf.
- **Teddy's Bar and Grill** • 96 Berry St [N 8th St]
  718-384-9787 • $
  Best bar food ever. Hipster and Polish locals unite.
- **Vinnie's** • 148 Bedford Ave [N 9th St]
  718-782 7078 • $
  Heavenly pizza with a side of puns.
- **Walter Foods** • 253 Grand St [Roebling St]
  718-387-8783 • $$$
  Spiffed-up American classics in a warmly lit bistro.
- **Yola's Café** • 524 Metropolitan Ave [Union Ave]
  718-486-0757 • $
  Terrific, authentic Mexican in a claustrophobic
  atmosphere.
- **Zenkichi** • 77 N 6th St [Wythe Ave]
  718-388-8985 • $$
  Amazing izakaya suitable for a tryst.

Map 2 · **Williamsburg**

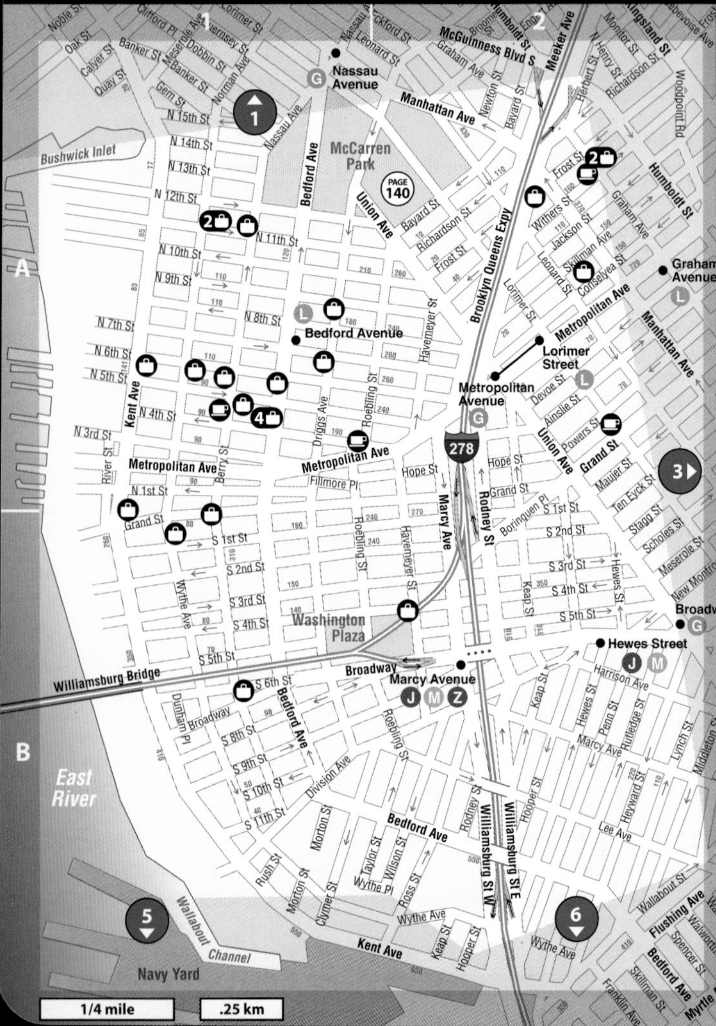

N

Noble St
Oak St
Clifford Pl
Lorimer St
Guernsey St
Dobbin St
Banker St
Eckford St
Leonard St
McGuinness Blvd S
Humboldt St
Newel St
Diamond St
Jewel St
Kingsland Ave
Nassau Ave
Meeker Ave
Woodpoint Rd
Quay St
Gem St
Franklin St
Calyer St
Graham Ave
Kent St
Nassau Avenue

G

N 15th St
N 14th St
N 13th St
N 12th St
N 11th St
Bedford Ave
Manhattan Ave
Manhattan Avenue
McCarren Park
PAGE 140
Union Ave
Bayard St
Richardson St
Frost St
Withers St
Jackson St
Stillman St
Conselyea St
Leonard St
Lorimer St
Devoe St
Ainslie St
Humboldt St
Graham Ave
Graham Avenue

Bushwick Inlet

A

N 10th St
N 9th St
N 8th St
N 7th St
N 6th St
N 5th St
N 4th St
N 3rd St
Kent Ave
Berry St
Wythe Ave
River St
Bedford Avenue

L

Metropolitan Ave

Driggs Ave
Roebling St
Havemeyer St

Metropolitan Avenue

Brooklyn Queens Expy

Metropolitan
Avenue

G

278

Lorimer
Street

L

Metropolitan Ave
Powers St
Grand St

Grand St

Hope St
N 1st St
Grand St
Fillmore Pl
S 1st St
S 2nd St
S 3rd St
S 4th St
S 5th St

Borinquen Pl
Rodney St
Marcy Ave

Maujer St
Ten Eyck St
Stagg St
Scholes St
Meserole St
Montrose Ave

3

Broadway

G

Hewes St
Hewes Street

J M

Washington
Plaza

Broadway
Marcy Avenue

J M Z

S 6th St
S 7th St
S 8th St
S 9th St
S 10th St
S 11th St

Williamsburg Bridge

Division Ave
Broadway
Berry St
Bedford Ave

Harrison Ave
Hooper St
Hewes St
Penn St
Rutledge St
Lynch St
Heyward St
Lee Ave

B

East
River

Dunham Pl
Rush St
Morton St
Roebling St
Havemeyer St
Keap St
Hooper St
Rodney St
Williamsburg St W
Williamsburg St E
Wallabout Ave
Flushing Ave
Bedford Ave
Wilson St
Ross St
Taylor St
Clymer St
Wythe Ave
Wythe Pl
Spencer St

5

6

Wallabout Channel

Navy Yard

Kent Ave
Wythe Ave
Wallabout St
Hooper St
Keap St
Franklin Ave

| 1/4 mile | .25 km |

Amarcord has a nicely edited selection of vintage clothes and bags; Beacon's Closet and Buffalo Exchange require some stamina to turn up great pieces (but they're in there). Vinyl collectors are in luck near the Bedford L (Academy, Earwax, Soundfix), and food geeks can find wall-to-wall gadgets at Whisk and Brooklyn Kitchen.

☕ Coffee

- **Blue Bottle Coffee** • 160 Berry St [N 5th St]
  718-534-5488
  SF Bay Area coffee genius comes to the hood.
- **Caffe Capri** • 427 Graham Ave [Frost St]
  718-383-5744
  Classic café with incredible cannolis.
- **Gimme Coffee** • 495 Lorimer St [Powers St]
  718-388-7771
  Coffee genius from Ithaca comes to Brooklyn.
- **Oslo** • 133 Roebling St [N 4th St]
  718-782-0332
  Modern coffee shop.

🛍 Shopping

- **Academy Annex** • 96 N 6th St [Wythe Ave]
  718-218-8200
  Bins and bins of new and used LPs.
- **Amarcord** • 223 Bedford Ave [N 4th St]
  718-963-4001
  Well-edited vintage goodies, many pieces direct from Europe.
- **Beacon's Closet** • 88 N 11th St [Wythe Ave]
  718-486-0816
  Rad resale with lots of gems.
- **Bedford Cheese Shop** • 229 Bedford Ave [N 5th]
  718-599-7588
  Best cheese selection in the borough.
- **The Brooklyn Kitchen** • 100 Frost St [Meeker]
  718-389-2982
  Awesome butcher shop and gourmet cooking supplies next to the BQE.
- **Buffalo Exchange** • 504 Driggs Ave [N 9th St]
  718-384-6901
  Recycled clothing chain's first NYC store.
- **Built By Wendy** • 46 N 6th St [Kent Ave]
  718-384-2882
  Brooklyn outpost of NYC-based independent label.
- **Earwax Records** • 218 Bedford Ave [N 5th St]
  718-486-3771
  Record store with all the indie classics.
- **Emily's Pork Store** • 426 Graham Ave [Withers]
  718-383-7216
  Broccoli rabe sausage is their specialty.
- **Future Perfect** • 115 N 6th St [Berry St]
  718-599-6278
  The coolest assemblage of cutting-edge housewares and indie furnishings.

- **KCDC Skateshop** • 90 N 11th St [Wythe Ave]
  718-387-9006
  Shop and gallery featuring locally designed gear.
- **Marlow & Daughters** • 95 Broadway [Berry St]
  718-388-5700
  Gorgeous (yes, expensive) cuts for the discerning carnivore.
- **The Mini-Market** • 218 Bedford Ave [N 5th St]
  718-218-7849
  Hodge-podge of tchotchkes and fun clothes.
- **Roulette** • 188 Havemeyer St [S 3rd St]
  718-218-7104
  Choice vintage housewares at affordable prices.
- **Savino's Quality Pasta** •
  111 Conselyea St [Manhattan Ave]
  718-388-2038
  Homemade ravioli.
- **Sodafine** • 119 Grand St [Berry St]
  718-230-3060
  Hot little numbers with big price tags.
- **Sound Fix Records** • 44 Berry St [N 11th St]
  718-388-8090
  Independent record store with a café/ performance space in back.
- **Spoonbill & Sugartown** •
  218 Bedford Ave [N 5th St]
  718-387-7322
  Art, architecture, design, philosophy, and literature. New and used.
- **Sprout** • 44 Grand St [Kent Ave]
  718-388-4440
  Contemporary home and garden store.
- **Spuyten Duyvil Grocery** • 132 N 5th St [Bedford]
  718-384-1520
  Belgium beer lovers' bar sells the goods in Williamsburg's mini mall.
- **Treehouse** • 430 Graham Ave [Frost Ave]
  718-482-8733
  Quirky, one-of-a-kind clothing and jewelry.
- **Two Jakes** • 320 Wythe Ave [Grand St]
  718-782-7780
  Furniture: Mod, metal, misc.
- **Ugly Luggage** • 214 Bedford Ave [N 5th St]
  718-384-0724
  Small storefront packed with antiques.
- **Uva Wines** • 199 Bedford Ave [N 5th St]
  718-963-3939
  The staff knows and loves their small, meticulous selection.
- **Whisk** • 231 Bedford Ave [N 3rd St]
  718-218-7230
  Kitchen boutique stocked with basic gear and beyond.

Map 2

For anyone wondering where the old Lower East Side went, this neighborhood might be part of the answer. Sure, new lofts dot the roads around the outlying L stops, but for the most part it's factories and bodegas, longstanding residences, and a few corners where it's best to keep your guard up. What the area lacks in Williamsburg-proper niceties, it makes up for with (relatively) cheaper rents and a genuine sense of diversity, possibility, and artistic community. All of which pales next to the real draw in this area: Awesome. Tacos.

East Williamsburg is still actively industrial. The hulking **Pfizer Pharmaceutical Plant** finally stopped running in recent years, but the blocks are filled with factories and warehouses that make everything from concrete to wontons (just follow the shifting scents in the air to find what's what). If it's hints of history you're after, a hike south of Metropolitan will turn up plenty of shuttered giants still bearing signs of the area's past as a textile and food production hub. Along the way, check out the **Williamsburg Houses** (1937)—one of the first NYC housing projects, the massive, early modern complex has been preserved as an architectural landmark.

All of that spare factory space has helped turn this part of Brooklyn into a booming artist colony; the geography is particularly inviting for those working with large-scale installation pieces and heavy materials. Collectives such as **3rd Ward**, **Chez Bushwick**, and **House of Yes** offer extensive rehearsal and workspaces for rent, fostering the development and exhibition of emerging painters, photographers, woodworkers, and even aerialists (no joke).

Excellent galleries are also thick on the ground: **Ad Hoc Art** puts up can't-miss collections of street and underground works, while **Asterisk** and **Grace Space** host outsider bands and performance artists, respectively. The **NUTUREart** gallery, now permanently located on Grand, is a vital stop for up-and-coming curators.

In between exhibits and openings, don't forget that the best way to see street art is out on the street. Keep your eyes open for amazing **graffiti murals**—especially near Boerum Street at Graham Avenue—and Banksy-style stencil works that pop up on abandoned walls and windows.

East Williamsburg was once the place for out of the way Italian joints (**Carmine's** is still a local institution), but an influx of Latin American immigrants over the past decade has created a stronghold of Salvadoran, Ecuadorian, and Mexican delights. **Bahia** makes freshly-made pupusas that are impossible to walk past; heavily-mirrored **Barzola** is a must for ceviche loyalists. If you have a date in tow, **Mesa Coyoacan** can't be beat for atmosphere.

If you're looking to drink the most for your dollar, this neighborhood's got your back. Two bucks will get you a beer at the **Lock Inn** or the super-dark **King's County**, also notable for its well-stocked whiskey shelf. For a value-added dive bar experience, head to **Don Pedro**; after dark the tiny Ecuodorian restaurant deals in stiff cocktails and underground bands. **Market Hotel** is the best last stop for a night out in East Williamsburg—the crumbling DIY venue is rife with warehouse-party energy.

Empty industrial areas make for plentiful art spaces (**3rd Ward**, **Asterisk**, **House of Yes**), and there's always an exhibition worth checking out before finding a barstool. The divey **Wreck Room** serves 'em stiff and cheap; local fav **duckduck** is so cozy and low-key it's like drinking on your own porch.

Bars

- **3rd Ward** • 195 Morgan Ave [Stagg St]
718-715-4961
Art shows and parties in East-burg's industrial wilderness.
- **Beauty Bar** • 921 Broadway [Melrose St]
347-529-0370
Same manicure-and-mixed drink fun as the Manhattan one.
- **Boulevard Tavern** •
579 Meeker Ave [N Henry St]
718-389-3252
Low-key dive with supposed ghosts in the room.
- **Bushwick Country Club** •
618 Grand St [Leonard St]
718-388-2114
"Muffy, I've got a feeling we're not in Greenwich anymore."
- **Don Pedro** • 90 Manhattan Ave [Boerum St]
718-218-6914
Lively local watering hole that frequently hosts local bands.
- **duckduck** • 161 Montrose Ave [Graham Ave]
Badly needed neighborhood bar.
- **Flushing Farms** • 970 Flushing Ave [Bogart St]
Café and performance space with a cool little lawn/garden/patch of sand.
- **Harefield Road** •
769 Metropolitan Ave [Graham Ave]
718-388-6870
Spacious, unpretentious spot for microbrews and hot toddies.
- **House of Yes** • 342 Maujer St [Morgan Ave]
A design & performance space for everyone from musicians to acrobats.

- **Kings County** • 286 Seigel St [White St]
718-418-8823
Cheap local bar for a whiskey fix.
- **Legion** • 790 Metropolitan Ave [Humboldt St]
Williamsburgers hang where war vets used to drown their sorrows.
- **Lock Inn** • 949 Grand St [Catherine St]
718-302-0810
Converted scooter shop with cheap beers.
- **The Market Hotel** •
1142 Myrtle Ave [Broadway]
DIY rock shows in a hidden, dilapidated space.
- **Office Ops** • 57 Thames St [Morgan Ave]
718-418-2509
The Rock and Rollerskate party should not be missed.
- **Pumps** • 1089 Grand St [Metropolitan Ave]
718-599-2474
Pump it up.
- **Sweet Ups** • 277 Graham Ave [Grand St]
718-384-3886
Great neighborhood bar with karaoke on Tuesdays.
- **Tandem** •
236 Troutman St [Knickerbocker Ave]
718-386-2369
Eclectic space with small plates and old-fashioned cocktails.
- **Wreck Room** •
940 Flushing Ave [Evergreen Ave]
718-418-6347
Get completely "over-served" at this live music spot.

Map 3 · **East Williamsburg**

Yes, you can find great tacos in New York, all it takes is a few minutes on an L train. Awesome specimens can be had at **Antojitos Mexicanos** and **Kiosco Piaxtla**, while **Grand Morelos** dishes rice and beans 24/7. For artisanal pizza, it's **Motorino** or **Roberta's**, two of Brooklyn's finest.

🍴 Restaurants

- **Antojitos Mexicanos** •
  107 Graham Ave [McKibben St]
  718-384-9076 • $
  Best Mexican food in the 'hood.
- **Bahia** • 690 Grand St [Manhattan Ave]
  718-218-9592 • $$
  Try the mouth-watering pupusas.
- **Barzola** • 197 Meserole St [Bushwick Ave]
  718-381-4343 • $$
  Ecuadorian fare in mirrored splendor.
- **BFP East** • 119 Ingraham St [Porter Ave]
  347-223-4211 • $
  A cafe & bar addition to the Brooklyn Fire
  Proof mini-empire.
- **Boulevard Cafe** •
  253 Bushwick Ave [Montrose Ave]
  718-381-2442 • $
  The prettiest cafe for blocks around, and good
  breakfast to boot.
- **Carmine's** • 358 Graham St [Conselyea St]
  718-782-9659 • $
  Amazing slices.
- **El Brillante Restaurant** •
  159 Graham Ave [Montrose Ave]
  718-782-3322 • $
  Friendly Spanish-American luncheonette.
- **El Matador** • 795 Grand St [Humboldt St]
  718-599-2959 • $$
  Tiny Spanish spot that's worth the trek beyond
  the BQE.
- **Gaby's Bakery** •
  238 Knickerbocker Ave [Starr St]
  718-418-8821 • $
  Low-price pasteleria. Stick to the sweetbreads
  & generous-sized doughnuts.
- **Garden Grill** • 318 Graham Ave [Devoe St]
  718-384-8668 • $
  Classic diner grub with good donuts.
- **Grand Morelos** • 727 Grand St [Graham St]
  718-218-9441 • $$
  24-hour Mexican diner/bakery.
- **Il Passatore** • 14 Bushwick Ave [Devoe St]
  718-963-3100 • $$
  Rustic, affordable pastas and pizzas for a price.
- **Kiosco Piaxtla** • 258 Graham St [Maujer St]
  718-388-2957 • $
  Tasty mole dishes.
- **Latin Cuisine** • 804 Grand St [Bushwick Ave]
  718-302-6146 • $$
  Good Colombian fare.

- **Life Café NINE83** • 983 Flushing Ave [Bogart]
  718-386-1133 • $$
  Same as Life on Ave B with excellent happy
  hour.
- **Lily Thai** • 615 Grand St [Leonard St]
  718-218-7522 • $
  Extensive menu with good lunch specials.
- **Loco Burrito** •
  243 Bushwick Ave [Montrose Ave]
  718-456-9114 • $$
  A place for the new unadventurous hipsters.
- **Long Lai Thai Cuisine** •
  214 Knickerbocker St [Troutman St]
  718-418-8555 • $$
  On a street of Latin food, this is
  Knickerbocker's Thai food oasis.
- **Los Primos** • 704 Grand St [Graham Ave]
  718-486-8449 • $$
  Authentic Latin spot with tasty seafood.
- **Manna's Restaurant** • 829 Broadway [Park St]
  718-218-8575 • $
  Pay-by-the-pound soul food buffet.
- **Mesa Coyoacan** •
  372 Graham Ave [Conselyea]
  718-782-8171 • $$$
  Upscale Mexican that's worth the pesos. Tasty!
- **Mojito Loco** • 102 Meserole St [Leonard St]
  718-963-2960 • $$
  Yummy Latin fusion. Love the corn.
- **Motorino** • 319 Graham Ave [Devoe St]
  718-599-8899 • $$
  Awesome Neapolitan pizza with seasonal
  toppings.
- **Olive Valley** • 43 Bogart St [Moore St]
  718-894-1800 • $
  Cheap falafel in an ocean of cheap Latin
  American.
- **Pacific Ocean House** • 84 Manhattan Ave
  [McKibben St]
  718-388-3371 • $$
  The only sushi in this neck of the woods.
- **Phorum** • 50 Starr St [Wilson Ave]
  718-417-7830 • $$
  Unexpected wine bar, brunch too.
- **Roberta's** • 261 Moore St [White St]
  718-417-1118 • $$
  Solid wood-oven pizza in an industrial setting.
- **Sel de Mer** • 374 Graham Ave [Conselyea St]
  718-387-4181 • $$
  Seaside fare in East Willyburg.

Bagels, Coffee, & Shopping

For all-day shopping, the best bet is to head back towards the BQE, but there are some stops to make on the way: **The Vortex** and **Urban Jungle** hold thrift-store treasures for anyone willing to put in the effort; local vendors line the **Moore Street Market**, recently saved from closure (again).

 Bagels

- **The Bagel Store** •
  754 Metropolitan Ave [Graham Ave]
  718-782-5856
  The basics, hot and cheap.

Coffee

- **The Archive** • 49 Bogart St [Grattan St]
  718-381-1944
  Coffee, free WiFi, and video rental.
- **Café Nijasol** • 173 Montrose Ave [Humboldt]
  718-599-1612
  Friendly neighborhood café serving coffee, breakfast, and sandwiches.
- **Little Skip's** • 941 Willoughby [Myrtle Ave]
  718-484-0980
  Cool little café with great espresso.
- **Lula Bean** • 797 Grand St [Bushwick Ave]
  718-599-5852
  Killer coffee this far down Grand St? Who knew.
- **Potion Café** •
  248 McKibben St [Bushwick Ave]
  718-628-5470
  Just coffee. Nice.

Shopping

- **Alondra Record Shop** •
  206 Knickerbocker Ave [Troutman St]
  718-417-3388
  Always sound-battling the other record store across the street.
- **Artist & Craftsman** •
  761 Metropolitan Ave [Graham Ave]
  718-782-7765
  Art supplies.
- **Baggu** • 109 Ingraham St [Porter Ave]
  858-952-1032
  Stylish, reusable grocery bags for when you finally go green.
- **Blue Angel Wines** • 638 Grand St [Leonard St]
  718-388-2210
  Excellent selection of bottles under 20 bucks.
- **Bottle Shoppe** • 353 Graham St [Conselyea]
  718-388-4122
  Neighborhood staple for vino.

- **Brooklyn Natural** • 49 Bogart St [Grattan St]
  718-381-0650
  Upscale deli—check out the new late-night delivery menu.
- **Brooklyn Vintage** • 260 Moore St [Bogart St]
  917-501-9998
  A cure for mid-century overkill: flawless pieces from the 30s and 40s.
- **Brooklynski** • 351 Graham Ave [Conselyea St]
  718-389-0901
  Quirky little gifts for cool Brooklynites.
- **Busura World Fashion** •
  1065 Broadway [Union Ave]
  Sick of sifted, high-price "thrift"? Look no further.
- **Food Bazaar** • 21 Manhattan Ave [Varet St]
  718-532-0320
  Excellent fish, produce and beer selections.
- **Fortunato Brothers** •
  289 Manhattan Ave [Devoe St]
  718-387-2281
  Old-school pastry and espresso shop.
- **GreenDepot** • 1 Ivy Hill Rd [Varick Ave]
  718-782-2991
  Al Gore would shop here if he lived in Brooklyn.
- **Khim's Millennium Market** •
  324 Graham Ave [Devoe St]
  718-302-4152
  Overpriced organic and natural groceries.
- **Khim's Millennium Market** •
  260 Bushwick Ave [Johnson Ave]
  718-497-7068
  Overpriced organic and natural groceries.
- **Leo's** • 207 Knickerbocker Ave [Troutman St]
  718-456-1054
  Always winning the sound battle with Alondra's across the street.
- **Moore Street Market** •
  110 Moore St [Humboldt St]
  718-384-1371
  Latino fresh food for 50+ years (multi-vendor).
- **Urban Jungle** •
  118 Knickerbocker Ave [Flushing Ave]
  718-497-1331
  Hangar-like thrift store that's ripe for the picking.
- **The Vortex** • 222 Montrose Ave [Bushwick Ave]
  718-609-6066
  Hidden treasures waiting to be found.
- **Zukkie's** • 279 Bushwick Ave [Johnson Ave]
  718-456-0048
  Some good finds amongst the junk.

Neighborhood Overview

Map 4

Bushwick used to be synonymous with crime and urban blight, but nowadays there's not too much anxiety on a late-night walk home. This neighborhood has been on the rise since rent in Williamsburg started sky rocketing, and Bushwick's close location and low-rent lured students and artists into what used to be—and, in many pockets, continues be—a family-oriented, predominantly Latino community.

Get ready for a lot of grey—much of what's considered "residential" to the Williamsburg expats of Bushwick's artist community are warehouses and factories renovated into loft spaces. But Bushwick isn't completely color-starved. Commissioned murals like the one on the corner of Central and Myrtle break up the monotony of uneven sidewalks and just-functional architecture. Get up onto any rooftop to appreciate a skyline that can move even the most jaded local. Bits of nature like Maria Hernandez Park also provide residents with some much-needed green (no, not that kind). A fair warning for any over-nighters: come armed with clean sheets. The city-wide resurgence of bedbugs has hit Bushwick particularly hard.

As a residential neighborhood, Bushwick is fully functional. Youngsters out past bedtime might not be able to get their midnight skinny latte (sorry, yuppies: no Starbucks for miles), but the main thoroughfares—Wilson Avenue, Central Avenue, Knickerbocker Avenue, and Broadway—provide every service imaginable. Ninety-nine cent stores compete with music stores, pawn shops, and laundromats. ("The best" of any of these businesses is usually determined by how long it takes to walk there.) Sick of those con men across the river who charge $80 for a trim, not including tip? In Bushwick, a cut from a unisex hair salon for around $10 to $20 is never more than three steps away.

Bushwick shows its family roots in the mind-boggling number of churches of all different denominations scattered throughout the neighborhood, many merely humble storefronts among the milieu of bodegas and take-out Chinese. For a historic parish, visit **St. Barbara's** for beautiful, if out-of-place, architecture and a thriving religious community. But residents, beware the bells: they have a tendency to interrupt a hungover Sunday morning sleep.

Folks who want to bring a piece of their faith home can visit any number of the botanicas selling articulos religosos around the area, such as **Botanica Sauteria and Magic**, stocked with candles, incense, and saint-themed aerosol sprays (really!). Besides, no Bushwick home is complete without at least one glass candle-holder depicting a Catholic saint.

Nobody will ever go hungry in Bushwick—the neighborhood is cluttered with chain stores of Kennedy Fried Chicken and other knock-offs of this knock-off franchise (notice the acronym?). Cheap gems like **Tortilleria Mexicana Los Hermanos** provide good food for the thrifty, but higher-class sit-down fare is limited to stand-out **Northeast Kingdom**.

Bushwick may not rival Chelsea in gallery quantity, but shows what the mainstream won't, and serves it up with substantially less stick-up-the-ass attitude. **Norte Maar** showcases performance art and other media, while nomadic acts like **Parlour** exhibit in living rooms across the neighborhood. Caffeine junkies can get their fix at the **Wyckoff Starr**.

Map 4 • **Bushwick**

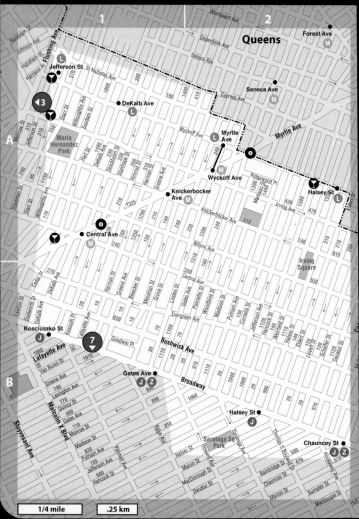

Bushwick's venues are never pretentious but prepare to come out smelling like Pabst and weed smoke. Drop by the **Bushwick Starr** to see Manhattan-caliber performance art. Bring ear plugs for the lo-fi squeals of **Silent Barn**; give those ears a rest at an acoustic set in **Northeast Kingdom's** cozy basement lounge.

Bars

- **The Bushwick Starr** • 207 Starr St [Irving Ave]
  Get up close with the latest art & performance acts in the area.
- **Gotham City Lounge** •
  1293 Myrtle Ave [Central Ave]
  917-710-7123
  Heaven for grown-up geeks: booze & comic memorabilia.
- **Northeast Kingdom** •
  18 Wyckoff Ave [Troutman St]
  718-386-3864
  Perfectly executed downstairs bar with live music some nights.
- **Silent Barn** • 9-15 Wyckoff Ave [Hancock St]
  Raucous DIY music venue.

Billiards

- **Image Bar Lounge & Billiards** •
  5419 Myrtle Ave [Woodbine St]
  718-366-0091
  Drink specials & pool specials.
- **Ridgewood Billiards** •
  1379 Myrtle Ave [Himrod St]
  718-573-6488
  Standard billiard hall.

Map 4 • **Bushwick**

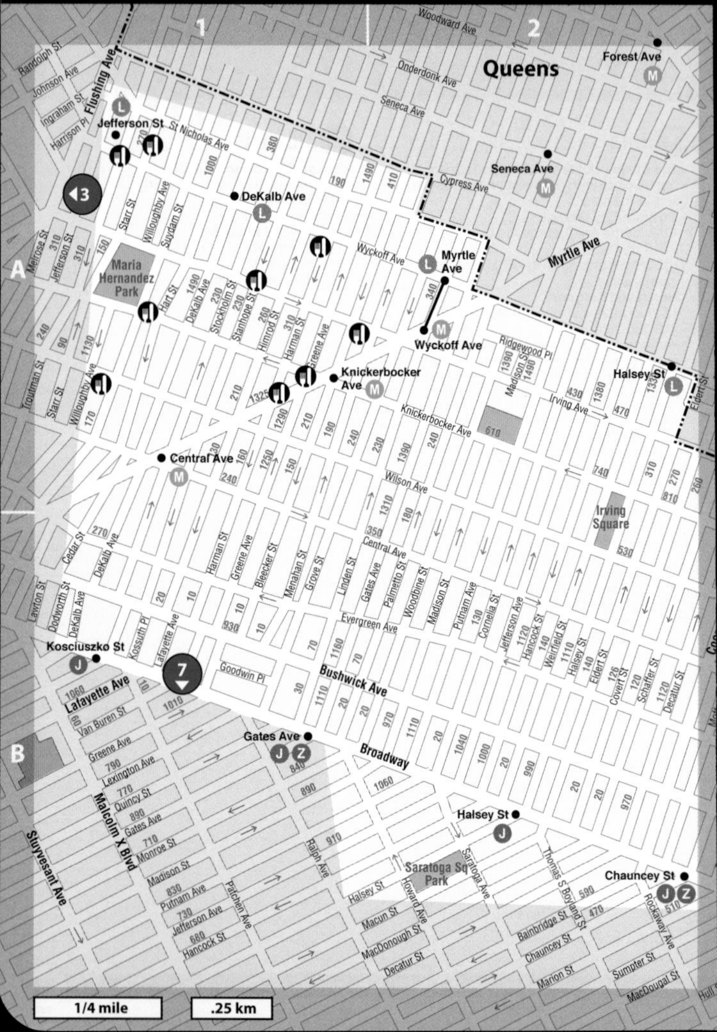

N

1   Woodward Ave   2

Randolph St
Johnson Ave
Ingraham St
Harrison Pl
Flushing Ave

Onderdonk Ave

Seneca Ave

Queens

Forest Ave
Ⓜ

L Jefferson St
St Nicholas Ave

380
1000

190

1490
410

Seneca Ave
Ⓜ

◀3

Starr St
Willoughby Ave
Suydam St
150
310
310

DeKalb Ave
L

Cypress Ave

Myrtle Ave

Maria
Hernandez
Park

Wyckoff Ave

Myrtle
Ave
L

A

Melrose St
Jefferson St
240
90
1130

DeKalb Ave
Stockholm St
Stanhope St
1490
210

Hart St
Harman St
310

Greene Ave

Wyckoff Ave
Ⓜ

240

Myrtle Ave
Ridgewood Pl

1390
1440
Irving Ave

430
1360
Halsey St
L

Fulton St

Troutman St
Willoughby Ave
Starr St
170

210

1320
1290
210

Knickerbocker
Ave
Ⓜ

Knickerbocker Ave
190
240
230
1390
240

610

Madison St

470
260
270

Central Ave
Ⓜ
240

Wilson Ave
1310
160

350
190

310
240

Cedar St
DeKalb St
270
20

Harman Ave
Greene Ave
Bleecker St
Menahan St
Grove St
150

Central Ave

Irving
Square

Lawton St
Dodworth St
DeKalb Ave

Linden St
Palmetto St
Woodbine St
Madison St
Putnam Ave
Cornelia St
Jefferson Ave
Hancock St
Weirfield St
Halsey St
Eldert St
Covert St

530

Evergreen Ave
930
10
70

130
1110
140
1120
126
1120

Kosciuszko St
J

Lafayette Pl
Lafayette Ave
1060

Van Buren St

Greene Ave
790
Lexington Ave
770
Quincy St
890
Gates Ave
719
Monroe St

Goodwin Pl

Bushwick Ave
30
1110
20

20
970
1110

7

1010

Gates Ave
J Z
BAR.

Broadway
890

20
1840
1000
20

1060

B

Malcolm X Blvd

Stuyvesant Ave

Madison St
830
Putnam Ave
730
Jefferson Ave
680
Hancock St

Ralph Ave

Halsey St
910

Halsey St
J

20
970

Halsey St
Howard Ave

Saratoga
Park

Sophia Ave

Macon St

MacDonough St

Decatur St

Thomas S Boyland St

Chauncey St
J Z

590
470

Bainbridge St
Chauncey St

Marion St

Sumpter St

Rockaway Ave

MacDougal St

1/4 mile   .25 km

Map 4

Except for **Northeast Kingdom**, people looking for Michelin stars should keep it to that other borough. Fortunately, their cuisine is so inventive and so good that we're not really complaining (yet). Chinese take-out and Latin American cuisine dominate the scene; check out **La Isla Cuchifritos** for Puerto Rican soul food 24/7 or for tasty pies try **Verde Coal Oven Pizza**.

🍴Restaurants

- **Alizee Coffee Shop** •
146 Wilson Ave [Suydam St]
347-432-9319 • $
Fresh eggs, fried bacon, done the right way:
on a buttered roll.
- **Chimu Express** • 180 Irving Ave [Stanhope St]
718-443-0787 • $
Generous portions of Peruvian food from
rotisserie chicken to skirt steak.
- **El Charro Bakery** •
1427 Myrtle Ave [Knickerbocker Ave]
718-452-1401 • $
Busy on the weekends, but some of the best
sweetbread around.
- **Fortunata's II** •
305 Knickerbocker Ave [Hart St]
718-497-8101 • $
Pizza, ice cream, and one killer meatball sub.
- **La Isla Cuchifritos** •
1439 Myrtle Ave [Knickerbocker Ave]
718-417-0668 • $
Fried dough stuffed with meat—and more
meat. Mmmm.
- **Mr. BBQ Churrascaria** •
178 Wyckoff Ave [Greene Ave]
718-628-0866 • $
Carnivores, rejoice.
- **Northeast Kingdom** •
18 Wyckoff Ave [Troutman St]
718-386-3864 • $$
Cozy, hip ski lodge-style eatery in gritty nabe.
- **Tortilleria Los Hermanos** •
271 Starr St [Wyckoff Ave]
718-456-3422 • $
Fantastic tacos tucked away in a tortilla
factory.
- **Verde Coal Oven Pizza** •
254 Irving Ave [Bleecker St]
718-381-8800 • $$
Hidden oven discovered behind a wall! Good
neighborhood spot.

Bagels, Coffee, & Shopping

Map 4

Associated is everyone's grocery staple but check out **Angel's Fruit Market** across the street for the freshest produce and a wide variety of Mexican sodas. **Rincon Musical** provides low-price instruments and a wide variety of cuatro guitars. Hungry locals can sate their sweet tooth on the cheap at **El Charro** and **Gaby's Bakery**.

 Coffee

- **Dunkin' Donuts** •
1556 Broadway [Weirfield St]
718-574-4539
Decent coffee served in gigantic Styrofoam cups.
- **Dunkin' Donuts** •
1443 Myrtle Ave [Knickerbocker Ave]
718-418-0733
Decent coffee served in gigantic Styrofoam cups.
- **Dunkin' Donuts** •
137 Wyckoff Ave [DeKalb Ave]
718-418-2483
Decent coffee served in gigantic Styrofoam cups.
- **Wyckoff Starr** • 30 Wyckoff Ave [Starr St]
718-484-9766
Nice little coffee shop in desolate surroundings.

 Shopping

- **Angel's Fruit Market** •
272 Knickerbocker Ave [Willoughby Ave]
718-366-7664
Freshest produce and an assortment of specialty items.
- **Associated Supermarket** •
1291 Broadway [Lexington Ave]
718-443-7913
Join the Association.
- **Botanica Sauteria and Magic** •
1485 Myrtle Ave [Menahan St]
718-366-6939
Articulos religiosos & other label-in-Spanish oils.
- **Bravo's Bike Repair** •
187 Wilson Ave [Dekalb Ave]
718-602-5150
Affordable repair, knowledgeable staff. Helps if usted habla espanol.
- **C-Town** • 346 Central Ave [Menahan St]
718-452-4313
No-frills market way cheaper than your local bodega.
- **C-Town** • 72 Wyckoff Ave [Suydam St]
718-417-8010
No-frills market way cheaper than your local bodega.

- **C-Town** • 1781 Broadway [Pilling St]
718-453-3232
No-frills market way cheaper than your local bodega.
- **Food Bazaar Supermarket** •
1759 Ridgewood Pl [Madison St]
718-381-8338
A huge selection of fresh produce, aisles of canned goods, and a large selection of frozen foods.
- **Green Village** • 276 Starr St [St Nicholas Ave]
718-599-4017
Piles of resale items for you to spend the day rummaging through.
- **Kenco Retail Shops** •
1451 Myrtle Ave [Bleecker St]
718-456-8705
Absolutely everything.
- **Key Food** • 1533 Broadway [Hancock St]
718-453-7000
No-frills market way cheaper than your local bodega.
- **My Dream Party** •
203 Wilson Ave [Stanhope St]
718-443-3275
Need wedding invites—and after the wedding, kid's birthday plates? Voilà.
- **Rincon Musical** •
398 Knickerbocker Ave [Himrod St]
718-574-0621
Come get your cuatro guitar and bachata greatest hits CD here.
- **Velo Brooklyn Bushwick Bike Shop** •
1342 Dekalb Ave [Central Ave]
347-405-7966
Fair prices and no attitude? No, you're not dreaming.

Map 3 • Brooklyn Heights/DUMBO/Downtown

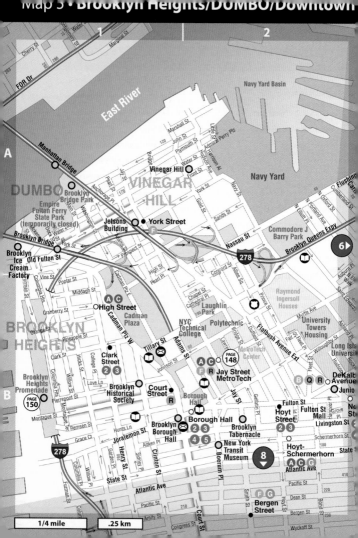

Three 'nabes for the price of one here; or, in the case of The Heights or DUMBO, two 'nabes for the price of four. Yes, Brooklyn Heights really is that expensive, but there's a reason—it's one of the most sublimely beautiful neighborhoods in all of New York, as it features jaw-dropping city views along its **Promenade**, two friendly retail strips on Montague and Henry Streets, views of the iconic **Brooklyn Bridge**, and some of the city's oldest and most beautiful brownstones and clapboard homes, especially around the "fruit street" area of Orange, Cranberry, and Pineapple, but even heading all the way south along Henry and Hicks Streets until the neighborhood ends at busy Atlantic Avenue.

By the time one hits Court Street heading east from Brooklyn Heights, however, you can chuck the sublime right out the window. Downtown Brooklyn is the borough's central nervous system, and features several courthouses, **Brooklyn's Borough Hall**, Metrotech Center (a small area which encompasses the **New York City College of Technology**, a large Marriott hotel, **Polytechnic Institute of New York University**, and, possibly most importantly, a **TKTS Booth**), Brooklyn Law School, the **Fulton Street Mall**, which features some of the highest commercial rents in all of NYC and is jam-packed with lunchtime shoppers, and, finally, a warren of subways that can take you to any other point in New York City, seemingly within minutes. If all this sounds like it would be hard to find some peace and quiet here, you'd be right. As Borough President Marty Markowitz would say, "fuggedaboutit."

The third neighborhood in this trilogy, DUMBO, easily distances itself from both The Heights and Downtown by being a warehouse-turned-artists' studios-turned-expensive-condo community. Like Brooklyn Heights, DUMBO (Down Under the Manhattan Bridge Overpass for you newbies) features killer views of downtown Manhattan from both its state park (**Empire-Fulton Ferry**, currently under renovation) and city park (**Brooklyn Bridge Park**), and its housing—converted lofts, many with exquisite city views—is too expensive for anyone who is reading (or writing!) this book. Unlike this area's other two 'nabes, however, retail in DUMBO, while growing, is still on the thin side, and many shops close fairly early (for New York) at night. As DUMBO truly only has one subway stop (the York Street F), it can get a little desolate, especially late at night. And while this all sounds like it is a quiet, idyllic little neighborhood, there's only one problem with the quiet—the CONSTANT rumble of the B, D, Q, J, M, and Z trains overhead on the **Manhattan Bridge**. Perhaps DUMBO's residents are able to block this out after a while, but to us, it should be an automatic 10% housing discount (yeah right).

For true peace and quiet, you'd have to head east about five blocks from DUMBO to check out one of our favorite of New York's micro-neighborhoods, **Vinegar Hill**. Literally only three blocks wide and two blocks long, Vinegar Hill is bordered by a power plant to the north, the **Navy Yard** to the East, the Farragut Houses to the South, and DUMBO to the West. Its cobblestone streets have vestiges of 19th-century Navy housing and an ex-retail strip along Hudson Street, although this could be changing as one of the city's newest great restaurants, **Vinegar Hill House**, is going gangbusters on this two-block strip; will the rest of the commercial-to-residential housing along Hudson get re-converted as well? Time will tell.

Map 3 • Brooklyn Heights/DUMBO/Downtown

1   **2**

Cherry St

FDR Dr

Water St

East River

Navy Yard Basin

Marshall St
John St
Plymouth St
Water St
Front St
York St

Admiral Perry Plz
Little St
Hudson Ave

Jay St
Bridge St
Pearl St

Anchorage Pl

Gold St
Navy St

Sands St

Navy Yard

**VINEGAR
HILL**

DUMBO

Brooklyn
Bridge Park

Empire
Fulton Ferry
State Park
(temporarily c)

Washington St

Water St
York St

Prospect St

High St

Pearl Pl

York Street
F

Nassau St

Concord St

Cumberland St

N Oxford St

N Portland Ave

N Elliott Pl

Flushing Ave

**Commodore J
Barry Park**

6

Old Fulton St

Furman St

Columbia St

Vine St

Poplar St

Middagh St

Cranberry St

Orange St

Pineapple St

Clark St

Cadman Plz W

Cadman Plz E

Middagh St

**BROOKLYN
HEIGHTS**

Cadman
Plaza

High Street

278

Chapel Pl
Cathedral Pl

Laughlin
Park

NYC
Technical
College

Polytechnic

Prince St

Bridge St

Jay St

Flatbush Avenue Ext

Myrtle Ave

**Raymond
Ingersoll
Houses**

Willoughby St

**University
Towers
Housing**

Auburn Pl

St Edwards St

Ashland Pl

Rockwell Pl

Fair St

**Long Is
Univers**

Tillary St

Adams St

Johnson St

MetroTech
Center

PAGE
148

**A C
F R**
**Jay Street
MetroTech**

B Q R

**Long Is
Univers**

**DeKalb
Avenue**

N

**Clark
Street**
2 3

College Pl

Henry St

Hicks St

Monroe Pl

Clinton St

Love Ln

**BROOKLYN
HEIGHTS
PAGE
150**

Pierrepont St

Montague St

Remsen St

Grace Ct

Joralemon St

Aitken Pl

**Court
Street**
R

Boerum Pl

**Borough
Hall**

Borough Hall
2 3
4 5

Fulton St

**Hoyt
Street**
2 3

Livingston St

Schermerhorn St

**Hoyt-
Schermerhorn**
A C G
Atlantic Ave

State

Hunts La

Garden Pl

Sidney Pl

Willow Pl

Columbia Pl

State St

Atlantic Ave

Pacific St

Clinton St

Court St

Smith St

Hoyt St

278

8

F G

**Bergen
Street**

Dean St

Bergen St

Wyckoff St

Bond St

Pacific St

Congress St

Amity St

1/4 mile   .25 km

By 8 pm, teeming Downtown Brooklyn is a ghost town; you'll either need to head north to DUMBO or west to The Heights to wet your whistle. Two DUMBO options are bustling **Water Street Bar** and newly relocated **Galapagos Art Space**, both of which you can hit after a performance at brilliant **St. Ann's Warehouse**. In The Heights, **Henry Street Ale House** is a good complement to catching a flick at cozy **Heights Cinemas**.

Bars

- **68 Jay Street Bar** • 68 Jay St [Front St]
  718-260-8207
  Arty local bar.
- **Eamonn's** • 174 Montague St [Clinton St]
  718-596-4969
  Standard Irish-American pub.
- **Galapagos Art Space** • 16 Main St [Water St]
  718-222-8500
  Hip, arty entertainment emporium. Building is
  LEED certified.
- **Henry Street Ale House** •
  62 Henry St [Cranberry St]
  718-522-4801
  Cozy, dark space with good selections on tap.
- **Jack the Horse Tavern** •
  66 Hicks St [Cranberry St]
  718-852-5084
  Outstanding upscale pub/New American
  cuisine, great feel.
- **O'Keefe's** • 62 Court St [Livingston St]
  718-855-8751
  Sports bar (large Mets following). Surprisingly
  decent food.
- **reBar** • 147 Front St [Pearl St]
  718-797-2322
  Belgian beer hub upstairs from Coffee Box.
- **Speak Low** • 81 Washington St [York St]
  718-222-1569
  Asian-themed basement bar.
- **St Ann's Warehouse** • 38 Water St [Dock St]
  718-254-8779
  Be careful not to cut yourself on the edginess.
- **Water Street Bar** • 66 Water St [Main St]
  718-625-9352
  Roomy Irish pub.

Movie Theaters

- **Pavilion Brooklyn Heights** •
  70 Henry St [Orange St]
  718-596-7070
  Intimate, classy, and just about perfect.
- **Regal Court Street Stadium 12** •
  108 Court St [State St]
  718-246-8170
  Audience participation-friendly megaplex.
- **reRun Gastropub Theater** •
  147 Front St [Jay St]
  718-797-2322
  Small cinema inside reBar serving up booze
  and indie films.

Theaters/Performing Arts

- **Bargemusic** •
  Fulton Ferry Landing [Old Fulton St]
  718-624-2083
  Ah, classical music on the East River.
- **Galapagos Art Space** • 16 Main St [Water St]
  718-222-8500
  Hip, arty entertainment emporium. Building is
  LEED certified.
- **St Ann's Warehouse** • 38 Water St [Dock St]
  718-254-8779
  Be careful not to cut yourself on the edginess.

Map 3 • Brooklyn Heights/DUMBO/Downtown

East River

Navy Yard Basin

FDR Dr

Cherry St
Water St

Marshall St

A

DUMBO
Brooklyn
Bridge Park

Empire
Fulton Ferry
State Park
(temporarily closed)

Plymouth St

Navy Yard

VINEGAR
HILL

Navy St

Admiral Perry Plz

Water St
Front St

Harrison Al

York St

Gold St

Sands St

● York Street

Commodore J
Barry Park

Brooklyn Queens Expy

6 ▶

Anchorage Pl

Jay St

Bridge St

Pearl St

Pearl St

Old Fulton St

Vine St
Poplar St

Front St

Water St

York St

Furman St

Columbia Hts

Nassau St

Concord St

Chapel St

High St

Pearl St

St Edwards St

I-278

Raymond
Ingersoll
Houses

Myrtle Ave

University
Towers
Housing

Auburn Pl

North Portland Ave

North Oxford St

North Elliott Pl

Cumberland St

Carlton Ave

Adelphi St

Clermont Ave

Vanderbilt Ave

Ashland Pl

Fort Greene Pl

Flushing Ave

Long Is
Univers

Middagh St

Cranberry St

High Street
Cadman
Plaza

Laughlin
Park

NYC
Technical
College

Polytechnic

MetroTech
Center

PAGE
148

Flatbush Avenue Ext

Clark St

Clark Street
2 3

Pineapple St

Orange St

Pineapple St

Hicks St

Henry St

Clinton St

Willow St

BROOKLYN
HEIGHTS

Johnson St

A C
F R Jay Street
MetroTech

Fair St

Willoughby St

DeKalb
Avenu

B Q R

Brooklyn
Heights
Promenade

PAGE
150

Pierrepont St

Montague St

Love Ln

Montague Ter

Court
Street
R

Borough
Hall

● Borough Hall

Duffield St

Gold St

Bridge St

Lawrence St

Fulton
Street

Hoyt
Street
2 3

Hanover Pl

Livingston St

Bond St

Schermerhorn St

Remsen St

2

Joralemon St

Hunts Ln

Grace Ct

Aitken Pl

2 3
4 5

Boerum Pl

Hoyt-
Schermerhorn
A C G

State

Smith St

Bond St

I-278

Henry St

Sidney Pl

Clinton St

State St

Atlantic Ave

Pacific St

Dean St

8 ▼

Atlantic Ave

Pacific St

Bergen St

F G

Bergen
Street

Wyckoff St

Furman St

Columbia Pl

Willow Pl

Congress St

Amity St

Court St

Bergen St

1/4 mile   .25 km

Our favorite places here are mostly unfortunately in the "special occasion" category due to price—for instance, The Heights' cozy gastropub **Jack the Horse**, game-oriented old-school **Henry's End**, and superb newcomer **Vinegar Hill House**. Otherwise, wait in line for great pizza at **Grimaldi's**, grab fast food on **Fulton Street Mall**, or hit classic **Junior's** for hangover food.

🍴 Restaurants

- **Bubby's** • 1 Main St [Plymouth St]
  718-222-0666 • $$
  It's all about the pie.
- **DUMBO General Store** •
  111 Front St [Adams St]
  718-855-5288 • $$
  Food and drink for artists. And condo dwellers.
- **Fascati Pizzeria** • 80 Henry St [Orange St]
  718-237-1278 • $
  Excellent slice pizza.
- **Five Front** • 5 Front St [Old Fulton St]
  718-625-5559 • $$
  Tasty newcomer with a beautiful garden.
- **Five Guys** • 138 Montague St [Henry St]
  718-797-9380 • $
  Burger joint with tasty fries and free peanuts while you wait.
- **Grimaldi's** • 19 Old Fulton St [Doughty St]
  718-858-4300 • $
  Excellent, though not the best, NY pizza.
- **Hale & Hearty Soup** • 32 Court St [Remsen St]
  718-596-5600 • $$
  Super soups.
- **Heights Café** • 84 Montague St [Hicks St]
  718-625-5555 • $$$
  Decent dining near the Promenade.
- **Henry's End** • 44 Henry St [Middagh St]
  718-834-1776 • $$$
  Inventive, game-oriented menu.
- **Iron Chef House** • 92 Clark St [Monroe Pl]
  718-858-8517 • $$
  Dependable sushi and cozy atmosphere.
- **Jack the Horse Tavern** •
  66 Hicks St [Cranberry St]
  718-852-5084 • $$$$
  Outsanding upscale pub/New American cuisine, great feel.
- **Junior's Restaurant** •
  386 Flatbush Avenue Ext [St Johns Pl]
  718-852-5257 • $
  American with huge portions. Cheesecake.
- **Lantern Thai** • 101 Montague St [Hicks St]
  718-237-2594 • $$
  Mediocre Thai. The Montague curse.
- **Miso** • 40 Main St [Front St]
  718-858-8388 • $$$
  Japanese fusion cuisine.
- **Morton's the Steakhouse** •
  399 Adams St [Willoughby St]
  718-596-2700 • $$$$
  In case Luger's is booked…
- **Noodle Pudding** • 38 Henry St [Middagh St]
  718-625-3737 • $$
  Northern Italian fare.
- **Park Plaza Restaurant** •
  220 Cadman Plaza W [Clark St]
  718-596-5900 • $
  NFT-approved neighborhood diner.
- **Pete's Downtown** • 2 Water St [Old Fulton St]
  718-858-3510 • $$
  Italian food and a view.
- **Queen Ristorante** • 84 Court St [Livingston St]
  718-596-5954 • $$$$
  Good white-tablecloth, bowtied-waiter Italian joint
- **Rice** • 81 Washington St [York St]
  718-222-9880 • $$
  Tasty Asian for less.
- **River Café** • 1 Water St [Old Fulton St]
  718-522-5200 • $$$$$
  Great view, but overrated.
- **Siggy's Good Food** • 76 Henry St [Orange St]
  718-237-3199 • $$
  Organic café.
- **Superfine** • 126 Front St [Pearl St]
  718-243-9005 • $$
  Mediterranean-inspired menu, bi-level bar, local art and music. NFT pick.
- **Sushi Gallery** • 71 Clark St [Henry St]
  718-222-0308 • $$
  Sushi Express, reasonable prices.
- **Teresa's** • 80 Montague St [Hicks St]
  718-797-3996 • $
  Polish-American comfort food. Come hungry.
- **Toro Restaurant** • 1 Front St [Old Fulton St]
  718-625-0300 • $$
  Spanish-Asian fusion.
- **Vinegar Hill House** •
  72 Hudson Ave [Water St]
  718-522-1018 • $$$
  Excellent wood-fired meats and veggies served in old-timey setting.

Map 5 • Brooklyn Heights/DUMBO/Downtown

Need something—anything—quick and cheap? The **Fulton Street Mall** area is your answer, with a **Macy's**, famous **Sid's Hardware**, and tons of other discount shops. In DUMBO, you can get great books at **powerHouse**, chocolate at **Jacques Torres**, and pastries at **Almondine**. In the Heights, browse excellent women's clothing at **Tango** on Montague.

 Bagels

- **Montague Street Bagels** •
  108 Montague St [Henry St]
  718-237-2512
  The only game in town.

Coffee

- **Almondine Bakery** • 85 Water St [Main St]
  718-797-5026
  Grab a cup and check out the view.
- **Iris Cafe** •
  20 Columbia Pl [Joralemon]
  718-722-7395
  Very tiny. Very Brooklyn.

Shopping

- **Almondine Bakery** • 85 Water St [Main St]
  718-797-5026
  Pastry smells waft to the street.
- **Barnes & Noble** • 106 Court St [State St]
  718-246-4996
  Chain bookstore.
- **Bridge Fresh Market** • 68 Jay St [Water St]
  718-488-1993
  Organic grocer.
- **Brooklyn Ice Cream Factory** •
  1 Water St [Old Fulton St]
  718-246-3963
  Get your ice cream fix on the Brooklyn waterfront.
- **Cranberry's** • 48 Henry St [Cranberry St]
  718-624-3500
  Oldtime deli/grocery of rationally priced comestibles.
- **Design Within Reach** •
  76 Montague St [Hicks St]
  718-643-1015
  Not really, but the stuff IS cool.
- **Egg Organics** • 68 Jay St [Water St]
  212-685-1490
  Clothes for mommy and baby.
- **Halcyon** • 57 Pearl St [Water St]
  718-260-9299
  Vinyl for DJ fanatics.
- **Half Pint** • 55 Washington St [Front St]
  718-875-4007
  Ditch Gap Kids!

- **Heights Prime Meats** • 59 Clark St [Henry St]
  718-237-0133
  Butcher.
- **Housing Works-Brooklyn Thrift Shop** •
  122 Montague St [Henry St]
  718-237-0521
  Our favorite thrift store.
- **Jacques Torres Chocolate** • 66 Water St [Main]
  718-875-9772
  The Platonic ideal of chocolate.
- **Lassen & Hennigs** • 114 Montague St [Henry]
  718-875-6272
  Specialty foods and deli.
- **Macy's** • 422 Fulton St [Hoyt St]
  718-875-7200
  Less crazed than Herald Square by about 1700%.
- **Modell's** • 360 Fulton St [Red Hook Ln]
  718-855-1921
  Sports. Get your Cyclones stuff here!
- **Montague Street Video** •
  138 Montague St [Clinton St]
  718-875-1715
  Good selection serving the Heights.
- **Peas & Pickles** • 55 Washington St [Front St]
  718-488-8336
  DUMBO's first grocery.
- **Pomme** • 81 Washington St [York St]
  718-855-0623
  Pricey imports for baby hipsters. Haircuts, too.
- **powerHouse Arena** • 37 Main St [Water St]
  718-666-3049
  One of our favorite gallery/bookstores.
- **Recycle-A-Bicycle** • 35 Pearl St [Plymouth St]
  718-858-2972
  Bikes to the ceiling.
- **Sid's Hardware & Homecenter** •
  345 Jay St [Myrtle Prom]
  718-596-1300
  It's famous, believe it or not.
- **Stewart/Stand** • 165 Front St [Jay St]
  718-407-4197
  Another very cool design shop for DUMBO.
- **Super Runners Shop** • 123 Court St [State St]
  718-858-8550
  Running sneaks and the like.
- **Tango** • 145 Montague St [Henry St]
  718-625-7518
  Jodie loves the clothes here. 'Nuff said.
- **TKTS Booth** • 1 Metrotech Center [Johnson St]
  Shhh…don't tell anyone there's one in Brooklyn!
- **West Elm** • 75 Front St [Main St]
  718-875-7757
  Cool home décor at reasonable prices.

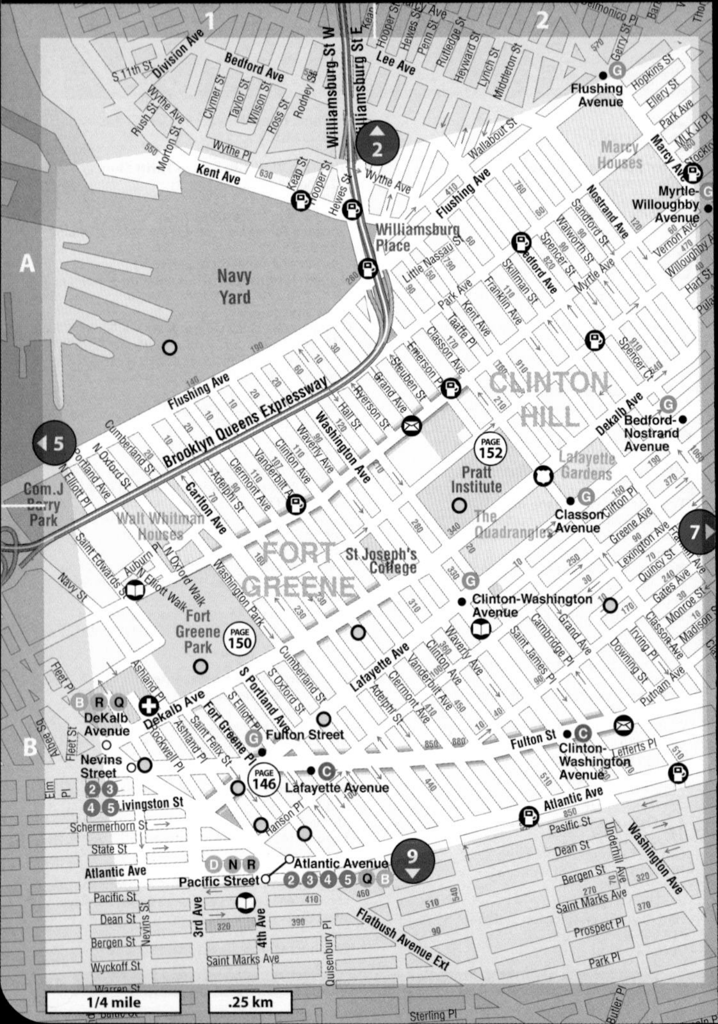

Map 6 • **Fort Greene / Clinton Hill**

N

1

2

S 11th St

Division Ave

Bedford Ave

S 10th St

Williamsburg St W

Williamsburg St E

Lee Ave

Hooper St

Hewes St

Penn St

Rutledge St

Heyward St

Lynch St

Middleton St

Bartlett St

Hopkins St

Ellery St

Park Ave

G Flushing Avenue

Taylor St

Wilson St

Ross St

Wythe Ave

Kent Ave

Rush St

Clymer St

Morton St

Wythe Pl

930

Hewes St

Keap St

Harrison Ave

Flushing Ave

Marcy Ave

MLK Jr Pl

Vernon Ave

Marcy Houses

2

Williamsburg Place

Willoughby Ave

Myrtle-Willoughby Avenue G

Wallabout St

Little Nassau St

Park Ave

Kent Ave

Franklin Ave

Skillman St

Spencer St

Sanford St

Nostrand Ave

Bedford Ave

Myrtle Ave

Willoughby Ave

Vernon Ave

G

Spencer Ct

A

Navy Yard

Flushing Ave

Clason Ave

Taaffe Pl

Emerson Pl

Steuben St

Brand Place

Ryerson St

Hall St

CLINTON HILL

Lafayette Gardens

DeKalb Ave

Bedford-Nostrand Avenue G

5

Brooklyn Queens Expressway

Washington Ave

Waverly Ave

Clinton Ave

Vanderbilt Ave

Adelphi St

Clermont Ave

Carlton Ave

N. Oxford St

N. Portland Ave

N. Elliott Pl

Com. J Barry Park

Navy St

Saint Edwards St

Walt Whitman Houses

Auburn Pl

Fort Greene Park

PAGE 150

Pratt Institute

PAGE 152

The Quadrangle

Classon Avenue G

Greene Ave

Clinton Ave

Lexington Ave

Quincy St

Gates Ave

7

FORT GREENE

St Joseph's College

Clinton-Washington Avenue G

Waverly Ave

Cambridge Pl

Grand Ave

Saint James Pl

Downing St

Monroe St

Madison St

Putnam Ave

Irving Pl

Gates Ave

Ashland Pl

Rockwell Pl

Fort Greene Pl

S Oxford St

S Portland Ave

Cumberland St

Carlton Ave

Adelphi St

Clermont Ave

Vanderbilt Ave

Lafayette Ave

B

B R Q DeKalb Avenue +

DeKalb Ave

Fulton Street G

Fulton St C Clinton-Washington Avenue

Fulton St

Clinton Ave

Waverly Ave

Cambridge Pl

Grand Ave

Lafferts Pl

Nevins Street

2 3

4 5 6 Livingston St

PAGE 146

Lafayette Avenue

Hanson Pl

Lafayette Ave

Atlantic Ave

Washington Ave

Schermerhorn St

State St

Atlantic Ave

D N R Pacific Street

Atlantic Avenue 9

2 3 4 5 Q

Pacific St

Dean St

Atlantic Ave

Saint Marks Ave

Pacific St

Dean St

Bergen St

Wyckoff St

Warren St

3rd Ave

4 Ave

Nevins St

Elm Pl

Fleet St

Elm Pl

Flatbush Avenue Ext

Quenbury Ave

Prospect Pl

Park Pl

Saint Marks Ave

Dean St

Bergen St

Saint Marks Ave

Dinberg Pl

Sterling Pl

1/4 mile   .25 km

Fort Greene is simply one of New York's perfect neighborhoods—the population is diverse, it's geographically close to Manhattan, it's got a stellar park, tons of restaurants, a farmer's market, a flea market, beautiful tree-and-brownstone-lined streets, historic buildings, subway access, a world-class performing arts complex—the list goes on.

Even Fort Greene's historic aspect is diverse, since its landmark buildings run the gamut from religious to cultural to economic to civic to military. What's more, many of these buildings now serve more than one purpose. To start with, check out the Underground Railroad murals at the **Lafayette Avenue Presbyterian Church**. The **Brooklyn Masonic Temple** not only houses the Masons but has an indie rock concert series that runs regularly. The **Brooklyn Academy of Music** (BAM) has two live performance spaces, movie theaters, a cafe, a bookstore, and regularly runs film festivals as well as its famous "Next Wave" festival of dance, opera, music, and theater. The **Williamsburg Savings Bank Building** is one of the tallest structures in Brooklyn and has now been converted to condos. The Brooklyn Navy Yard now houses businesses as well as Steiner Studios. And shoppers flock to hulking Atlantic Terminal Mall, which sits above a massive Long Island Railroad Station.

On weekends, Fort Greene Park is rollicking with a bustling farmer's market, playgrounds, cricket, soccer, park rangers, and local community groups (Fort Greene, for instance, has a peace and justice group, a historic association, a community council, a CSA, a bi-annual newspaper, an environmental group, a Food Co-Op planning commission, and its very own New York Times blog). Just a few blocks away, the **Brooklyn Flea** is a major shopping (and now eating!) destination, complete with tons of Etsy-type crafts vendors, a pupusa stand, and a bang-on portable wood-oven pizza stand.

But that's only half the story here, because Fort Greene's "sister" neighborhood, Clinton Hill, also has a lot going for it. Clinton Hill, for instance, hosts bucolic **St. Joseph's College** and famous **Pratt Institute**, where, on its grounds, you can see world-class sculpture and check out its famous Power Plant. Several historic churches also dot the Clinton Hill landscape, which is filled with beautiful brownstones as well as some massive single-family homes on Washington Street.

Clinton Hill is home to an African community that has set up a number of restaurants and shops in the neighborhood (chief among them being the restaurant and live music venue **Grand Dakar** as well as **Kush**, **Joloff**, and **Soule**), and it's also home to a whole row of artists' studios on Lexington Avenue, ending at Danny Simmons' **Corridor Gallery** on Grand and Lexington. The now-partially-dismantled **Broken Angel** building on the corner of Quincy and Downing was famously highlighted in Dave Chappelle's Block Party, film (Baby Mama) and TV (Rescue Me) shoots take place regularly; Clinton Hill has arrived, clearly, as even local coffee/food nexus **Choice Market** has had its BLT profiled by the Food Network.

The only downside to Clinton Hill is the serious crime which continues to happen in the neighborhood, from the mugging/skull-bashing of Pratt students to drug deals gone bad, and even a police shooting of an unarmed man in 2009. So: be wary. Edginess, which Clinton Hill has in abundance, comes with a price.

Map 6 • Fort Greene / Clinton Hill

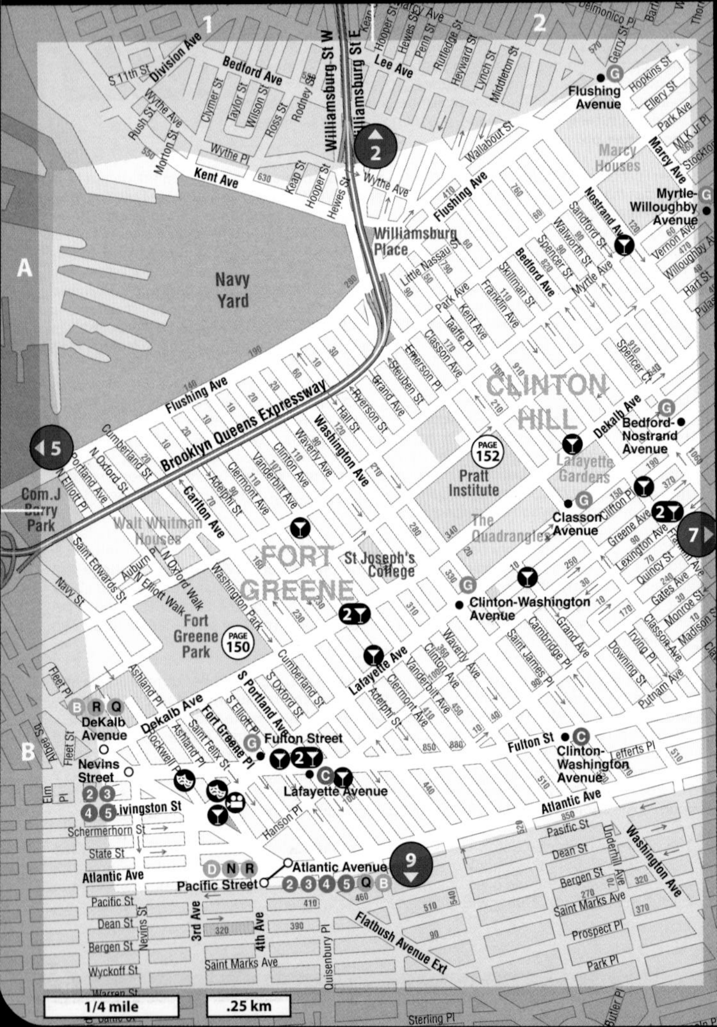

N

1
2

Delmonico Pl

S 11th St
Division Ave
Bedford Ave
Williamsburg St W
Williamsburg St E
Lee Ave
Hooper St
Hewes St
Penn St
Rutledge St
Heyward St
Lynch St
Middleton St
Hopkins St
Ellery Pl
M.K.A. Pl
Harman Pl

Wythe Ave
Taylor St
Wilson St
Ross St
Rodney St
Keap St

Flushing Avenue
G

Clymer St
Marcy Houses

Morton St
Wythe Pl
Kent Ave
Kent Ave
Kapp St
Hooper St
Hewes St
630

Nostrand Ave
Myrtle-Willoughby Avenue
G

Williamsburg Place
Wythe Ave
Little Nassau St
Park Ave
Kent Ave
Taffe Pl
Franklin Ave
Sandford St
Walworth St
Spencer St
Bedford Ave
Skillman St
Myrtle Ave
Vernon Ave
Willoughby Ave
Hart St

Navy Yard

Flushing Ave
Harrison Ave
Grand Ave
Steuben Pl
Classon Pl
Clinton Ave
Spencer St

CLINTON HILL

Dekalb Ave
Bedford-Nostrand Avenue
G

5
Com. J Barry Park

Brooklyn Queens Expressway
Cumberland Pl
N Oxford St
N Portland Ave
Carlton Ave
Washington Ave
Waverly Ave
Vanderbilt Ave
Clermont Ave

PAGE 152
Pratt Institute

Lafayette Gardens
The Quadrangles

Classon Avenue
G
Lexington Ave
2
7

Walt Whitman Houses
Auburn Pl
N Elliott Walk
Park Ave

FORT GREENE

St Joseph's College

Clinton-Washington Avenue
G

Greene Ave
Quincy St
Gates Ave

Navy St
St Edwards St

Fort Greene Park
PAGE 150

Cumberland St
S Oxford St
S Portland Ave
S Elliott Pl
Lafayette Ave
Adelphi St
Clermont Ave
Vanderbilt Ave
Clinton Ave
Waverly Ave
St James Pl
Cambridge Pl
Grand Ave
Downing St
Irving Pl
Putnam Ave
Monroe St
Madison St

Fleet Pl
Ashland Pl
R Q
DeKalb Avenue
B

Dekalb Ave
Fort Greene Pl
S Elliott Pl
Ashland Pl

Fulton Street
2
Fulton St
Clinton-Washington Avenue
G

Nevins Street
2 3 4 5
Livingston St
Lafayette Avenue
C

Schermerhorn St
State St
Hanson Pl

Atlantic Ave

Elm Pl
Nevins St
Atlantic Ave
D N R
Pacific Street

Atlantic Avenue
2 3 4 5 **Q B**
9

Pacific St
Dean St
Bergen St
Wyckoff St
Warren St

3rd Ave
4th Ave
Flatbush Avenue Ext
Ouenberburgh Pl

Saint Marks Ave
Prospect Pl
Park Pl

Sterling Pl

| 1/4 mile | .25 km |

The scene here has gotten some great new additions, including **Sweet Revenge** (great backyard) and **Brooklyn Public House** (great beer selection), to go along with stalwarts **Frank's, Alibi, Rope, Stonehome**, and **Sweet Revenge**. All are great before or after a movie at **BAM Rose Cinemas** or a performance at the **Masonic Hall**.

 Bars

- **The Alibi** • 242 Dekalb Ave [Vanderbilt Ave]
  718-783-8519
  Real bar neighborhood bar.
- **Amarachi Lounge** • 325 Franklin [Clifton Pl]
  646-641-4510
  DJs, dancing, drinks…fun time will be had by all.
- **BAMcafé** • 30 Lafayette Ave [Ashland Pl]
  718-623-7811
  Fine food, cocktails, and live music in a classy cavernous space.
- **Brooklyn Masonic Temple** •
  317 Clermont Ave [Lafayette Ave]
  718-638-1256
  Masons + Indie Rock = smiles all around.
- **Brooklyn Public House** •
  247 Dekalb Ave [Vanderbilt Ave]
  347-227-8976
  Lots of beers, with food, open 'till 2 am. Perfect.
- **Der Schwarze Kolner** •
  710 Fulton St [S Oxford St]
  347-841-4495
  German beer hall, w/ food. Ft. Greene now almost perfect.
- **Frank's Cocktail Lounge** •
  660 Fulton St [S Elliott Pl]
  718-625-9339
  When you need to get funky.
- **Grand Dakar** • 285 Grand Ave [Clifton Pl]
  718-398-9900
  Occasional live music; skip the jazz but check out the African sets.
- **One Last Shag** •
  348 Franklin Ave [Lexington Ave]
  718-398-2472
  Cocktails and kitschy setting. The Pratt kids love this place.
- **Project Parlor** • 742 Myrtle Ave [Sanford St]
  347-497-0550
  Cozy bar with surprisingly huge backyard in shabby environs.

- **Rope** • 415 Myrtle Ave [Clinton Ave]
  718-522-2899
  Unprepossessing locals bar.
- **Rustik** • 471 Dekalb Ave [Franklin Ave]
  347-406-9700
  Neighborhood tap draws cozy clientele.
- **Stonehome Wine Bar** •
  87 Lafayette Ave [S Portland Ave]
  718-624-9443
  Dark cave for serious oenophiles.
- **Sweet Revenge** •
  348 Franklin Ave [Lexington Ave]
  718-398-2472
  Great locals bar with patio, free grill, and Guinness on tap.

Movie Theaters

- **BAM Rose Cinemas** •
  30 Lafayette Ave [St Felix St]
  718-636-4100
  First-run films plus excellent classics and foreign selections.

Theaters/Performing Arts

- **Harvey Lichtenstein Theater** •
  651 Fulton St [Rockwell Pl]
  718-636-4100
  BAM-tastic! Except for the balcony seats.
- **Howard Gilman Opera House** •
  30 Lafayette Ave [St Felix St]
  718-636-4100
  Gorgeous setting for BAM's top works.

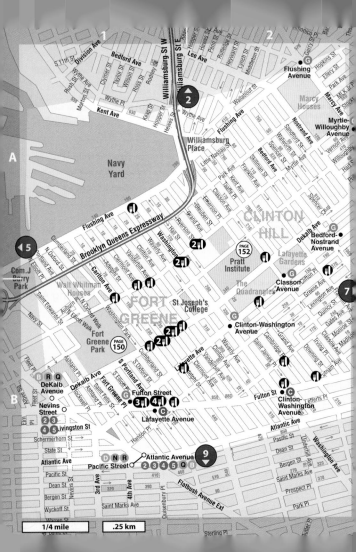

Restaurants

It's all here, folks: Italian (**Locanda** and **Scopello**), French (**Chez Lola**, **Chez Oskar**, **Cafe Lafayette**), BBQ (**Smoke Joint**), Japanese (**Yamashiro**), tapas (**Olea**), hip (**General Greene** and **No. 7**), African (**Kush**), Middle Eastern (**Black Iris**), burgers (**67 Burger**), and Mexican (**Castro**). Full yet?

🍴Restaurants

- **67 Burger** • 67 Lafayette Ave [S Elliott Pl]
  718-797-7150 • $
  Super-cool stop for a quick bite before your movie at BAM.
- **abistro** • 154 Carlton Ave [Myrtle Ave]
  718-855-9455 • $$
  Three words: Senegalese Fried Chicken.
- **Bati** • 747 Fulton St [S Portland Ave]
  718-797-9696 • $$
  Friendly (aren't they all?) Ft. Greene Ethiopian. Good pre-BAM option.
- **Black Iris** • 228 Dekalb Ave [Clermont Ave]
  718-852-9800 • $$
  Middle Eastern; good lamb, terrible chicken, excellent Zaatar bread.
- **Cafe Lafayette** • 99 S Portland Ave [Fulton St]
  718-624-1605 • $$
  French goodness near BAM; small, intimate.
- **Castro's Restaurant** • 511 Myrtle Ave [Grand]
  718-398-1459 • $$
  Burritos delivered con cervezas, if you like.
- **Chez Lola** • 387 Myrtle Ave [Clermont Ave]
  718-858-1484 • $$$
  French, inventive specials; a Ft. Greene favorite.
- **Chez Oskar** • 211 Dekalb Ave [Adelphi Ave]
  718-852-6250 • $$$
  French cuisine in a good neighborhood bistro.
- **Choice Market** • 318 Lafayette Ave [Grand]
  718-230-5234 • $
  Excellent sandwiches, baked goods, burgers, etc. served w/ maddening slowness.
- **Five Spot** • 495 Myrtle Ave [Ryerson St]
  718-852-0202 • $$$
  Hoppin' soul food joint w/ live entertainment.
- **The General Greene** •
  229 Dekalb Ave [Clerrmont Ave]
  718-222-1510 • $$
  Two words: candied bacon.
- **Habana Outpost** • 757 Fulton St [S Portland]
  718-858-9500 • $
  Grilled corn and free movies in a solar-powered restaurant.
- **Ici** • 246 Dekalb Ave [Vanderbilt Ave]
  718-789-2778 • $$$
  Beautiful new addition to FG restaurant scene, and worth the splurge.
- **Il Porto** • 37 Washington Ave [Flushing Ave]
  718-624-2965 • $$
  Cute Italian/pizzeria in front of the Navy Yard.

- **Kif** • 219 Dekalb Ave [Adelphi St]
  718-852-7273 • $$$
  Moroccan mash-up beloved by locals.
- **Kush** • 17 Putnam Ave [Grand Ave]
  718-230-3471 • $$
  West African café and restaurant; killer short ribs.
- **Locanda Vini & Olii** •
  129 Gates Ave [Cambridge Pl]
  718-622-9202 • $$$$$
  Rustic but marvelous neighborhood Italian. Marvelous décor.
- **Luz** • 177 Vanderbilt Ave [Myrtle Ave]
  718-246-4000 • $$$
  Yuppie interior with requisite brunch.
- **Madiba** • 195 Dekalb Ave [Carlton Ave]
  718-855-9190 • $$$
  South African—Bunny Chow, need we say more? Shebeen with live music.
- **Maggie Brown** • 455 Myrtle Ave [Washington]
  718-643-7001 • $$
  Food by the fireplace; great burgers.
- **Nice Pizza** • 340 Franklin Ave [Greene]
  718-222-5800 • $$
  French pizza. It's Nice as in the city in France.
- **Night of the Cookers** • 767 Fulton St [S Oxford]
  718-797-1197 • $$$
  Hip bistro with southern accents.
- **No. 7** • 7 Greene Ave [Fulton St]
  718-522-6370 • $$$
  Hip killer postmodern goodness in Ft. Greene.
- **Olea** • 171 Lafayette Ave [Adelphi St]
  718-643-7003 • $$
  Friendly, buzzing neighborhood tapas/ Mediterranean. Get the bronzino.
- **Scopello** • 63 Lafayette Ave [S Elliott Pl]
  718-852-1100 • $$
  Sicilian chic in stylish surroundings. Get the octopus.
- **The Smoke Joint** • 87 S Elliot Pl [Lafayette Ave]
  718-797-1011 • $$
  Spend the $16 and get the short rib. Thank us later.
- **Soule** • 920 Fulton St [Washington Ave]
  718-399-7200 • $$
  Everything from king crab to roti to curry goat to blackened salmon. Tons of sides.
- **Umi Nom** • 433 Dekalb Ave [Classon Ave]
  718-230-3933 • $$
  Filipino-heavy Asian fusion done right.
- **Yamashiro** • 466 Myrtle Ave [Washington Ave]
  718-230-3313 • $$$
  Good sushi; try the spicy titanic roll.

Map 6

Map 6 • Fort Greene / Clinton Hill

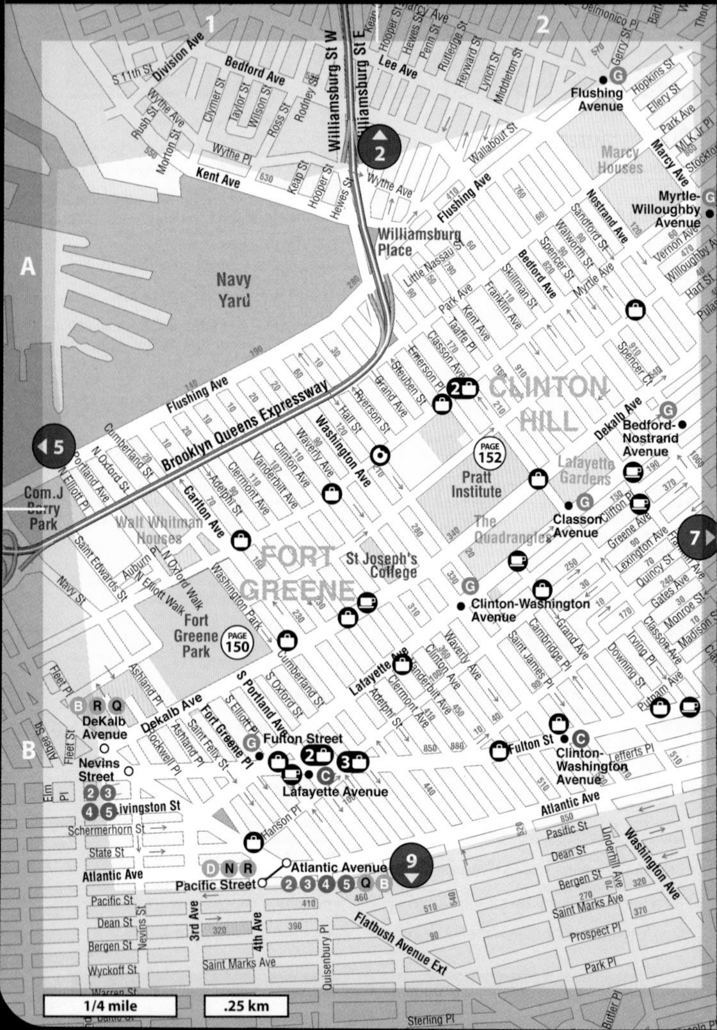

N

1

2

S 11th St
Division Ave
Bedford Ave
Wythe Ave
Clymer St
Taylor St
Wilson St
Ross St
Rodney St
Keap St
Hooper St
Hewes St
Penn St
Rutledge St
Heyward St
Williamsburg St W
Williamsburg St E
Lee Ave
Lynch St
Middleton St

Morton St
Rush St
Wythe Ave
Kent Ave
Wythe Pl
Kent Ave
Hooper St
Keap St
Wallabout St

Flushing Ave

Flushing Avenue

Navy Yard

Williamsburg Place

Little Nassau St
Park Ave
Kent Ave
Taaffe Pl
Franklin Ave
Skillman St
Steuben St
Emerson Pl
Grand Ave

CLINTON HILL

Flushing Ave
Brooklyn Queens Expressway

Washington Ave
Hall St
Ryerson St

Nostrand Ave
Sandford St
Walworth St
Spencer St
Marcy Ave
Myrtle Ave

Myrtle-Willoughby Avenue

Marcy Houses

Hopkins St
Ellery Pl
Park Ave
M.K. Jr Pl
Stockton St

Vernon Ave
Willoughby St
Hart St

Bedford Ave

Spencer St

5

Com. J Barry Park

Clinton Ave
Waverly Ave
Clermont Ave
Vanderbilt Ave
Adelphi St
Carlton Ave

N Portland Ave
N Oxford St
Cumberland St

Walt Whitman Houses

Saint Edwards St

Auburn Pl
N Elliott Pl
Elliott Walk

Fort Greene Park
PAGE 150

Cumberland St

S Portland Ave
S Oxford St
S Elliott Pl
Fort Greene Pl
S Elliott Pl
Carlton Ave

Lafayette Gardens

Lafayette Ave
Dekalb Ave
Willoughby Ave
Greene Ave
Lexington Ave
Quincy St
Gates Ave
Monroe St
Madison St

Classon Ave
Clinton-Washington Avenue

Bedford-Nostrand Avenue

Dekalb Ave

Pratt Institute
PAGE 152

The Quadrangles

St Joseph's College

FORT GREENE

Waverly Ave
Clifton Pl
Cambridge Pl
Grand Ave
St James Pl
Downing St
Irving Pl
Classon Ave

7

Dekalb Ave
R Q

Nevins Street
2 3

Fort Greene Pl
Ashland Pl
Rockwell Pl

Fulton Street
2 4
C
3

Lafayette Avenue

Fulton St
Clinton-Washington Avenue

Jefferts Pl

Atlantic Ave

Elm Pl
Fleet St
Fleet Pl

4 5 6 Livingston St
Schermerhorn St
State St

Atlantic Ave
Pacific St

Flatbush Ave
Hanson Pl

D N R
Atlantic Avenue
2 3 4 5 B Q
Pacific Street

9

3rd Ave
4th Ave

Pacific St
Dean St
Bergen St
Wyckoff St
Warren St

Nevins St
Quincunbury Pl
Flatbush Avenue Ext

Dean St
Bergen St
Saint Marks Ave
Prospect Pl
Park Pl

Washington Ave
Underhill Ave

Saint Marks Ave
Sterling Pl

1/4 mile   .25 km

Map 6

Hit either **Greene Grape Provisions** or **Choice Greene** for gourmet groceries to go along with that nice bottle of wine from **Olivino**, **Greene Grape**, **Gnarly Vines**, or **Thirst**. Pick up artist supplies at the **Pratt Store**, books at newly minted **Greenlight Books**, mid-century antiques at **Yu Interiors**, and freshly made donuts at **Dough**.

🥯 Bagels

- **Bergen Bagels on Myrtle** • 486 Myrtle Ave [Hall]
  718-789-9300
  Easily the best bagels in the 'hood.

☕ Coffee

- **Bedford Hill** • 343 Franklin Ave [Greene]
  718-636-7650
  Sweet little spot with good pastries.
- **Choice Market** • 318 Lafayette Ave [Grand Ave]
  718-230-5234
  Absolute epicenter of Clinton Hill.
- **Dough** • 305 Franklin Ave [Lafayette Ave]
  347-533-7544
  The perfect coffee partner: amazing doughnuts!
- **Marquet** • 680 Fulton St [S Portland Ave]
  718-596-2018
  French bakery w/ sit-down food, too.
- **Outpost** • 1014 Fulton St [Downing St]
  718-636-1260
  Important Fulton-area coffee shop.
- **Tillie's** • 248 Dekalb Ave [Vanderbilt Ave]
  718-783-6140
  Top local Ft. Greene coffee shop.

🛍️ Shopping

- **Bargains R Us** • 976 Fulton St [Grand Ave]
  Simultaneously one of the handiest and one of the sketchiest places to shop in Brooklyn.
- **Bespoke Bicycles** • 64 Lafayette Ave [S Elliott]
  718-643-6816
  Small bike shop, service, sales, repairs.
- **Blue Bass Vintage** • 431 Dekalb Ave [Classon]
  347-750-8935
  Thrift store with wide selection and rummage sale feel.
- **Brooklyn Flea** • 176 Lafayette Ave [Clermont]
  Already-famous flea market with rotating vendors & killer food.
- **Cake Man Raven Confectionary** •
  708 Fulton St [Hanson Pl]
  718-694-2253
  Get the red velvet cake!
- **Choice Greene** • 214 Greene Ave [Grand Ave]
  718-230-1219
  Cheese, game, produce. The gentrification of Fort Greene is complete.

- **Dope Jams** • 580 Myrtle Ave [Classon Ave]
  718-622-7977
  Soul, funk, hip-hop, but no dope.
- **Gnarly Vines** • 350 Myrtle Ave [Carlton Ave]
  718-797-3183
  Cool Myrtle wine merchant.
- **Green in BKLYN** • 432 Myrtle Ave [Clinton]
  718-855-4383
  One-stop shop to help you live an eco-friendly lifestyle.
- **The Greene Grape** • 765 Fulton St [S Oxford]
  718-797-9463
  Ft. Greene wine nexus.
- **Greene Grape Provisions** •
  753 Fulton St [S Portland Ave]
  718-233-2700
  Excellent gourmet meat-cheese-fish trifecta.
- **Greenlight Bookstore** •
  686 Fulton St [S Portland Ave]
  718-246-0200
  Ft. Greene's newest and immediately best bookstore.
- **Lit Fuse Cyclery** •
  409 Willoughby Ave [Walworth St]
  347-442-1672
  Hipster neighborhood fixer-up shop, repairs cheap, attitude great.
- **The Midtown Greenhouse Garden Center** •
  115 Flatbush Ave [Hanson Pl]
  718-636-0020
  Fully stocked with plants and gardening supplies.
- **Olivino** • 905 Fulton St [Clinton Ave]
  718-857-7952
  Micro-sized wine shop.
- **Pratt Institute Bookstore** •
  550 Myrtle Ave [Emerson Pl]
  718-789-1105
  Art supplies, books, ephemera.
- **Sister's Community Hardware** • 900 Fulton St
  [Washington Ave]
  718-399-7023
  Best music in a hardware store you'll ever hear.
- **Thirst Wine Merchants** •
  187 Dekalb Ave [Carlton Ave]
  718-596-7643
  Brilliant wine and alcohol selection, plus bar.
- **White Elephant Gallery** • 572 Myrtle Ave
  [Classon Ave]
  718-789-9423
  Mindset is key. It could be treasure.
- **Yu Interiors** • 15 Greene Ave [Cumberland St]
  718-237-5878
  Modern furniture, bags, and candles.

Map 7 · **Bedford-Stuyvesant**

Somewhere between the tough streets immortalized in hip-hop and the hot-topic chatter of gentrification and hipster-invasion lies the real Bedford-Stuyvesant, one of North Brooklyn's largest, most storied neighborhoods. The diversity of Bed-Stuy's blocks—from brownstone to project highrise, nail salon to wine bar—is slowly being matched by its population. Partly revitalized and yet still bearing the brunt of decades of economic struggle, today's Bed-Stuy offers an interesting mix of transition and history in one of the borough's most fascinating areas.

A mash-up of the nineteenth-century-founded Bedford and Stuyvesant Heights neighborhoods, Bed-Stuy also includes the communities of Ocean Hill and Weeksville, the latter of which was one of the first free African-American communities in the US, and includes the **Hunterfly Road Houses** (1840s-1880s). The greater Bed-Stuy demographic remains predominantly African-American, and is to this day a touchstone of hip-hop culture, though Jay-Z has long since upgraded to TriBeCa from his roots in the Marcy houses.

Bed-Stuy is home to hundreds of stunning brownstone and greystone homes, typically three- to four- stories high and ranging in condition from condemned to immaculately restored. Much of the Stuyvesant Heights end of the neighborhood is landmarked, including the anomalous and expansive **Akwaaba Mansion** (1860s), an Italianate home now converted into a high-end bed and breakfast. And did you know you could landmark a tree? The **Magnolia Grandiflora** in **Von King Park** is one of the city's rare examples. Visit in the springtime when its marzipan-like petals begin to explode. Don't overlook (as if you could) the amazing stature of two of the neighborhood's former armories on Marcus Garvey Boulevard at Jefferson, and on Bedford Avenue at Atlantic. They're now homeless shelters, but they look like medieval castles right in the heart of the 'hood.

Though not a nightlife destination (depending on your idea of nightlife), Bed-Stuy has cultivated several fantastic locals' spots, from the unusual like Larry's **Liquid Love** to old-fashioned supper clubs like **Brown Sugar** and **Sugar Hill**. And while the new shining stars of Lewis Avenue's commercial strip—**Peaches**, **Saraghina**, and **Therapy Wine Bar** begin to draw people just that much farther out on the A train, the real local treasures are Caribbean spots like **A&A Doubles King** and **Ali Trinidad Roti**. Get there before the doubles—Trini chickpea curry pockets served in greasy mini roti pockets and wrapped in twisty wax paper—run out in the early afternoon.

Strolls around the neighborhood itself can be sometimes iffy—"block to block" is the usual term used to describe the neighborhood—but Bed-Stuy is most truly appreciated as a whole, taking in the gentrified new businesses alongside the RIP murals thrown up 'round the side of sketchy bodegas. Biking in the neighborhood is a great way to tour around, and major routes of the NYC bike system go northbound up Throop Avenue (towards Williamsburg) and southbound down Tompkins Avenue (past the park and along the growing fashion and coffee businesses on that avenue).

Though the skinny jeans set sticks to the Bushwick borderlands under the J/M/Z train (**Goodbye Blue Monday**), Bed-Stuy offers an array of supper/nightclubs (**Sugar Hill**, **Brown Sugar**) and cozy locals (**Liquid Love**). You'll find you need to be buzzed in to some of the bars around here—but you're free to leave whenever you're done with your Heineken.

 Bars

- **Bodega** • 1089 Broadway [Dodworth St]
  Small, sweaty music venue in—what else—a former bodega.
- **Brown Sugar** •
  433 Marcus Garvey Blvd [Macon St]
  718-919-4163
  Bar, grill, open mike, karaoke.
- **Goodbye Blue Monday** •
  1087 Broadway [Dodworth St]
  718-453-6343
  An antique shop and café with live music nightly.
- **The Jazz Spot** •
  375 Kosciuszko St [Marcus Garvey Blvd]
  718-453-7825
  Hot food and tasty jazz in a café atmosphere.
- **Liquid Love** • 1165 Bedford Ave [Putnam Ave]
  718-783-9129
  A sophisticated meeting place.
- **Sistas' Place** • 456 Nostrand Ave [Hancock St]
  718-398-1766
  Jazz, poetry, and open mic nights.
- **Therapy Wine Bar** •
  364 Lewis Ave [Halsey St]
  718-513-0686
  Casual, chill by-the-glass boîte.
- **Tip Top Bar & Grill** •
  432 Franklin Ave [Madison St]
  718-857-9744
  Good, cheap dive.

Map 7 • Bedford-Stuyvesant

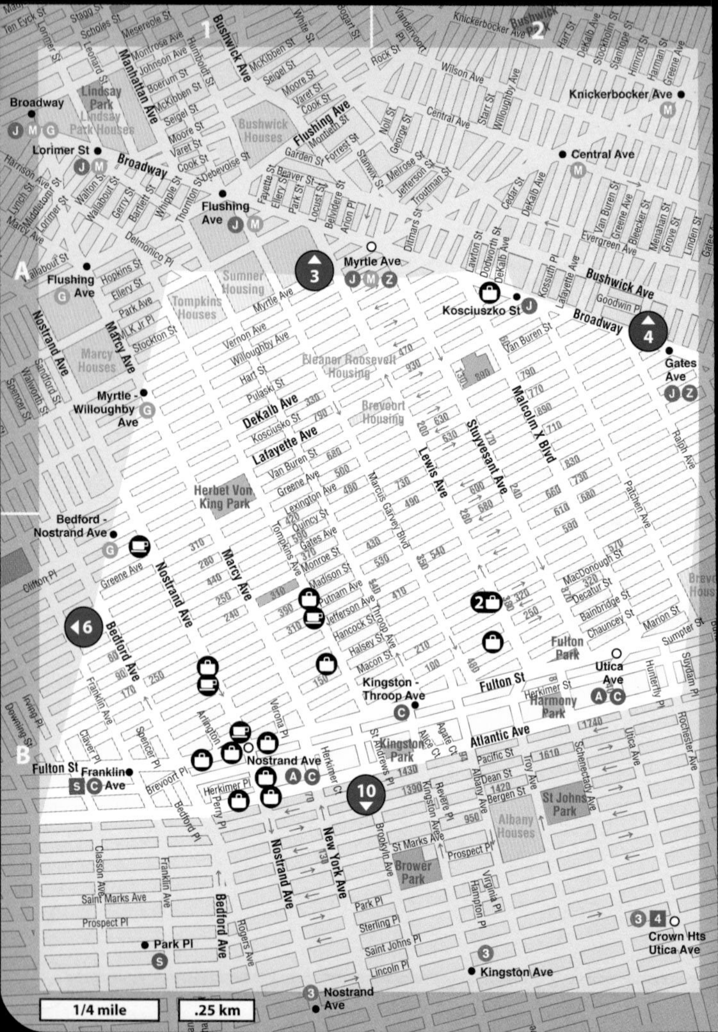

Ⓝ

1

2

Stagg St
Scholes St
Ten Eyck St
Meserole St
Montrose Ave
Johnson Ave
Manhattan Ave
Bushwick Ave
McKibbin St
Moore St
Siegel St
Seigel St
Boerum St
Varet St
Cook St
Knickerbocker Ave
Wilson Ave
Starr St
Willoughby Ave
Central Ave
Jefferson Ave
Troutman St
Suydam St
Stanhope St
Hart St
Linden St
Grove St

Rock St
White St
Bogart St

Lindsay Park
Lindsay Park Houses

Broadway
Ⓙ Ⓜ Ⓖ

Lorimer St
Ⓛ

Broadway
Ⓜ

Bushwick Houses

Flushing Ave
Ⓙ Ⓜ

Flushing Ave
Ⓐ

Hopkins St
Ellery St
Park Ave
Stockton St

Tompkins Houses

Sumner Housing

Myrtle Ave
3
Myrtle Ave
Ⓙ Ⓜ Ⓩ

Kosciuszko St
Ⓙ

Central Ave
Ⓜ

Knickerbocker Ave
• Knickerbocker Ave

• Central Ave

Bushwick Ave
Goodwin Pl
Broadway

Gates Ave
4
Ⓙ Ⓩ

Marcy Houses

Myrtle – Willoughby Ave
Ⓖ

Vernon Ave
Willoughby Ave
Pulaski St
DeKalb Ave
Kosciuszko St
Lafayette Ave
Van Buren St
Greene Ave
Lexington Ave
Quincy St
Gates Ave
Monroe St
Madison St
Putnam Ave
Jefferson Ave
Hancock St
Halsey St
Macon St
Fulton St

Eleanor Roosevelt Housing
Brevoort Housing

Malcolm X Blvd
Stuyvesant Ave
Lewis Ave
Marcus Garvey Blvd
Tompkins Ave
Throop Ave

MacDonough St
Decatur St
Bainbridge St
Chauncey St
Marion St

Herbert Von King Park

Bedford – Nostrand Ave
Ⓖ

Greene Ave
Nostrand Ave
Marcy Ave

6

Clifton Pl
Bedford Ave
Franklin Ave

Fulton St
Franklin Ave
Ⓢ Ⓒ

Nostrand Ave
Ⓐ Ⓒ

Kingston – Throop Ave
Ⓒ

Fulton Park

Utica Ave
Ⓐ Ⓒ

Harmony Park

Herkimer Pl
Herkimer St

Fulton St

Kingston Park

Atlantic Ave

Pacific St
Dean St
Bergen St

St Johns Park

Albany Houses

Brevoort Pl
Arlington Pl

10

Kingston Ave
Ⓒ

New York Ave
Brooklyn Ave
Kingston Ave
Albany Ave
Troy Ave

St Marks Ave
Prospect Pl

Brower Park

Park Pl

Saint Marks Ave
Prospect Pl

Park Pl
• Park Pl
Ⓢ

Sterling Pl
Saint Johns Pl
Lincoln Pl

Classon Ave
Bedford Ave

Nostrand Ave
Ⓢ

Kingston Ave
3
• Kingston Ave

3
Nostrand Ave

3 4
Crown Hts
• Utica Ave

Bed-Stuy's evolving culinary landscape now extends well beyond Crown Fried Chicken (though there are still a few dozen outlets to choose from in the neighborhood) to Neapolitan pizza (**Saraghina**), Trinidadian roti (**Ali's**), Southern (**Peaches HotHouse**), gourmet bar food (**Do Or Dine**), or grab some treats from "The King of Doubles" (**A&A Bake & Doubles**).

Restaurants

- **A&A Bake & Doubles •**
481 Nostrand Ave [Macon St]
718-230-0753 • $
A neighborhood favorite—no one leaves without their doubles.
- **Ali's Roti Shop •** 1267 Fulton St [Macon St]
718-783-0316 • $
West Indian roti.
- **Athom Café •** 1096 Broadway [Dodworth St]
646-881-5834 • $
French café offering sandwiches, salads, and pastries.
- **Common Grounds •**
376 Tompkins Ave [Putnam Ave]
718-484-4368 • $
Community-minded coffee house serving waffles, pastries, and panini.
- **Dabakh Malick Resaurant •**
1191 Fulton St [Bedford Ave]
718-399-1588 • $$
Senegalese steam table for the adventurous hungry.
- **Do or Dine •** 1108 Bedford Ave [Lexington]
718-684-2290 • $$$
Fancy/tasty/awesome drunk food that goes down easy.

- **Food 4 Thought Cafe •**
445 Marcus Garvey Blvd [MacDonough St]
718-443-4160 • $$
Rastafarian astrology cafe. With turkey burgers!
- **Peaches •** 393 Lewis Ave [MacDonough St]
718-942-4162 • $$$
Southern cooking from the guys who own Smoke Joint.
- **Peaches HotHouse •**
415 Tompkins Ave [Hancock St]
718-483-9111 • $$$
Get thee some Nashville-style Hot Chicken!
- **Riccardo's Pizza •**
528 Nostrand Ave [Fulton St]
718-638-6924 • $
Best pizza in the Stuy, period. Pops is no joke with a pie.
- **Saraghina •** 435 Halsey St [Lewis Ave]
718-574-0010 • $
Bed-Stuy gets on the wood-fired 'za bandwagon.
- **SugarHill Supper Club •**
609 Dekalb Ave [Nostrand Ave]
718-797-1727 • $$
Downtown soul(food).

Map 7 • Bedford-Stuyvesant

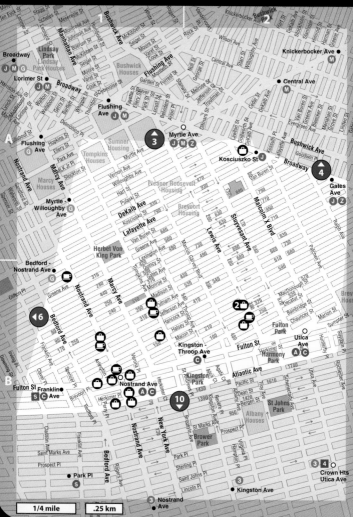

1/4 mile   .25 km

Even in a neighborhood full of anomalies, a thriving independent bookstore (**Brownstone Books**) is still a surprise, but the Lewis Avenue strip keeps on blooming (and even has a flower shop, **Creative Blossoms**). For basic goods, the Fulton Street retail strip has all you'll ever need.

Coffee

- **Aida's Cafe de Java** •
508 Nostrand Ave [Macon St]
718-230-0390
Cozy café on cozier Nostrand Ave.
- **Common Grounds** •
376 Tompkins Ave [Putnam Ave]
718-484-4368
Community-minded coffee house serving waffles, pastries, and panini.
- **Sistas' Place** • 456 Nostrand Ave [Hancock St]
718-398-1766
Best known for its coffee, tea, and juices, but the crowd stays for the jazz, poetry and open mike nights.
- **Tiny Cup** • 279 Nostrand Ave [Clifton Pl]
718-399-9200
NFT-approved coffee.

Shopping

- **Andrew Fish Market** •
1228 Fulton St [Bedford Ave]
718-623-6774
You pick it, they cook it. Fried to perfection on the spot.
- **Birdell's Records** •
535 Nostrand Ave [Herkimer St]
718-638-4504
If it's been recorded, they have it.
- **Brooklyn Weinstein Paint & Home Center** •
420 Tompkins Ave [Halsey St]
718-638-7207
Paint the town whatever color you choose.
- **Brownstone Books** •
409 Lewis Ave [Decatur St]
718-953-7328
Excellent neighborhood bookshop.

- **Creative Blossoms** • 370 Lewis Ave [Macon St]
347-240-9720
Fresh flowers, plants and wares for the backyard-blessed.
- **Exotic Homes & Gardens** •
1213 Atlantic Ave [Nostrand Ave]
718-230-1536
Home decor in Bed-Stuy. Exotic.
- **Foot Locker** • 1258 Fulton St [Nostrand Ave]
718-399-6979
For all your footwear needs.
- **La Table Exquise** •
370 Tompkins Ave [Putnam Ave]
718-200-6757
Parisian artisanal, natural bakery. They're actually French!
- **Legacy Awards** •
695 Nostrand Ave [Atlantic Ave]
718-774-0785
Custom t-shirts and personal engravings. "World's Greatest Lover" indeed.
- **Lion's Den** • 1113 Broadway [Dekalb Ave]
347-442-1344
Rasta-wear, second-hand speakers, and passable knock-off perfume.
- **Little Red Boutique** • 374 Lewis Ave [Macon]
718-443-1170
The accessory and candle racket hard at work here.
- **Original Barber Shop** •
385 Nostrand Ave [Putnam Ave]
718-638-3470
Old techniques are still in use at this tidy little shop.
- **Tony's Country Life** •
1316 Fulton St [Nostrand Ave]
718-789-2040
Best health emporium in the 'hood with a friendly and helpful staff.

Map 8 • BoCoCa / F

Map 8

Sorry for the "BoCoCa" thing, folks, but we just can't fit "Boerum Hill / Cobble Hill / Carroll Gardens" along with "Red Hook" on the header bar. Crusty oldtimers will say "I remember when this area was just called "South Brooklyn"—what the hell is Cobble Hill?" Well, Mr. Crusty Oldtimer, this is what happens when neighborhoods are old, become economically stable, and have real estate agents trying to package their wares.

First up: Cobble Hill, which is kind of the bastard child of Brooklyn Heights—waterfront but without the Promenade, very-nice-but-not-stunning brownstones, and just a hair more inconvenient regarding subway access. However, taking into account the retail options on Atlantic Avenue and Court Street's northern third, along with a few cute places tucked away on Clinton and Henry Streets, Cobble Hill's dining, shopping, and nightlife are far and away superior to The Heights. Equally important, perhaps, is that Cobble Hill features one of the quaintest small parks in all of New York—if you've ever seen **Cobble Hill Park** right after a snowfall, for instance, you'll know what we're talking about.

Boerum Hill, forever immortalized in Jonathan Lethem's Motherless Brooklyn, has a rather unique floor plan in that is much wider East-West than North-South; Boerum Hill extends east all the way to Fourth Avenue, and encompasses more retail along the Atlantic Avenue corridor, as well as Smith Street's northern half. Boerum Hill has come a long, long way in the past twenty years, as evidenced by Smith Street's high commercial rents (say goodbye to porn video, furniture rental, and dollar stores) and the ongoing renovation of many of its brownstones.

In Italian enclave Carroll Gardens, on the other hand, you don't get the feeling that the neighborhood ever took that big of a nosedive; first and second-generation working-class folk at least occupied and maintained their wide brownstones with their unique "garden" frontages, while pruning their fig and pear trees in their backyards. Now many of these owners are either condo-izing their brownstones or selling outright to Manhattanites who realize that Carroll Gardens is perhaps the perfect neighborhood—decent schools, a centralized park, a 20-minute subway ride to Manhattan, quick access to the BQE and the Brooklyn-Battery Tunnel, and a ludicrous amount of retail on lower Court and Smith Streets. There are still several old-school Italian shops and eateries that hold their own against the influx of hip restaurants on lower Court Street and the design shops of Smith Street.

And yes, then there is Red Hook. Cut off from the rest of the universe due to a lack of subway access and Robert Moses' Brooklyn-Queens Expressway, peppered with derelict industrial sites (re: the **Red Hook Grain Terminal**), and simply just bereft of good-quality housing stock, Red Hook has nonetheless—after a few early-millennium fits and starts—turned the corner, possibly for good. There is still no subway, and housing remains a mystery, but two big-box retailers—**Fairway** and **Ikea** (some sort of Scandinavian furniture place...perhaps you've heard of it?) have chosen to make Red Hook their home, which will only bring more and more new and exciting retail to Van Brunt Street, at least until Starbucks, Urban Outfitters, and the chain-yogurt-store-of-the-month move in. The vibrant sports-and-food-stall scene at the **Red Hook Ball Fields** during summer is not to be missed. And did we mention the view of New York Bay from **Louis J Valentino Park**? It rocks.

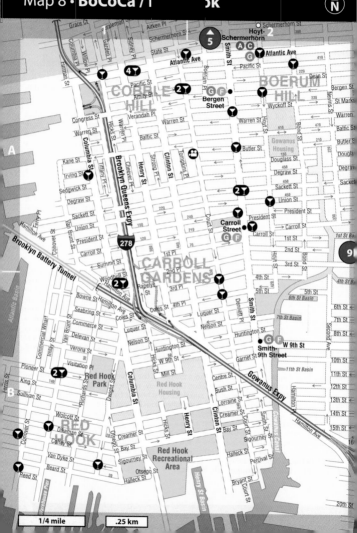

Nightlife

Map 8

Each of the 'nabes here have their stalwarts—in Boerum Hill, it's classic **Brooklyn Inn** or jukebox-savvy **The Boat**. In Cobble Hill, you can drink at several places on Atlantic (**Floyd**, **Montero**, **Last Exit**) before checking out newcomer **Henry Public**. In Carroll Gardens, it's **Gowanus Yacht Club** in summer and **Brooklyn Social** in winter, and in Red Hook, **Bait and Tackle** and newbie **Fort Defiance** compete with classic dive **Sunny's**.

Bars

- **Abilene** • 442 Court St [3rd Pl]
  718-522-6900
  Cozy and unpretentious. Drink specials galore.
- **Bar Great Harry** • 280 Smith St [Sackett St]
  718-222-1103
  There's a blog devoted to the draft beer section.
- **Black Mountain** • 415 Union St [Hoyt St]
  718-522-4340
  Try the Lebanese wine!
- **Boat** • 175 Smith St [Wyckoff St]
  718-254-0607
  Dank, dark and friendly. Nice tunes to boot.
- **Botanica** • 220 Conover St [Coffey St]
  718-797-2297
  Classy looking joint.
- **Brooklyn Inn** • 148 Hoyt St [Bergen St]
  718-522-2525
  When you're feeling nostalgic.
- **Brooklyn Social** • 335 Smith St [Carroll St]
  718-858-7758
  Old boy's lounge revamped. Cocktails still the same. NFT Pick.
- **Building on Bond** • 112 Bond St [Pacific St]
  347-853-8687
  Coffee by day, alcohol by night. Perfect.
- **Clover Club** • 210 Smith St [Baltic St]
  718-855-7939
  Charming den of cocktails and conversation.
- **Cody's** • 154 Court St [Dean St]
  718-852-6115
  Great sports bar. Seriously.
- **Downtown Bar & Grill** • 160 Court St [Amity]
  718-625-2835
  Gets the package games. More beers than God intended for man.
- **Floyd** • 131 Atlantic Ave [Henry St]
  718-858-5810
  Indoor bocce ball court!
- **Fort Defiance** • 365 Van Brunt St [Dikeman St]
  347-453-6672
  Great cocktails, great beer, great pork chop.
- **Gowanus Yacht Club** • 323 Smith St [President]
  718-246-1321
  Dogs, burgers, and beer. Love it.
- **Henry Public** • 329 Henry St [Atlantic Ave]
  718-852-8630
  From those that brought us Brooklyn Social.
- **home/made** • 293 Van Brunt St [Pioneer St]
  347-223-4135
  Wine-soaked snacking on the waterfront.

- **The Jakewalk** • 282 Smith St [Sackett St]
  347-599-0294
  The important things in life: wine and whiskey.
- **Jalopy** • 315 Columbia St [Hamilton Ave]
  718-395-3214
  Live music from rockabilly to out jazz; banjos in the window.
- **Kili** • 81 Hoyt St [State St]
  718-855-5574
  Nice space and chilled vibe.
- **Last Exit** • 136 Atlantic Ave [Henry St]
  718-222-9198
  Still trying to win trivia night. $10 pails of PBR.
- **Montero's Bar and Grill** • 73 Atlantic Ave [Hicks]
  718-624-9799
  A taste of what things used to be like.
- **Moonshine** • 317 Columbia St [Hamilton Ave]
  718-852-8057
  You supply the meat; they supply the grill.
- **PJ Hanley's** • 449 Court St [4th Pl]
  718-834-8223
  Booze since 1874.
- **Red Hook Bait & Tackle** •
  320 Van Brunt St [Pioneer St]
  718-797-4892
  Kitschy, comfy pub with cheap drinks and good beers on tap.
- **Roebling Inn** • 97 Atlantic Ave [Hicks St]
  718-488-0048
  Good vibe at this sister tavern of the Brooklyn Inn.
- **Rocky Sullivan's** • 34 Van Dyke St [Dwight St]
  718-246-8050
  The six-point portfolio is on tap-a Red Hook must.
- **Sugar Lounge** • 147 Columbia St [Irving St]
  718-643-2880
  Hammocks, hummus, and happy people.
- **Sunny's** • 253 Conover St [Reed St]
  718-625-8211
  No longer pay-what-you-wish, but still cheap and good.
- **Waterfront Ale House** • 155 Atlantic Ave [Clinton]
  718-522-3794
  Renowned burgers and sizable beer list.

Movie Theaters

- **Cobble Hill Cinemas** • 265 Court St [Butler St]
  718-596-9113
  Great indie destination, though theaters are small.

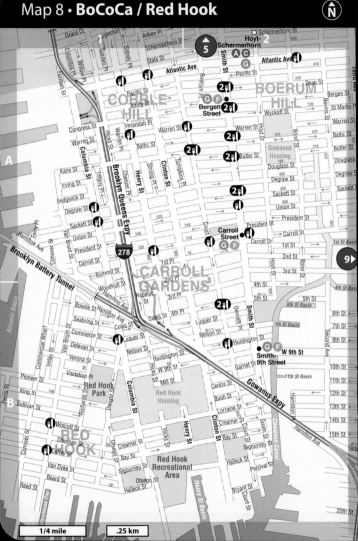

Map 8 • BoCoCa / Red Hook

Restaurants

There's more good food here than in some entire states, trust us—from Michelin-noted **Ki Sushi**, **Saul**, and **The Grocery** to brick-oven goodness at **Lucali**, hearty German fare at **Prime Meats**, Southern at **Seersucker**, killer brunch at **Buttermilk Channel** and **Frankie's 457**, Middle Eastern havens **Bedouin Tent** and **Hadramout**, late-night French at **Bar Tabac**, and old-school Italian at **Ferdinando's**.

Map 8

🍴 Restaurants

- **Alma** • 187 Columbia St [Degraw St]
718-643-5400 • $$$
Top NYC Mexican with great views of Lower Manhattan.
- **Atlantic Chip Shop** • 129 Atlantic Ave [Henry]
718-855-7775 • $$
Heart attack on a plate.
- **Bar Tabac** • 128 Smith St [Dean St]
718-923-0918 • $$$
Open late; fabulous frites, burgers, et al.
- **Bedouin Tent** • 405 Atlantic Ave [Bond St]
718-852-5555 • $
Two words: lamb sandwich. No, four: best lamb sandwich ever.
- **Bocca Lupo** • 391 Henry St [Warren St]
718-243-2522 • $$$
Postmodern panini by day and (late) night. We love NYC.
- **Brucie** • 234 Court St [Baltic St]
347-987-4961 • $$$
Lunch = scallop sandwich. Dinner = Italian delights
- **Buttermilk Channel** • 524 Court [Huntington]
718-852-8490 • $$$
Oysters, sausages, fried chicken, waffles, burgers, ahhh.
- **Char No. 4** • 196 Smith St [Baltic St]
718-643-2106 • $$
Worship (and eat) at this temple of whisky and bourbon.
- **DeFonte's Sandwich Shop** •
379 Columbia St [Luquer St]
718-625-8052 • $
Crazy-ass Italian hero shop.
- **Ferdinando's Focacceria** • 151 Union St [Hicks]
718-855-1545 • $
Sicilian specialties you won't find anywhere else! Get the panelle special.
- **Fragole** • 394 Court St [Carroll St]
718-522-7133 • $$
Fresh and cozy Italian. An absolute gem.
- **Frankie's 457** • 457 Court St [Luquer St]
718-403-0033 • $$
Fantastic meatballs. Cool space. Killer brunch.
- **The Good Fork** • 391 Van Brunt St [Coffey St]
718-643-6636 • $$$
Yep. It's good. VERY good.
- **The Grocery** • 288 Smith St [Sackett St]
718-596-3335 • $$$$
Magnificent. Reservations recommended.

- **Hadramout** • 172 Atlantic Ave [Clinton St]
718-852-3577 • $
Great Yemeni diner—order the salta and don't fear the fenugreek foam!
- **Hanco's** • 85 Bergen St [Smith St]
718-858-6818 • $
Banh Mi for people who won't trek to Sunset Park.
- **Hope & Anchor** • 347 Van Brunt St [Wolcott]
718-237-0276 • $$
Great upscale diner.
- **Joya** • 215 Court St [Warren St]
718-222-3484 • $$
Excellent, inexpensive, but super-noisy Thai.
- **Ki Sushi** • 122 Smith St [Dean St]
718-935-0575 • $$
Affordable sushi in sleek surroundings; Michelin-starred.
- **Lucali** • 575 Henry St [Carroll St]
718-858-4086 • $$
One man makes every perfect pizza by hand. Be prepared to wait.
- **Mile End**• 97 Hoyt St [Atlantic Ave]
718-852-7510 • $$
Jewish deli, Montreal-style. Two words: smoked meat.
- **Prime Meats** • 465 Court St [Luquer St]
718-254-0327 • $$$
German delights like wurst and sauerbraten take center stage.
- **Quercy** • 242 Court St [Baltic St]
718-243-2151 • $$$$
Sister restaurant to La Luncheonette in Manhattan, and equally sublime.
- **Saul** • 140 Smith St [Bergen St]
718-935-9844 • $$$
Romantical and delicioso.
- **Seersucker** • 329 Smith St [Carroll St]
718-422-0444 • $$
Fried Southern goodness, with a Brooklyn twist of course.
- **Sherwood Café/Robin des Bois** •
195 Smith St [Warren St]
718-596-1609 • $$
Mellow French vibe—best croque monsieur in town.
- **Watty & Meg** • 248 Court St [Kane St]
718-643-0007 • $$
Great new eclectic spot 50 yards from Cobble Cinemas. You know what to do.
- **Zaytoons** • 283 Smith St [Sackett St]
718-875-1880 • $$
Excellent Middle Eastern pizzas and kebabs.

Map 8 · **BoCoCa / Red Hook**

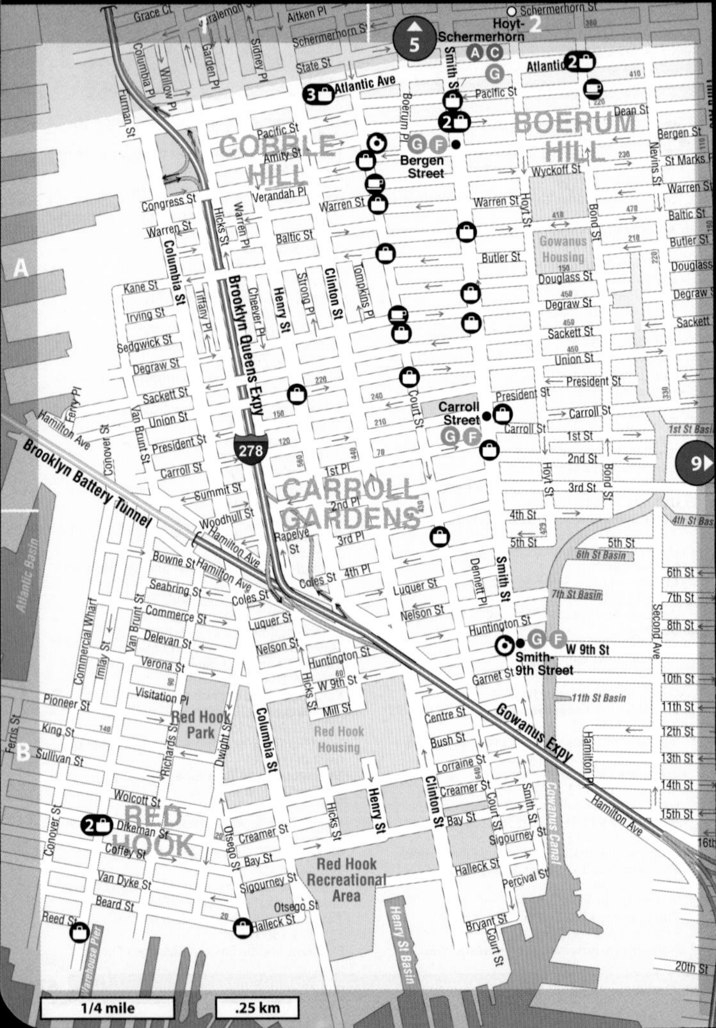

N

Grace Ct
Aitken Pl
Schermerhorn St
Hoyt-
Schermerhorn St
5
A C
G
Atlantic
Atlantic Ave
Pacific St
3
Columbia Pl
Willow Pl
Sidney Pl
Boerum Pl
Smith St

BOERUM
HILL

Dean St
Bergen St
Nevins St
St Marks Pl
Warren St
Baltic St
Butler St
Douglass
Sackett

COBBLE
HILL
Pacific St
Amity St
Verandah Pl
Warren St
Bergen
Street
Congress St

Baltic St
Wyckoff St
Warren St
Butler St

Gowanus
Housing
Douglass St
Degraw St
Sackett St
Union St

Kane St
Irving St
Sedgwick St
Degraw St
Sackett St
Union St
President St
Carroll St

President St
Carroll St
1st St
2nd St
3rd St

Carroll
Street
G F

Hamilton Ave
Van Brunt St
Conover St

Brooklyn Battery Tunnel

278

1st Pl
2nd Pl

CARROLL
GARDENS

Summit St
Woodhull St
Bowne St
Hamilton Ave
Seabring St
Commerce St
Van Brunt St
Delevan St
Verona St
Pioneer St
King St
Sullivan St

A

Columbia St
Hicks St
Henry St
Clinton St
Tompkins Pl
Strong Pl
Cheever Pl

Brooklyn Queens Expy

Rapelye
3rd Pl
Coles St
4th Pl
Luquer St
Nelson St
Huntington St
W 9th St
Mill St

Court St
Smith St
Hoyt St
Bond St

4th St
5th St
6th St Basin
7th St Basin

Smith St
Dennett Pl
Nelson St
Huntington St

Smith-
9th Street
G F
W 9th St

Garnet St
11th St Basin

9

1st St Bas

4th St Bas

6th St
7th St
8th St
10th St
11th St
12th St
13th St
14th St
15th St
16th

Second Av

B

Ferris St
Conover St
Sullivan St

2

RED
HOOK

Dikeman St
Coffey St
Van Dyke St
Reed St

Red Hook
Park

Columbia St

Red Hook
Housing

Henry St

Bowne St
Creamer St
Bay St
Sigourney St
Otsego St
Beard St
Halleck St

Red Hook
Recreational
Area

Centre St
Bush St
Lorraine St
Creamer St
Clinton St
Bay St
Sigourney St
Percival St
Bryant St
Court St

Gowanus Expy

Hamilton Ave

Gowanus Canal

Henry St Basin

20th St

Atlantic Basin
Commercial Wharf
Imlay St
Van Brunt St

1/4 mile   .25 km

Bagels, Coffee, & Shopping

We dare you to walk Atlantic, Smith, and Court without buying anything—for instance, food destinations **Sahadi's, Staubitz, D'Amico's, Caputo's, Fish Tales, Smith & Vine, Stinky,** and the **Pork Store,** or hip **Swallow, Environment 337, Enamoo, Flight 001,** or **Dear Fieldbinder,** for another. Then window shop on Atlantic for all your antique needs.

Bagels

- **Court Street Bagels** • 181 Court St [Bergen]
  718-624-3972
  A line out the door every weekend.
- **Line Bagels** • 476 Smith St [W 9th St]
  718-422-0001
  Rob likes it. So should you.

Coffee

- **Building on Bond** • 112 Bond St [Pacific St]
  347-853-8687
  NFT's quasi-office and hang out space.
- **Cafe Pedlar** • 210 Court St [Warren St]
  718-855-7129
  Stumptown Coffee is served here. That's all you need to know.
- **D'Amico Foods** • 309 Court St [Degraw St]
  718-875-5403
  The neighborhood spot for fresh beans.

Shopping

- **A Cook's Companion** • 197 Atlantic Ave [Court]
  718-852-6901
  A fantastic shop with everything for your kitchen (except the boring).
- **American Beer Distributors** •
  256 Court St [Kane St]
  718-875-0226
  International beer merchant. NFT pick.
- **Blue Marble** • 196 Court St [Wyckoff St]
  718-858-0408
  Organic ice cream and other treats.
- **Brooklyn Farmacy** • 513 Henry St [Sackett St]
  718-522-6260
  These old-school soda jerks are actually quite nice.
- **Caputo's Fine Foods** • 460 Court St [3rd Pl]
  718-855-8852
  Italian gourmet specialties. The real deal.
- **Dear Fieldbinder** • 198 Smith St [Baltic St]
  718-852-3620
  Designer duds and accessories. Who needs the LES?
- **Enamoo** • 109 Smith St [Pacific St]
  718-624-0175
  Plants, hipster t-shirts, pretty jewelry, and, um, vintage porn?

- **Environment337** • 337 Smith St [Carroll St]
  718-522-1767
  Another Smith Street hit.
- **Erie Basin** • 388 Van Brunt St [Dikeman St]
  718-554-6147
  Jewelry and stuff from the 19th and early 20th century.
- **Exit 9** • 127 Smith St [Dean St]
  718-422-7720
  Quirky gifts.
- **Fairway** • 480 Van Brunt St [Reed St]
  718-694-6868
  Best grocery store in Brooklyn. By far.
- **Fish Tales** • 191 Court St [Wyckoff St]
  718-246-1346
  The place for expensive, but fresh, fish.
- **Flight 001** • 132 Smith St [Dean St]
  718-243-0001
  Luggage, etc, for the pampered traveler.
- **G Esposito & Sons** • 357 Court St [President]
  718-875-6863
  Sopressata and sausages direct from the Godhead.
- **Ikea** • 1 Beard St [Otsego St]
  718-246-4532
  Everything you need for your 312 sq ft apt.
- **Malko Karkanni Bros.** • 174 Atlantic [Clinton]
  718-834-0845
  Cashew Baklava makes you believe again.
- **Mazzola Bakery** • 192 Union St [Henry St]
  718-643-1719
  Top bakery in CG.
- **Metal and Thread** • 398 Van Brunt St [Coffey]
  212-518-1411
  Exquisite jewelry and antique tools. Yes, antique tools.
- **Sahadi Importing Company** •
  187 Atlantic Ave [Court]
  718-624-4550
  Totally brilliant Middle Eastern supermarket--olives, cheese, bread, etc.
- **Smith & Vine** • 268 Smith St [Douglass St]
  718-243-2864
  If NFT owned a liquor store, this would be it.
- **Staubitz Meat Market** • 222 Court St [Baltic]
  718-624-0014
  Top NYC butcher.
- **Stinky** • 261 Smith St [Douglass St]
  718-522-7425
  I get it! It's a cheese store!
- **Swallow** • 361 Smith St [2nd St]
  718-222-8201
  An exquisite selection of glass, jewelry, & books.

Map 8

Map 9

Park Slope is an easy target. The streets are filled with overprotective moms, granola liberals, and spoiled kids, all of whom throw elbows for pedestrian authority. A joke is that lefty New Yorkers come to the Slope to spawn and breed, and it's about seven-eighths true. But you know what? It's not just a haven for places like the **Park Slope Food Co-op** (the largest customer-owned establishment in America, or, the biggest socialist experiment in America, take your pick). It's also got world-class dining and shopping options, incredible brownstone architecture, and is smack-up against one of the great city parks.

The 'Slope has had a slow and ever-developing history of...development. Whether you want to call this progress or gentrification is up to you. It's easy to understand why people flocked here, though. Bordered by Prospect Park on one side and including the lovely **Grand Army Plaza**, this entire neighborhood is nineteenth-century brownstone architecture at its best. The rows of houses all have distinct touches on their stoops, their fronts, and it's all very idyllic and photo-op ready. Mixed in almost every other block is a limestone church, giving the neighborhood a skyline of regal steeples. Suffice it to say that the neighborhood has a smattering of old school, with early twentieth century pubs and boutique butcher shops mixed in with the newest place to get an organic vanilla chai latte. But that brings us to the modern side.

And what a modern side it is. The number of cool shops, restaurants, and bars that are on 5th Avenue, 7th Avenue, and Flatbush Avenue is simply astounding. (If you look at these three streets on a map, it forms Pi, which we're sure means something, but we don't know what). There is so much retail on these three streets that you'd think there wouldn't be room for any more, but 4th Avenue and now even 3rd Avenue, near the scenic **Gowanus Canal**, have gotten into the act.

And the wave of development is expanding ever outward. On the northeast end of the neighborhood, Prospect Heights has been undergoing changes, turning Vanderbilt and Washington Avenues into bustling commercial hotspots. It's a new frontier that's a bit less familo-centric than the Slope, but, since Prospect Heights sports many lovely and relatively rare 3-story brownstones, we expect at least two kids in every brownstone by the end of the next decade.

On the southeastern end of the Slope is Windsor Terrace, which has attracted a new wave of young renters who can't afford Center Slope but still get great park access and a mini-retail strip along Prospect Park West. These renters mix in with the mostly blue-collar Irish long-term residents; Windsor Terrace also has an interesting mix of housing types and is another one of those oddly shaped neighborhoods that is scrunched in between other things (namely, Prospect Park and the Prospect Expressway).

Flatbush Ave

State St

Atlantic Ave

Pacific St

Dean St

1

6

2

10

B Q

Atlantic Avenue

Pacific Street

D N R

Dean St

Bergen St

Bergen St

Bergen Street

Vanderbilt Ave

Washington Ave

Grand Ave

PROSPECT HEIGHTS

St Mark's Pl

St Mark's Ave

Sterling Pl

Fourth Ave

Prospect Pl

Park Pl

Dulsenbury

Sterling Pl

St Johns Pl

Carlton Ave

7th Avenue

B Q

Park Pl

Sterling Pl

St Johns Pl

Lincoln Pl

Butler St

Fifth Ave

Sixth Ave

Seventh Ave

Grand Army Plaza

Plaza St E

Underhill Ave

A

Warren St

Baltic St

Butler St

Douglass St

Degraw St

Sackett St

Lincoln Pl

Berkeley Pl

Union St

Union Street

R

President St

Carroll St

Garfield Pl

Eighth Ave

Polhemus Pl

Fiske Pl

Montgomery St

Grand Army Plz

Flatbush Ave

West Dr

East Dr

Brooklyn Botanic Garden

PAGE 144

1st St

2nd St

3rd St

4th St

5th St

6th St

7th St

8th St

PARK SLOPE

Prospect Park W

PAGE 142

Prospect Park

8

Whitwell Pl

Denton Pl

1st St Basin

4th St Basin

4th Avenue-9th Street

F G

R

10th St

11th St

12th St

13th St

14th St

15th St

16th St

Third Ave

Fourth Ave

Fifth Ave

Sixth Ave

9th St

7th Avenue

F G

Seventh Ave

Eighth Ave

15th Street-Prospect Park

F G

W Lake Dr

Prospect Park SW

Prospect Avenue

R

Prospect Expy

Jackson Pl

Windsor Pl

Calder Pl

Windsor Pl

Prospect Ave

Prospect Park W

Howard Pl

Fuller Pl

Sherman St

10th Ave

11th Ave

WINDSOR TERRACE

B

278

11

1/4 mile

.25 km

27

17th St

18th St

12

17th St

18th St

13

Gourmet cocktails and beers have been sprouting up everywhere at spots like **Cornelius** and **Union Hall**. Support your local dive at **O'Connor's** and **Freddy's**. **The Bell House** now competes with **Southpaw** for rock shows, but **Barbes** has a fabulous mix of world music jammed into its tiny back room space. For something different, hit **Issue Project Room** near the Gowanus.

 Map 9

 Bars

• **Barbes** • 376 9th St [6th Ave]
347-422-0248
Smart-looking space with eclectic entertainment. Recommended.
• **Beast** • 638 Bergen St [Vanderbilt Ave]
718-399-6855
Great, great local vibe.
• **Beer Table** • 427 7th St [14th St]
718-965-1196
Like beer? Go here.
• **The Bell House** • 149 7th St [3rd Ave]
718-643-6510
Huge Gowanus live music venue + front bar; stellar.
• **Black Horse Pub** • 568 5th Ave [16th St]
718-788-1975
Where to watch footy.
• **Buttermilk Bar** • 577 5th Ave [16th St]
718-788-6297
A solid more-than dive.
• **Canal Bar** • 270 3rd Ave [President St]
718-246-0011
Dive near the Gowanus, but not into it.
• **Cherry Tree** • 65 4th Ave [Bergen St]
718-399-1353
Rowdy Irish pub with a stately backyard.
• **Commonwealth** • 497 5th Ave [12th St]
718-768-2040
So many beers, so little time.
• **Cornelius** • 565 Vanderbilt Ave [Pacific St]
718-398-6662
Unique liquor from small independent distilleries.
• **Draft Barn** • 530 3rd Ave [13th St]
718-768-0515
Gigantic medieval beer hall. Cool.
• **Flatbush Farm** • 76 St Marks Ave [6th Ave]
718-622-3276
Great bar, great food, great everything, really.
• **Freddy's Bar and Backroom** •
627 5th Ave [17th St]
718-622-7035
Freddy's lives! Fav drinking hole with live music.
• **The Gate** • 321 5th Ave [3rd St]
718-768-4329
Large outdoor area. Twenty beers on tap.
• **Great Lakes** • 284 5th Ave [1st St]
718-499-3710
Laid-back hipster dive. Great jukebox, cheap beer.

• **Hank's Saloon** • 46 3rd Ave [Atlantic Ave]
347-227-8495
Sweaty, hillbilly-esque.
• **Issue Project Room** • 232 3rd St [3rd Ave]
718-330-0313
Premier avant-garde music venue in cool factory building.
• **littlefield** • 622 Degraw St [4th Ave]
718-855-3388
Eco-friendly performance space: music, film, art. Sweet.
• **Loki Lounge** • 304 5th Ave [2nd St]
718-965-9600
Darts and billiards tone down the classic wood bar. Good music.
• **O'Connor's** • 39 5th Ave [Bergen St]
718-783-9721
Friendly dive in need of a designer.
• **Pacific Standard** • 82 4th Ave [St Marks Pl]
718-858-1951
Drinking and board games most certainly mix.
• **Park Slope Ale House** • 356 6th Ave [5th St]
718-788-1756
Good pub grub and beer selection.
• **Patio Lounge** • 179 5th Ave [Berkeley Pl]
718-857-3477
Verdant boozing.
• **Puppet's Jazz Bar** • 481 5th Ave [11th St]
718-499-2622
Jazz and wine preside in this wee club.
• **Soda** • 629 Vanderbilt Ave [Prospect Pl]
718-230-8393
Nice summer drinkin' spot. NFT pick.
• **Southpaw** • 125 5th Ave [Sterling Pl]
718-230-0236
Best live music in the Slope.
• **Starlite Lounge** • 1084 Bergen St [Flatbush]
718-771-3340
Oldest Black-owned, "non-discriminating" bar in the 'hood. Karaoke Thursdays.
• **Tavern on Dean** • 755 Dean St [Underhill Ave]
718-638-3326
Crayons and table paper mix really well with beer.
• **Union Hall** • 702 Union St [5th Ave]
718-638-4400
Quirky spot for indie shows and stuffed birds.
• **Washington Commons** •
748 Washington Ave [Park Pl]
718-230-3666
Rotating beer selection, late happy hour, and a great outdoor space.

Flatbush Ave

State St

Atlantic Ave

Pacific St

Pacific Street

Dean St

Dean St

Bergen St

Washington Ave

Vanderbilt Ave

Grand Ave

Bergen Street

Bergen St

Carlton Ave

St Mark's Ave

PROSPECT HEIGHTS

Prospect Pl

Park Pl

Sterling Pl

St Johns Pl

Lincoln Pl

7th Avenue

Sterling Pl

St Johns Pl

Lincoln Pl

Plaza St E

Fourth Ave

Fifth Ave

Sixth Ave

Seventh Ave

Dean St

Pacific Street

St Mark's Pl

Warren St

Baltic St

Butler St

Douglass St

Degraw St

Sackett St

Union Street

Carroll St

Garfield Pl

1st St

2nd St

3rd St

4th St

5th St

6th St

7th St

8th St

Prospect Pl

Park Pl

Sterling Pl

St Johns Pl

Lincoln Pl

Berkeley Pl

Union St

President St

Grand Army Plaza

Grand Army Plz

Brooklyn Botanic Garden

PAGE 144

Eighth Ave

Pollhemus Pl

Fiske Pl

Montgomery Pl

PARK SLOPE

PAGE 142

Prospect Park

Prospect Park W

West Dr

East Dr

Flatbush Ave

Third Ave

Whitwell Pl

Denton Pl

1st St Basin

4th St Basin

4th Avenue-9th Street

9th St

7th Avenue

10th St

11th St

12th St

13th St

14th St

15th St

16th St

Fifth Ave

Sixth Ave

Seventh Ave

Eighth Ave

15th Street-Prospect Park

Prospect Park SW

Prospect Park W

WINDSOR TERRACE

Prospect Avenue

Prospect Expy

Hamilton Ave

Jackson Pl

Webster Pl

Caldar Pl

Windsor Pl

Prospect Ave

17th St

18th St

17th St

18th St

Vanderbilt Ave

Howard Pl

Fuller Pl

Sherman St

11th Ave

278

27

1/4 mile

.25 km

Map 9

Where to begin? Our hands-down favorites: top Italian **Al Di La**, slow-food-friendly **Applewood**, French bistro **Belleville**, Portugese/Italian **Convivium Osteria**, top pizzeria **Franny's**, friendly Ethopian **Ghenet**, Australian outpost **Sheep Station**, warm and eclectic **Stone Park Cafe**, classic diner **Tom's**, and, of course, that little-known **Blue Ribbon** place.

🍴 Restaurants

- **12th Street Bar and Grill** •
1123 8th Ave [11th St]
718-965-9526 • $$$
Outstanding gourmet comfort fare.
- **Al Di La Trattoria** • 248 5th Ave [Carroll St]
718-783-4565 • $$$
Chandelier & brick-walled Italian. Super.
- **Applewood** • 501 11th Ave [7th Ave]
718-788-1810 • $$$
Elegant, cheerful slow food.
- **Beast** • 638 Bergen St [Vanderbilt Ave]
718-399-6855 • $$$
American tapas. An NFT favorite on Vanderbilt.
- **Belleville** • 332 5th Ave [3rd St]
718-832-9777 • $$$$
Fab bistro French; they've perfected entrecote.
- **Blue Ribbon Brooklyn** • 280 5th Ave [1st St]
718-840-0404 • $$$$
Brooklyn outpost of brilliant late-night
Manhattan eatery.
- **Brooklyn Fish Camp** •
162 5th Ave [Douglass St]
718-783-3264 • $$$
Mary's Fish Camp redux.
- **Cheryl's Global Soul** •
236 Underhill Ave [Lincoln Pl]
347-529-2855 • $$
Modern, international menu emphasizing
comfort.
- **ChipShop** • 383 5th Ave [6th St]
718-832-7701 • $
Brit boys dish fish, chips, and The Beatles.
- **Convivium Osteria** • 68 5th Ave [St Marks Pl]
718-857-1833 • $$$$
Delicious Italian with a Portuguese influence.
Rustic, warm setting.
- **Flatbush Farm** • 76 St Marks Ave [6th Ave]
718-622-3276 • $$
Local, seasonal, and delish.
- **Franny's** • 295 Flatbush Ave [Prospect Pl]
718-230-0221 • $$
Brilliant pizza, drop-dead fresh, NFT fave.
- **Gen Restaurant** •
659 Washington Ave [St Marks Ave]
718-398-3550 • $$$
Delicious, fresh Japanese cuisine and laid-back
service.
- **Ghenet** • 348 Douglass St [4th Ave]
718-230-4476 • $$
Top NYC Ethiopian, hands-down.

- **Hanco's** • 350 7th Ave [10th St]
718-499-8081 • $
Banh mi and bubble tea hotspot.
- **Jpan Sushi** • 287 5th Ave [1st St]
718-788-2880 • $$$
Excellent, inventive special rolls; weird space.
- **La Taqueria** • 72 7th Ave [Berkeley Pl]
718-398-4300 • $
Easy y barato, meaning cheap. Autentico.
- **Moim** • 206 Garfield Pl [7th Ave]
718-499-8092 • $$$
Innovative Korean in a swanky setting.
- **Nana** • 155 5th Ave [Lincoln Pl]
718-230-3749 • $$
Absolutely delicious Pan-Asian.
- **Rawstar Vegan Live Cuisine** •
687 Washington Ave [Prospect Pl]
718-975-0304 • $$
Oh, baby I like it raw.
- **Rose Water** • 787 Union St [6th Ave]
718-783-3800 • $$$
Intimate, airy Mediterranean.
- **Scalino** • 347 7th Ave [10th St]
718-840-5738 • $$
Fresh Italian food mama would approve of.
- **Sheep Station** • 149 4th Ave [Douglass St]
718-857-4337 • $$
Australian craft beers and aussie-themed food.
Mate.
- **Smiling Pizzeria** • 323 7th Ave [9th St]
718-788-2137 • $
Good quick happy slices.
- **Stone Park Cafe** • 324 5th Ave [3rd St]
718-369-0082 • $$$$
Definitely a contender for best Park Slope
dining.
- **Taro Sushi** • 446 Dean St [5th Ave]
718-398-0872 • $$
Top sushi, cozy seating. Lunch specials
available Monday through Saturday.
- **Tom's** • 782 Washington Ave [Sterling Pl]
718-636-9738 • $$
Old-school mom-and-pop diner since 1936. A
cholesterol love affair.
- **The V-Spot** • 156 5th Ave [Degraw St]
718-622-2275 • $$
Loads of "meat" options, good for the veggie
initiate.
- **Watana** • 420 7th Ave [14th St]
718-832-1611 • $$
Best Thai food on the slope. BYOB.

Flatbush Ave

State St

Atlantic Ave

Pacific St

Dean St

Pacific Street

Bergen St

Pacific St

Dean St

Bergen St

Bergen Street

St Mark's Ave

Atlantic Avenue

Washington Ave

Grand Ave

PROSPECT HEIGHTS

7th Avenue

Sterling Pl

St Johns Pl

Lincoln Pl

Vanderbilt Ave

Prospect Pl

Park Pl

Sterling Pl

St Johns Pl

Lincoln Pl

Berkeley Pl

Union St

President St

Carroll St

Garfield Pl

1st St

2nd St

3rd St

4th St

5th St

6th St

7th St

8th St

St Mark's Pl

Warren St

Baltic St

Butler St

Douglass St

Degraw St

Sackett St

Union Street

Whitwell Pl

Denton Pl

Grand Army Plaza

Grand Army Plz

Brooklyn Botanic Garden

Montgomery St

Plaza St E

Flatbush Ave

West Dr

East Dr

PARK SLOPE

Eighth Ave

Prospect Park W

Prospect Park

4th Avenue-9th Street

9th St

7th Avenue

10th St

11th St

12th St

13th St

14th St

15th St

16th St

Fourth Ave

Fifth Ave

Sixth Ave

Seventh Ave

Prospect Avenue

15th Street-Prospect Park

Prospect Park SW

WINDSOR TERRACE

W Lake Dr

Sherman St

Tenth Ave

Howard Pl

Prospect Expy

Jackson Pl

Webster Pl

Calder Pl

Windsor Pl

Prospect Ave

17th St

18th St

Hamilton Ave

Third Ave

1st St Basin

4th St Basin

Duisburry Pl

Carlton Ave

Vanderbilt Ave

Park Pl

Fiske Pl

Polhemus Pl

Plaza St E

Butler Pl

278

27

11

12

13

48

6

10

PAGE 144

PAGE 142

1/4 mile

.25 km

Bagels, Coffee, & Shopping

For food (and beer), the main spots are **Bierkraft**, **Bklyn Larder**, **Blue Apron**, **Blue Marble**, **Grab**, **Russo's**, and **United Meat**. Stellar gift/jewelry stores to check out are **Clay Pot**, **Cog and Pearl**, **Matter**, **Rare Device**, and **Razor**. **Beacon's Closet** is still a clothing destination, **Dixon's** is a classic bike shop, and get your capes and lasers at **Brooklyn Superhero Supply**.

Map 9

🥯 Bagels

- **Bagel Hole** • 400 7th Ave [12th St]
  718-788-4014
  Smaller bagels, good nova.
- **Bergen Bagels** • 473 Bergen St [6th Ave]
  718-789-7600
  Good Brooklyn standard.
- **Terrace Bagels** • 224 Prospect Park W [Windsor]
  718-768-3943
  Possibly Brooklyn's best.

☕ Coffee

- **Café Grumpy** • 383 7th Ave [12th St]
  718-499-4404
  Gourmet java comes to strollerland.
- **Gorilla Coffee** • 97 5th Ave [Park Pl]
  718-230-3244
  Milk, two sugars, and a shot of hipness.
- **Joyce Bakeshop** • 646 Vanderbilt Ave [Park Pl]
  718-623-7470
  Prospect Heights goodness.
- **Patisserie Colson** • 374 9th Ave [6th Ave]
  718-965-6400

🛍 Shopping

- **Beacon's Closet** • 92 5th Ave [Warren St]
  718-230-1630
  Rad resale with lots of gems.
- **Bierkraft** • 191 5th Ave [Union St]
  718-230-7600
  Cheese, chocolate, & nearly 1000 varieties of beer.
- **Bklyn Larder** • 228 Flatbush Ave [Bergen St]
  718-783-1250
  Take home a taste of Franny's every night.
- **Blue Apron Foods** • 814 Union St [7th Ave]
  718-230-3180
  Euro-style cheese, charcuterie, and imported goodies.
- **Blue Marble Ice Cream** •
  186 Underhill Ave [St Johns Pl]
  718-399-6926
  Delicious even in February.
- **Brooklyn Superhero Supply** •
  372 5th Ave [5th St]
  718-499-9884
  Capes, treasure maps, and bottled special powers. Also, McSweeney's publications.

- **Clay Pot** • 162 7th Ave [Garfield Pl]
  718-788-6564
  Hand-crafted gifts, jewelry.
- **Cog and Pearl** • 190 5th Ave [Berkeley Pl]
  718-623-8200
  World's coolest crafts, jewelry, art.
- **Dixon's Bicycle Shop** • 792 Union St [7th Ave]
  718-636-0067
  Classic, friendly, family-owned bike shop.
- **Four & Twenty Blackbirds** • 439 3rd Ave [8th]
  718-499 2917
  Seasonal pies (and other treats) baked fresh daily. Delicious goodness!
- **Grab** • 438 7th Ave [15th St]
  718-369-7595
  Cheese, bread, charcuterie…ah, what goodness.
- **Gureje** • 886 Pacific St [Underhill Ave]
  718-857-2522
  West African flavored clothing, with a music club in the back!
- **JackRabbit Sports** • 151 7th Ave [Garfield Pl]
  718-636-9000
  Mecca for runners, swimmers, and cyclists.
- **Leaf and Bean** • 83 7th Ave [Berkeley Pl]
  718-638-5791
  Coffees and teas.
- **Loom** • 115 7th Ave [President St]
  718-789-0061
  Irresistible gifts and housewares.
- **Matter** • 227 5th Ave [President St]
  718-230-1150
  Design shop for the modern home.
- **Pie Shop** • 211 Prospect Park West [16th St]
  718-788-2448
  Handmade meat pies from Down Under.
- **Razor** • 329 5th Ave [4th St]
  718-832-0717
  Designer gear can make anyone look sharp.
- **Russo's Fresh Mozzarella** • 363 7th Ave [11th]
  718-369-2874
  Homemade pasta and sauce. Yum.
- **Stitch Therapy** • 335 5th Ave [4th St]
  718-398-2020
  Luxurious yarns. Plus knitting classes.
- **Under The Pig Collectibles** •
  355 5th Ave [5th St]
  718-788-2135
  Items made well enough to survive both time and pig-girth.
- **United Meat Market** • 219 Prospect Park West [16th St]
  718-788-7227
  Butchered sheep flesh never tasted so good.

Prospect-Lefferts Gardens / Crown Heights

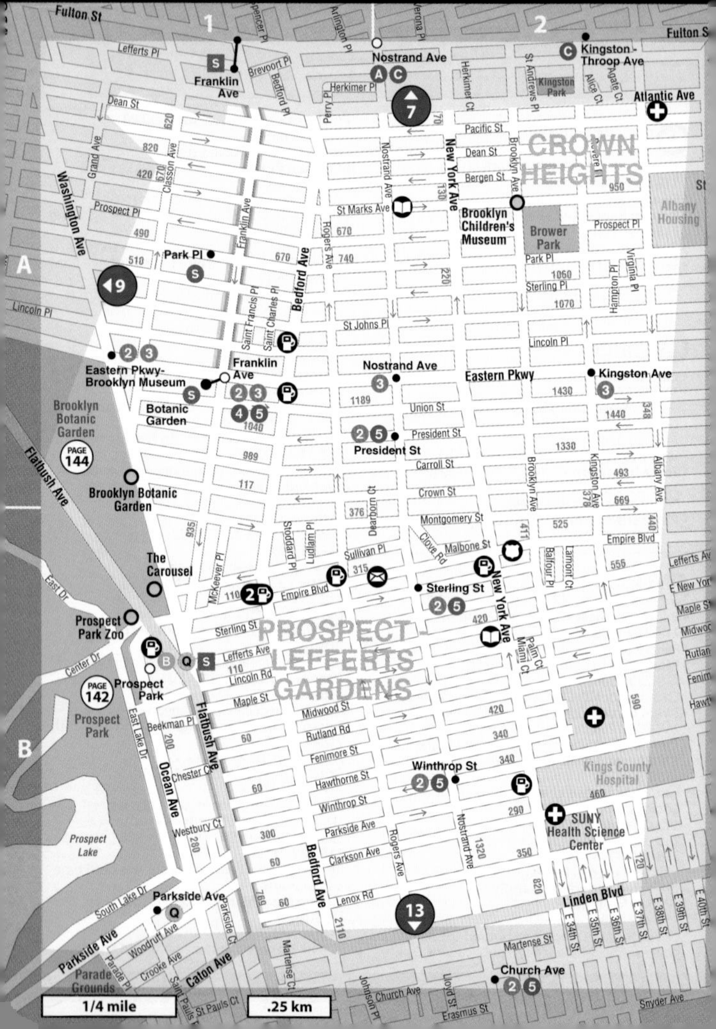

Neighborhood Overview

Map 10

Crown Heights and Prospect-Lefferts Gardens, formerly guarded secrets, are now two 'nabes that the rest of the world is starting to catch onto. Park Slope, the biggest brother of the "brownstoner" mentality, is on the other side of the park--and that is a blessing rather than a curse. Free you are from inflated rents, sort of. Welcome to family Brooklyn as it was meant to be.

The topography of the area is a familiar narrative to old-school Brooklyn. The neighborhoods began as bourgeois bedroom communities; hence the beautiful, late-nineteenth/early-twentieth century architecture and design, including tons of three-story limestone townhouses. Eastern Parkway, the Champs-Élysées of Brooklyn, is a tree-lined multi-lane esplanade that people both commute on and relax around. In the summer, you'll find a lot of frozen ices and fresh fruit stands adorning the area. Hidden in the neighborhoods are stylish mansions and houses, including those in the Lefferts Manor area. The area benefits from your own exploring, but as a hint you should have the camera ready.

One of the most trumpeted aspects of this area (we'll give you a dollar if you can tell us where Crown Heights ends and Prospect-Lefferts begins) is the proximity to the park, which should come at no surprise. Prospect Park is a perennially underutilized resource, but most locals would agree things would take a turn for the suck if it turned into an overrun tourist zone like that big park in Manhattan. While the Park Slope side has featured newer redevelopments like the Bandshell and playgrounds, the attractions here are oldies but goodies. The **Prospect Park Zoo** and the **Carousel** have been local mainstays without much fanfare, but you'd be surprised how the good ole stuff for family fun holds up. Furthering the family fun is the award-winning **Brooklyn Children's Museum**.

But the "crown jewel" of Crown Heights is without a doubt the **Brooklyn Botanic Garden**, a sublime destination filled with zen calm that makes you forget the city you left behind only five minutes ago. In springtime during the Cherry Blossom Festival, the Garden is packed, but it's well worth it to see this fabulous nature show. And, of course, tucked in the most northeastern corner of the Garden happens to be the **Brooklyn Museum**, which now has at least one show of international stature a year as well as sporting a new post-modern front.

Demographically, this is a family zone with populations mostly of Hasidic and Caribbean peoples. Worth checking out is the West Indian Day parade come September. Also, at 770 Eastern Parkway, the Lubavitch Hasidic movement bought a building they liked so much that they rebuilt it all over the world for their global communities. However, probably the biggest thing to come out of this area was the Crown Heights Riot, a racially charged conflict in the early '90s. It was Brooklyn back in the day of Do the Right Thing, where tensions were running high and the Hasidic and black communities were engaged in a conflict that bloodied up the streets. Gentrification and Giuliani have cleaned up said streets though, so while there are still some leftover tensions, the areas are much safer nowadays.

Crown Heights and Prospect-Lefferts Gardens are two beautiful, slightly unspoiled locales if you're looking for bedroom Brooklyn. The families are sweet, the Caribbean food amazing, the park access can't be overstated.

Prospect-Lefferts Gardens / Crown Heights

Neighborhood haunts abound here, usually with a West Indian flavor. Check out **Caribbean City** to dance the night away, or **Tavern on Nostrand** for a more relaxed beer. Newcomer **Franklin Park** provides the hipster/beer garden/patio vibe.

Nightlife

- **Abigail** • 807 Classon Ave [St Johns Pl]
  718-399-3200
  Nice restaurant/coffee shop/bar combo.
- **Franklin Park** • 618 St Johns Pl [Franklin Ave]
  718-975-0196
  Slick beer garden with nice patio.
- **The Inkwell Cafe** • 408 Rogers Ave [Sterling St]
  718-675-6145
  Drinks, jazz, comedy and karaoke...time to chill!
- **Maximillian Bells** •
  1146 Nostrand Ave [Rutland Rd]
  Reliable and lovable dive bar.
- **Wingate Field** •
  Brooklyn Ave & Winthrop St [New York Ave]
  718-469-1912
  Live music every now and then.

Fulton St

1

2

Fulton St

Lefferts Pl

Spencer Pl

Brevoort Pl

Arlington Pl

Verona Pl

Nostrand Ave

Kingston - Throop Ave

S

Franklin Ave

A C

Herkimer Pl

Herkimer Ct

St Andrews Pl

Kingston Park

Atlantic Ave

Dean St

820

Grand Ave

Classon Ave

Franklin Ave

Bedford Ave

Perry Pl

7

Pacific St

CROWN HEIGHTS

Washington Ave

820

New York Ave

Dean St

Bergen St

950

St J

420

Prospect Pl

St Marks Ave

Brower Park

Prospect Pl

Albany Housing

490

Franklin Ave

670

740

1050

Sterling Pl

Virginia Pl

Buffalo Ave

510

Park Pl

S

Park Pl

1070

19

Saint Francis Pl

Saint Charles Pl

Bedford Ave

Rogers Ave

St Johns Pl

Lincoln Pl

Lincoln Pl

A

Eastern Pkwy-Brooklyn Museum

2 3

Franklin Ave

Nostrand Ave

Eastern Pkwy

Kingston Ave

Brooklyn Botanic Garden

2 3

1189

1430

4 5

Botanic Garden

1040

Union St

1440

348

PAGE 144

989

220

President St

2 5

President St

Carroll St

1330

493

Albany Ave

Kingston Ave

Troy Ave

117

376

Dearborn Ct

Crown St

Montgomery St

525

669

Flatbush Ave

East Dr

McKeever Pl

Stoddard Pl

Ludlam Pl

Sullivan Pl

315

Clove Rd

Malbone St

411

Empire Blvd

556

Lefferts Ave

E New York Av

110

Empire Blvd

Sterling St

2 5

420

Maple St

Brooklyn Ave

New York Ave

Rutland

Midwood

PROSPECT LEFFERTS GARDENS

B Q S

Lefferts Ave

Lincoln Rd

Fenimor

Hawtho

PAGE 142

110

Maple St

420

590

Prospect Park

Beekman Pl

Midwood St

Flatbush Ave

Rutland Rd

340

2 1

Ocean Ave

Chester Ct

Fenimore St

Winthrop St

2 5

Kings County Hospital

450

Hawthorne St

Winthrop St

SUNY Health Science Center

Prospect Lake

300

60

Parkside Ave

290

Bedford Ave

Rogers Ave

350

Troy Ave

E 34th St

E 35th St

E 36th St

E 37th St

E 40th St

Westbury Ct

Clarkson Ave

Parkside Ave

Q

60

769

60

Lenox Rd

2110

13

Linden Blvd

South Lake Dr

Parkside Ave

320

Martense St

Center Dr

Woodruff Ave

Crooke Ave

Martense St

Church Ave

Church Ave

2 5

Parade Grounds

Caton Ave

Flatbush Ave

St Pauls Ct

Johnson Ave

Church Ave

Erasmus St

Lloyd St

Snyder Ave

1/4 mile

.25 km

Sit-down places like **Abigail** and **Chavella's** are few and far between, but the take-out is amazing. Caribbean food is the name of the game, so get some roti or jerk chicken at hotspots like **Culpepper's** and **Gloria's**. On Lincoln Road, the choice is obvious: the fish tacos at **Enduro**.

Restaurants

- **Abigail** • 807 Classon Ave [St Johns Pl]
  718-399-3200 • $$$
  Signs of life on Classon? Sweet.
- **Bombay Masala** •
  678 Franklin Ave [Prospect Pl]
  718-230-7640 • $$
  Surprisingly good Indian.
- **Bristen's** • 751 Franklin Ave [Sterling Pl]
  646-393-9421 • $
  Decent sammys. Good patio.
- **Brooklyn Exposure** •
  1401 Bedford Ave [St Marks Ave]
  718-783-8220 • $$$
  The classiest date place in the neighborhood.
- **Chavella's** • 732 Classon Ave [Park Pl]
  718-622-3100 • $$
  Insanely popular Mexican on Classon.
- **Culpepper's** • 1082 Nostrand Ave [Lincoln Rd]
  718-940-4122 • $
  Deliciousness from Barbados. Get the fish over cou cou and a side of coconut bread
- **D Ital Shak Health Food Restaurant & Bakery** • 989 Nostrand Ave [Empire Blvd]
  718-756-6557 • $
  Skip the fried chicken for these take-out veggie patties.
- **Enduro** • 51 Lincoln Rd [Flatbush Ave]
  718-282-7097 • $$$
  Go with a margarita, fish tacos, and guac.
- **Gloria's West Indian Food** •
  991 Nostrand Ave [Empire Blvd]
  718-778-4852 • $
  All the locals know Gloria's roti.
- **Golden Krust** •
  1014 Nostrand Ave [Empire Blvd]
  718-604-2211 • $
  West Indian chain with a bent toward home cooking.

- **Golden Krust** • 568 Flatbush Ave [Maple St]
  718-282-1437 • $
  West Indian chain with a bent toward home cooking.
- **Imhotep's Health & Living** •
  734 Nostrand Ave [Park Pl]
  718-493-2395 • $
  Cheap, healthy, organic takeout.
- **Irie Vegetarian** •
  804 Nostrand Ave [Lincoln Rd]
  718-493-2451 • $$
  Caribbean for herbivores.
- **King of Tandoor** •
  600 Flatbush Ave [Rutland Rd]
  347-533-6811 • $$
  The king of Lefferts Indian food, definitely.
- **Meytex Lounge** • 543 Flatbush Ave [Maple St]
  718-941-1093 • $
  You're Ghana love it.
- **Paradise Foods** • 843 Franklin Ave [Union St]
  718-953-2270 • $$
  Tasty, inexpensive West Indian.
- **Peppa's Jerk Chicken** •
  738 Flatbush Ave [Woodruff Ave]
  347-712-9341? • $
  Scrumptious and spicy.
- **Sushi Tatsu II** • 609 Franklin Ave [Dean St]
  718-398-8828 • $$
  Japanese. They deliver.
- **Sushi Tatsu III** •
  644 Flatbush Ave [Fenimore St]
  718-282-8890 • $$
  Third location is a charm.
- **Tavern on Nostrand** •
  813 Nostrand Ave [Union St]
  718-778-7160 • $$
  Tasty new American food with live jazz.
- **Trinidad Ali Roti Shop** •
  589 Flatbush Ave [Midwood St]
  718-462-1730 • $$
  Caribbean with style.

Fulton St

Lefferts Pl

1

Brevoort Pl

Nostrand Ave

2

Kingston-
Throop Ave

Fulton St

S

Franklin
Ave

A C

Atlantic Ave

Herkimer St

St Andrews Pl

Kingston
Park

Herkimer St

7

Pacific St

Dean St

Dean St

Bergen St

CROWN
HEIGHTS

820 Ave

420 Ave

Osborn Ave

Classon Ave

Prospect Pl

St Marks Ave

Prospect Pl

Albany
Housing

St J

490

670

Brower
Park

510

Park Pl

S

670

740

Park Pl

1050
Sterling Pl

1970

Virginia Pl

Buffalo Pl

Kingston Ave

9

Bedford Ave

St John's Pl

Lincoln Pl

Lincoln Pl

2 **3**

Eastern Pkwy-
Brooklyn Museum

Nostrand Ave

Eastern Pkwy

Kingston Ave

1430

3

S

Franklin
Ave

2 **3**

3

1189

1440

348

4 **6**

1040

Union St

Botanic
Garden

989

President St

2 **5**

1330

493

Brooklyn
Botanic
Garden

117

376

935

Dean Ct

Ludlam Pl

President St

Carroll St

Crown St

669

525

440

411

PAGE
144

McKeever Pl

110

Sullivan Pl

315

Montgomery St

Clove Rd

Malbone St

Empire Pl

556

Empire Blvd

Lamont Ct

Balfour Pl

Lefferts Ave

New York Ave

Maple Ave

Midwood St

Rutland Ave

Fenimore St

Hawthorne St

Flatbush Ave

East Dr

Sterling Ave

110

Sterling St

2 **5**

420

Kingston Ave

Brooklyn Ave

Albany Ave

590

PROSPECT
LEFFERTS
GARDENS

Center Dr

Q S

Prospect
Park

PAGE
142

Lefferts Ave

Lincoln Rd

Maple St

Midwood St

Rutland Rd

Fenimore St

426

340

Kings County
Hospital
469

Prospect
Park

Beekman Pl

200

Ocean Ave

60

Chester Ct

2

50

Winthrop St

Winthrop St

2 **5**

290

SUNY
Health Science
Center

Westbury Ct

60

300

Parkside Ave

350

Clarkson Ave

1320

60

Bedford Ave

789

Lenox Rd

2110

Rogers Ave

Nostrand Ave

820

Linden Blvd

E 34th St

E 35th St

E 37th St

E 38th St

E 39th St

Prospect
Lake

13

Martense St

South Lake Dr

Parkside Ave

Q

Parade
Grounds

Parkside Ave

Woodruff Ave

Crooke Ave

St Pauls Pl

St Pauls Ct

Caton Ave

Johnson Ave

Church Ave

Church Ave

2 **5**

Erasmus St

Snyder Ave

| 1/4 mile | .25 km |

There isn't exactly a shopping mecca here, though you can find fresh fruit and West Indian sundries everywhere. Off the beaten path are Jewish stores like **Judaica World** and get a whiff of the nearby Botanic Garden at **Barbara's**. For baked goods, hit **Allan's** or **Lily & Fig**, and, to wake up in the morning, **K-Dog & DuneBuggy** is the place.

Coffee

- **Abigail** • 807 Classon Ave [St Johns Pl]
  718-399-3200
  Start with coffee and stay all day.
- **Breukelen Coffee House** •
  764 Franklin Ave [St Johns Pl]
  718-789-7070
  Franklin Street godsend. Stumptown coffee, Balthazar treats. Sweet.
- **K-Dog & DuneBuggy** •
  43 Lincoln Rd [Flatbush Ave]
  718-282-7139
  Jane's local coffee shop. She says it's excellent.
- **The Pulp & The Bean** •
  809 Franklin Ave [Lincoln Pl]
  347-425-8642
  Coffee, tables, wi-fi.

Shopping

- **65 Fen** • 65 Fenimore St [Flatbush Ave]
  347-715-6001
  Great new Lefferts wine shop; very affordable.
- **Allan's Quality Bakery** •
  1109 Nostrand Ave [Maple St]
  718-774-7892
  Lines into the night.
- **Barbara's Flower Shop** •
  615 Nostrand Ave [Bergen St]
  718-773-6644
  Smells as good as the Botanic Garden.
- **Ethiopian Taste** •
  985 Nostrand Ave [Empire Blvd]
  718-744-0804
  Donna buys African CDs here. So should you.
- **Glass Shop** • 766 Classon Ave [Sterling Pl]
  Old glass workshop serving espresso in glass cups.
- **Judaica World** •
  329 Kingston Ave [Eastern Pkwy]
  718-604-1020
  Party time. Excellent.
- **Lily & Fig** • 727 Franklin Ave [Sterling Pl]
  718-636-0456
  It's cake time boys and girls.
- **Phat Albert's** • 495 Flatbush Ave [Lefferts Ave]
  718-469-2116
  Cheap is good.
- **Raskin's Fish Market** •
  320 Kingston Ave [President St]
  718-756-9521
  Worth the plunge, but hold your nose.
- **Scoops** • 624 Flatbush Ave [Fenimore St]
  718-282-5904
  Tasty ice cream.

Home of the bahn mi craze, the remains of Basquiat, and the highest and second-highest points in Brooklyn, Sunset Park is a neighborhood with a lot going on. Initially, Sunset Park might strike one as a little industrial looking with its bus depots, warehouses, and semis that noisily barrel down 3rd and 4th Avenues, but it's also a neighborhood that boasts some marvelous green space. The eponymous park affords one of the most breathtaking views in New York. Also home to an Olympic-sized public pool, Sunset Park manages to attract most of Brooklyn during the summer months. The hill in the center of the park is the perfect place to look down on it all while picnicking, catching a fireworks show or working off the cellulite. The nearby Tim Burton-esque **Green-Wood Cemetery** is home to the highest point in Brooklyn, not to mention some notable New York celebrities such as Boss Tweed and Leonard Bernstein. A day trip here meandering through its many paths should make your list of things to do in New York—some of the crypts are works of art in themselves; on occasionally the staff will open them for tours.

Like most neighborhoods in Brooklyn, Sunset Park has been attracting younger Manhattan transplants in search of more than just a cheap dim sum brunch and practically free margarita pitchers. That is: cheap rent. However, the neighborhood remains staunchly an immigrant one, though a few new establishments catering to a trendier set have come to roost.

Originally settled by Irish and Dutch immigrants, Sunset Park has since become one of the most diverse neighborhoods in New York, being comprised of Dominicans, Puerto Ricans, Mexicans, Chinese, Malaysian, Korean, and Vietnamese. The two largest populations, however, are Chinese and Mexican. On one side of the park there's Fifth Avenue, known as "Little Latin America," which is one of the largest Mexican-American neighborhoods in New York. Latin American restaurants, bodegas and bakeries line the avenue. In warmer months, older men in the community set up backgammon tables in front of their favorite delis. South and slightly east the park, there's Eighth Avenue, "Brooklyn's Chinatown," with Buddhist temples, Asian markets and dim sum spots galore. A smaller pocket of Vietnamese-Americans also call Sunset Park home, and the Vietnamese restaurant offerings in this part of Brooklyn are among the best in New York. Chinese New Year is celebrated here with verve, replete with parades, confetti and dragons. Though you'll find the respective main drags of "Brooklyn's Chinatown" and "Little Latin America" across the neighborhood from one another, everything in between is a melting pot. Just the way we like it.

North of all this multicultural goodness is a very narrow strip of housing and businesses sandwiched in between the river and the cemetery (named Green-Wood Heights), and north of that is a small portion of what is slowly being considered part of the "South Slope." There are a few good bars, restaurants, and shops opening up on Fifth and Sixth Avenues between the Prospect Expressway and the cemetery; this is definitely an area to watch in the coming years.

Melody Lanes draws even the most reluctant non-Sunset Parker out this way. Irish Haven, a basic pub where scenes from Scorcese's The Departed were filmed, has become equally popular. Check out sound gallery Diapason for avant-garde sound installations and performances. In the South Slope, hit either Korzo, Toby's, or Quarter.

Bars

- **Brooklyn's Tiki Bar** • 885 4th Ave [32nd St]
  718-768-2797
  Ample space in this trashy tiki.
- **Diapason** • 882 3rd Ave [33rd St]
  718-499-5070
  You have to take off your shoes to listen to the sound waves.
- **Feeney's Pub** • 6102 5th Ave [61st St]
  718-439-6020
  A sleepy, local, last resort.
- **Irish Haven** • 5721 4th Ave [58th St]
  718-439-9893
  Good Irish dive.
- **Korzo** • 667 5th Ave [20th St]
  718-285-9425
  Bar, lounge, food, Eastern European vibe.
- **Quarter Bar & Cafe** • 676 5th Ave [20th St]
  718-788-0989
  South Slope/Greenwood bar features D.U.B. pies and indeterminate hours.
- **Smolen Bar** • 708 5th Ave [22nd St]
  718-788-9729
  Dear Readers: This is a true dive bar. Enjoy.
- **Toby's Public House** • 686 6th Ave [21st St]
  718-788-1186
  Open 'till 4 am weekends. We love New York.

Bowling

- **Melody Lanes** • 461 37th St [5th Ave]
  718-832-2695
  NFT-approved bowling. The real deal.

Map 11 · Sunset Park / Green-Wood Heights

Bay St
Sjourney Smith St
Halleck St
Percival St
Clinton St
Bryant St
Court St

1

2

17th St
18th St
19th St
20th St
21st St
22nd St
23rd St
24th St

Prospect Ave
Prospect Ave

27

Prospect Expy

Tenth Ave

17th St
18th St

19th St

20th St

8

GREEN-WOOD HEIGHTS

9

Fifth Ave
Sixth Ave
Seventh Ave

2

25 St

D **N** **R**

25th St
26th St
27th St
28th St
29th St

Roosevelt Ct

Woodrow Ct

PAGE
138

Green-Wood
Cemetery

A

Gowanus Bay

Gowanus Expy

30th St
200
31st St
32nd St
33rd St
34th St
35th St
36th St

32nd St

Marginal St

250

D **N** **R**

36 St

37th St

650

37th St

38th St

BMT Yard

39th St
40th St
41st St
42nd St
43rd St
44th St

440

39th St

2

640

Ninth Ave

D

250

First Ave

Sunset
Park

750

830

940

12

Fort
Hamilton
Pkwy

D

45th St

R

540

2

740

830

Second Ave

Third Ave

46th St
47th St
48th St
49th St
50th St
51st St
52nd St

440

Fourth Ave

Fifth Ave

760

SUNSET
PARK

Sixth Ave

Seventh Ave

Eighth Ave

Ninth Ave

Tenth Ave

Fort Hamilton Pkwy

B

Bush
Terminal
Warehouses

Whale Sq

74

250

440

540

640

750

830

53 St

R

2

53rd St
54th St
55th St
56th St
57th St
58th St
59th St

540

640

640

640

640

750

850

3

LIRR
Yard

278

60th St
61st St
62nd St
63rd St
64th St

440

59 St

N **R**

550

550

62nd St
63rd St
64th St

640

750

850

Eighth Ave

N

Fort Hamilton
Ave

Fort Hamilton Pkwy

N Pkwy

14

65th St
66th St

Shore Road Dr

Wakeman Pl

Restaurants

Food is Sunset Park's specialty. Bahn mi doesn't get much better than **Ba Xuyen**, **8th Avenue Seafood** is one of the only worthwhile dim sum spots where you won't encounter brunch lines (**Pacificana** is one where you will, but it's worth the wait). For sloppy late-night hangover prevention, you can't beat **Tacos Matamoros**.

Restaurants

- **8th Avenue Seafood** • 4418 8th Ave [45th St]
718-633-6366 • $$
No brunch line!
- **Ba Xuyen** • 4222 8th Ave [42nd St]
718-633-6601 • $
Best bahn mi in Brooklyn.
- **Bubble Bee Cafe** • 5719 4th Ave [58th St]
718-439-6918 • $
The cheapest bahn mi and bubble tea.
- **Castillo Ecuatoriano** • 4020 5th Ave [40th St]
718-437-7676 • $$
Wide range of Ecuadoran platters.
- **El Tesoro Ecuatoriano Restaurant** •
4015 5th Ave [40th St]
718-972-3756 • $$
Ecuadorian grub, great seafood.
- **Elite Turkish Restaurant** •
805 60th St [8th Ave]
718-633-3535 • $$$
Great food. Must wear tuxedo for dinner.
- **Family Dumpling** • 5602 7th Ave [56th St]
718-492-0686 • $
Delicious beef pancake more than makes up
for surly owner.
- **International Restaurant** •
4408 5th Ave [44th St]
718-438-2009 • $$
Awesome Dominican-style breakfast.
- **J King Seafood Palace** •
618 62nd St [6th Ave]
718-833-3777 • $$
Massive dim sum parlor. Mandarin skills a plus.
- **Johnny's Pizzeria** • 5806 5th Ave [58th st]
718-492-9735 • $
Classic pizza joint.
- **Kakala Café** • 5302 8th Ave [53rd St]
718-437-9688 • $
Sweet, milky teas and oodles of noodles for
the "new generation."
- **King Star** • 6022 8th Ave [60th St]
718-492-6888 • $$
Surprisingly good Chinese.
- **Korzo** • 667 5th Ave [20th St]
718-285-9425 • $$
Eastern European pub grub.
- **La Gran Via Bakery** • 4516 5th Ave [45th St]
718-853-8021 • $
24-hour diabetes special.

- **Lanzhou Hand Pulled Noodles** •
5924 8th Ave [59th St]
718-492-7568 • $
Watch the theatrical master noodle puller
work his magic.
- **Mai Thai Thai Kitchen** • 4618 8th Ave [46th St]
718-438-3413 • $$
Spicy-hot pad thai with cool outdoor seating.
- **Mas Que Pan** • 5401 5th Ave [54th St]
718-492-0479 • $
Latino bakery with killer Cuban sandwiches.
- **Nyonya** • 5323 8th Ave [53rd St]
718-633-0808 • $$
Hokey interior; excellent Malaysian.
- **Pacificana** • 813 55th St [8th Ave]
718-871-2880 • $$
Filling the dim sum-sized hole in your heart.
Yum.
- **Piaxtla es Mexico Deli** • 505 51st St [5th Ave]
718-633-4816 • $
Cheap and delicious tacos and tortas.
- **Quarter Bar & Cafe** • 676 5th Ave [20th St]
718-788-0989 • $$
Cheese plates and savory pies.
- **Shi Wei Xian** • 5701 7th Ave [57th St]
718-567-7628 • $$
Quality Chinese.
- **Sunset Park Empanada Cart** •
5th Ave & 48th St • $
Munch and stroll.
- **Sunstone Tortillas Express Restaurant** •
5411 5th Ave [54th St]
718-439-8434 • $
The best and the cheapest of the
Chinese-operated Mexican.
- **Super Pollo Latino** • 4102 5th Ave [41st St]
718-871-5700 • $
Peruvian food famous for their chicken.
- **Tacos Matamoros** • 4508 5th Ave [45th St]
718-871-7627 • $
You can't get more Mexican than this!
- **Toby's Public House** • 686 6th Ave [21st St]
718-788-1186 • $$
4 words: Nutella and Ricotta Calzone. Trust us.
- **Yun Nan Flavour Snack Shop** •
775 49th St [8th Ave]
718-633-3090 • $
The name says it: flavorful Chinese snacks.
Cheap.

Map 11

Map 11 · Sunset Park / Green-Wood Heights

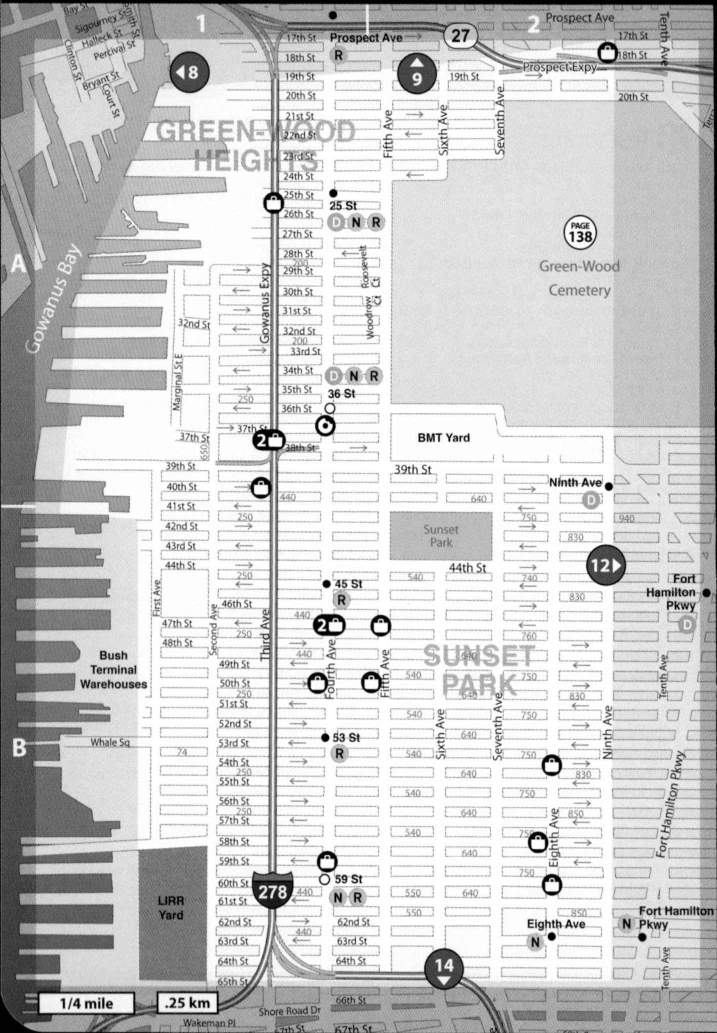

1

◄8

Bay St
Sigourney St
Halleck St
Percival St
Bryant St
Clinton St

GREEN-WOOD HEIGHTS

17th St
18th St
19th St
20th St
21st St
22nd St
23rd St
24th St
25th St
26th St
27th St
28th St
29th St
30th St
31st St
32nd St
33rd St
34th St
35th St
36th St

Prospect Ave

27

2 Prospect Ave

17th St
18th St

Prospect Expy

R

9

19th St
20th St

Fifth Ave
Sixth Ave
Seventh Ave

25 St
D **N** **R**

Woodrow Ct
Roosevelt Ct

PAGE 138

Green-Wood Cemetery

A

Gowanus Bay

Gowanus Expy

Marginal St E

32nd St

250

250

650

37th St

D **N** **R**

36 St

2

38th St

39th St
40th St
41st St
42nd St
43rd St
44th St

First Ave

440

250

250

250

BMT Yard

39th St

640

Ninth Ave
D

750

830

940

Sunset Park

44th St

640

740

750

830

12►

Fort Hamilton Pkwy

D

45 St

2

540

440

Second Ave

Third Ave

Fourth Ave

Fifth Ave

Sixth Ave

Seventh Ave

Eighth Ave

Ninth Ave

Tenth Ave

Fort Hamilton Pkwy

46th St
47th St
48th St
49th St
50th St
51st St
52nd St
53rd St
54th St
55th St
56th St
57th St
58th St
59th St
60th St
61st St
62nd St
63rd St
64th St
65th St

250

540

540

540

540

540

540

550

550

SUNSET PARK

640

640

640

640

640

640

760

648

750

750

830

850

750

53 St
R

59 St
N **R**

278

Eighth Ave
N

Fort Hamilton Pkwy
N

850

Tenth Ave

Bush Terminal Warehouses

B

Whale Sq

74

LIRR Yard

14

66th St
67th St

Shore Road Dr

Wakeman Pl

1/4 mile

.25 km

Map 11

Shopping in Sunset Park is more practical (**Rossman's Fruit and Vegetables**, **Costco**, **East Coast Beer**, **Hong Kong Supermarket**) than sexy, but bizarre magic-and-potion shop **Botanica 7 Potencias** will definitely make you think (rightly) that there is more to Sunset Park than meets the (inner) eye.

Bagels

• **Jerry Bagels** • 959 4th Ave [36th St]
718-832-4505
Homemade cream cheese!

Shopping

• **Boom Variety Gift Shop** •
4702 5th Ave [47th St]
718-492-6735
A selection to please the most discriminating dork.
• **Botanica 7 Potencias** • 4722 4th Ave [47th St]
718-439-3726
Secret little shop full of surprises.
• **Costco** • 976 3rd Ave [37th St]
718-965-7603
Where to shop if you have 4 kids and/or copious storage.
• **Don Paco Lopez Panaderia** •
4703 4th Ave [47th St]
718-492-7443
Mexico City-style bakery with amazing champurrado.
• **East Coast Beer Co** •
969 3rd Ave [37th St]
718-788-8000
For all your beer needs—kegs included.
• **Fabio's Tropical Ices** • 4918 4th Ave [50th St]
718-492-8644
Where small means extra large. Over 20 flavors.

• **Frankel's Discount Clothing** •
3924 3rd Ave [40th St]
718-768-9788
Less about fashion, more about character.
• **Full Doe Bakery** • 5905 4th Ave [59th St]
718-439-8880
Inexpensive Chinese goodies.
• **Hong Kong Supermarket** •
6023 8th Ave [60th St]
718-438-2288
Massive Asian grocery.
• **Movable Feast** •
284 Prospect Park West [18th St]
718-965-2900
Catering to your every need.
• **Petland Discounts** • 5015 5th Ave [50th St]
718-871-7699
Crap for your stupid pet.
• **Reef Aqiarium Inc** • 5415 8th Ave [54th St]
718-633-7850
Large selection of fish in Brooklyn Chinatown.
• **Rossman Fruit and Vegetable** •
770 3rd Ave [25th St]
718-788-3999
Try and spend $20 here.
• **Ten Ren Tea & Ginseng** •
5817 8th Ave [58th St]
718-853-0660
Lovely selection of teas.

Map 12 · **Borough Park**

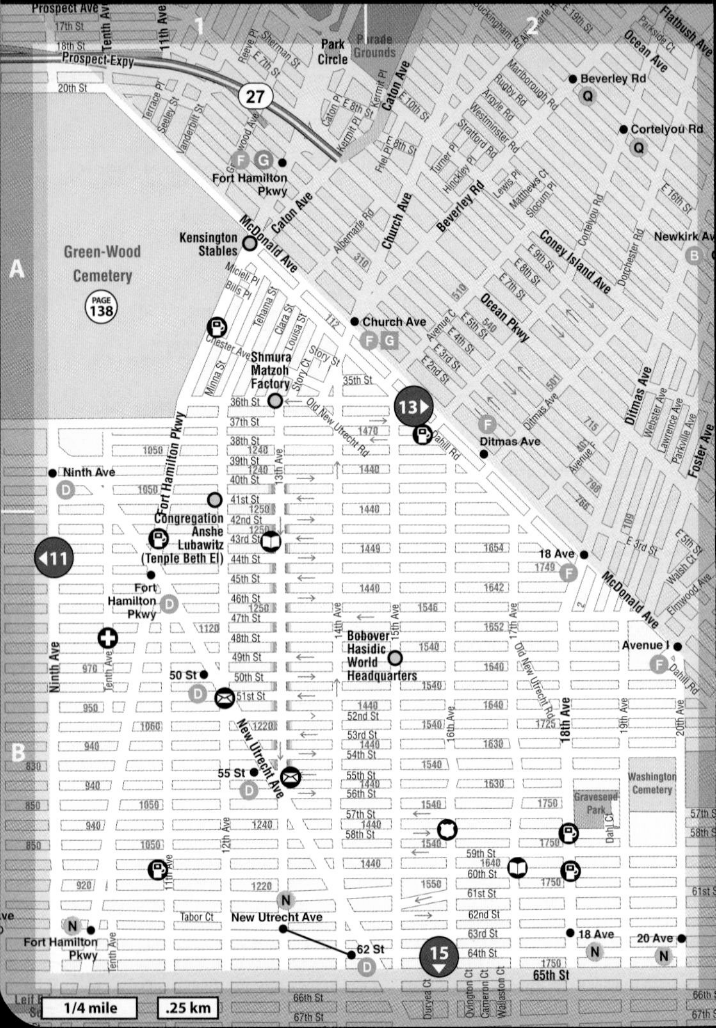

N

Prospect Ave
17th St
Tenth Ave
11th Ave
18th St
Prospect-Expy
20th St

Park Circle
Parade Grounds

27

Fort Hamilton Pkwy
F G

Kensington Stables

McDonald Ave
Caton Ave

Ocean Ave
Beverley Rd
Q

Cortelyou Rd
Q

Church Ave

Coney Island Ave
Ocean Pkwy

Newkirk Ave

Green-Wood Cemetery
PAGE 138

A

Church Ave
F G

Shmura Matzoh Factory

Old New Utrecht Rd
35th St
36th St
37th St
38th St
39th St
40th St

Fort Hamilton Pkwy
Chester Ave
Minna St
Clara St
Louisa St
Story St
Story Ct

13

Ditmas Ave
F

Ninth Ave
D

1050
1050
1240
1240
1240
1250

41st St
42nd St
43rd St
44th St
45th St
46th St
47th St
48th St
49th St
50th St
51st St
52nd St
53rd St
54th St
55th St
56th St
57th St
58th St
59th St
60th St
61st St
62nd St
63rd St
64th St
65th St
66th St
67th St

Congregation Anshe Lubawitz (Temple Beth El)

Fort Hamilton Pkwy
D

11

1440
1449
1440
1540
1440
1540
1640
1540
1640
1540
1630
1440
1630
1540
1640
1550
1750

1470
1440

Bobover Hasidic World Headquarters

15th Ave
16th Ave
17th Ave
18th Ave

18 Ave
1749
F

1654
1642
1652
1640

Avenue I
F

18 Ave
N

20 Ave
N

Dahill Rd

Washington Cemetery

Gravesend Park

1750
1750
1750

1750

Ninth Ave
970
950
1060
950
940
830
940
850
940
850
920

Tenth Ave
11th Ave
12th Ave

New Utrecht Ave
50 St
D

55 St
D

1120
1250
1440
1220
1220
1250
1240
1440
1440
1240

N
Fort Hamilton Pkwy

Tabor Ct
New Utrecht Ave
N

62 St
D

15

1/4 mile   .25 km

Map 12

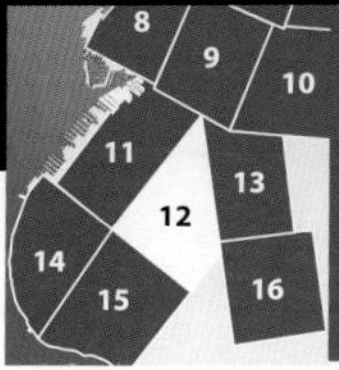

Williamsburg and Crown Heights have nothing on Borough Park (sometimes written Boro Park), home to the largest Orthodox Jewish population outside of Israel, including a burgeoning enclave of Hasidim. With ever-expanding boundaries, the neighborhood keeps growing, as do the families, with an average of six children per household. It's no wonder some have been calling it the "baby-boom of Brooklyn." These religious residents might garner attention on the subways for their wigs or their peyas, but in Borough Park, it's the non-Orthodox or Hasidic Jew that's the anomaly. You will certainly feel a little out of place here if you fall into that category; best to bring along that English-to-Yiddish dictionary. Yiddish, by the way, is everywhere. Along with Hebrew and Russian, it's widely spoken in the streets and shops, printed on signs, and an option on ATM menu screens.

Borough Park is a haven of family values and religious tradition. Some of the best times to visit are during the more festive holidays—either Sukkot or Purim. But on any given day, it's not unusual to see crowds numbering in the thousands spilling into the streets as a wedding lets out at a nearby synagogue. In contrast, by sundown on Friday for the Sabbath, the shtetl is virtually empty—no people, no lights, and no cars. One of the neighborhood's more important synagogues is the **Congregation Anshei Lubawitz**, a landmark neoclassical structure.

To move into this neighborhood, one would have better luck marrying into the community than finding something through a broker, but a few nights in **The Avenue Plaza Hotel** will give you a good dose of Borough Park culture. Catering mostly to Israelis who have come to visit relatives, or attend weddings or conferences, it's one of the few luxury hotel options in Brooklyn and a testament to Borough Park's importance as a hub of Orthodox and Hasidic practices.

But this is New York still, right? So where'd all the Starbucks go? Apart from banks, chain businesses are nearly non-existent, but you will find plenty of independently run shops, many of which cater to the religious needs of the community. Wig shops, kosher delis, and Judaica bookstores abound. Be aware that in keeping with the Sabbath, most shops are closed from sundown on Friday until sundown on Saturday. Bustling Thirteenth Avenue is the main shopping drag, and a good base from which to start exploring the neighborhood—it's the picture of wholesomeness and old world mercantilism with its shoe cobblers, furniture stores and bakeries. Borough Park boasts some fine discount shopping–and not just on the gefilte fish—designer housewares, china, clothes (albeit, modest ones) and furniture are among the cheapest to be found in New York City.

Around Passover, watch the lines crowd around the **Shmura Matzoh Factory**, one of the few bakeries in the United States that makes shmura matzoh, which is matzoh that has been shepherded and blessed by a Rabbi during every stage of the process from grain to unleavened bread.

Map 12 · Borough Park

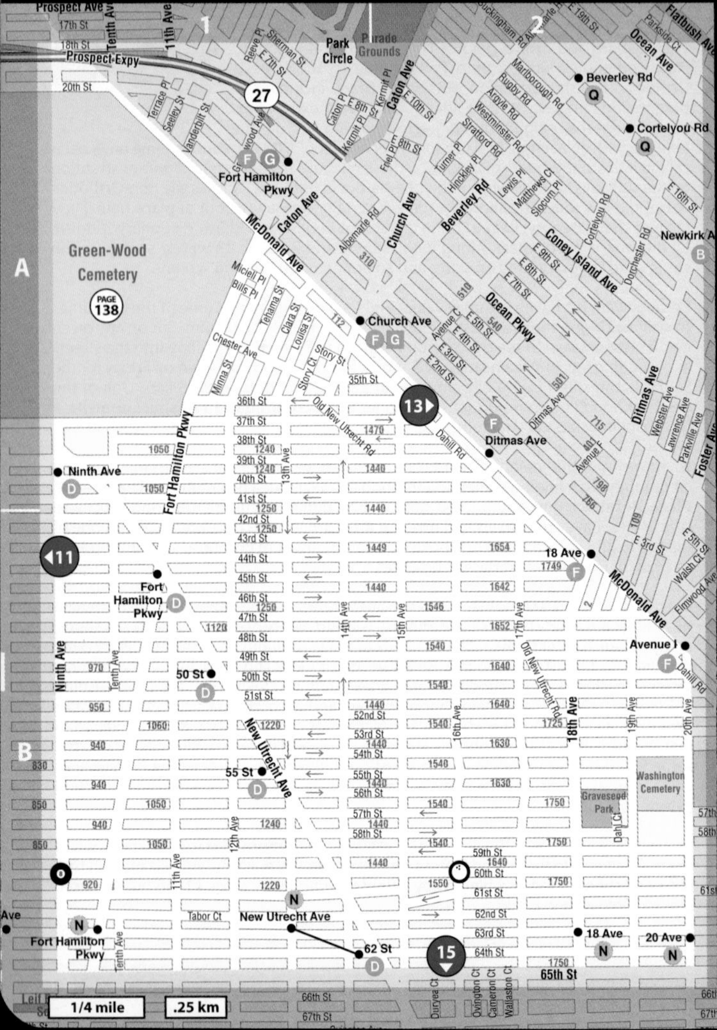

N

Prospect Ave
17th St
18th St
Prospect Expy
20th St

11th Ave
Tenth Ave

Reeve Pl
E 7th St
Sherman St

Park Circle

Parade Grounds

Buckingham Rd
E 16th St

2

Flatbush Ave
Marlborough Rd

Ocean Ave

27

Fort Hamilton Pkwy
F G

Terrace Pl
Seeley St
Vanderbilt St

Caton Pl
Caton Ave
Linden Ct

Caton Ave

Church Ave

McDonald Ave

Albemarle Rd
318
310

Beverley Rd

Rugby Rd
Argyle Rd
Westminster Rd
Stratford Rd
Field Pl
Turner Pl

Q Beverley Rd

Q Cortelyou Rd

Cortelyou Rd

Marlborough Rd

Lewis Pl
Matthews Ct
Highlawn Ave

Beverley Rd

E 4th St
E 3rd St

Coney Island Ave

Newkirk Ave

A

Green-Wood Cemetery

PAGE 138

Church Ave F G

Chester Ave

Minna St

Micieli Pl
Bills Pl

Tehama St
Clara St
Louisa St
Story St

Old New Utrecht Ave

E 2nd St
Ocean Pkwy

540
534
528

Church Ave

Ditmas Ave

Avenue C
518

715
735

Ditmas Ave

Dahill Rd

Dahill Rd

Waldorf Ct
Lawrence Ave
Parkville Ave

Foster Ave

36th St
37th St
38th St
39th St
40th St
41st St
42nd St
43rd St
44th St
45th St
46th St
47th St
48th St
49th St
50th St
51st St
52nd St
53rd St
54th St
55th St
56th St
57th St
58th St

13th Ave
14th Ave
15th Ave

18 Ave F
1749

18th Ave

E 3rd St

Old New Utrecht Ave

17th Ave

Elmore Pl

19th Ave
20th St

Avenue J F

B

Ninth Ave D

Fort Hamilton Pkwy

Ninth Ave
Tenth Ave
11th Ave

Fort Hamilton Pkwy D

50 St D

55 St D

1050
1050
970
950
1050
940
830
850
940
850

1050
1120
1250
1220
940
1050
1240

11

Fort Hamilton Pkwy D

1470
1240
1240
1440
1440
1440
1449
1440
1546
1540
1640
1440
1540
1640
1440
1540
1630
1440
1830
1440
1540
1440

1654
1642
1652
1725

Gravesend Park

Dahill Rd

1750
1750
1750

Washington Cemetery

58th

o

N Fort Hamilton Pkwy

Tenth Ave
11th Ave

920

Tabor Ct

New Utrecht Ave N

62 St D

920
1229
1240

59th St
60th St
61st St
62nd St
63rd St
64th St
65th St

1640
1550
1540

15

63rd St
Dorina Ct
Dahgren Pl
Calderon Ct
Wallabout St

18 Ave N

20 Ave N

1750

61st

1/4 mile   .25 km

66th St
67th St

Map 1

What were you expecting? Beyond the late-night discussions that go around at the falafel shops, there is little to be done here after dark. After all, six kids per household have to happen sometime. Your two choices are shooting pool at **60th Street Billiards** or bowling at **Maple Lanes**. That's some action, we guess...

 Billiards

• **60th Street Billiards** • 928 60th St [9th Ave]
718-436-5602
Shoot pool while you wait for your car to get fixed.

 Bowling

• **Maple Lanes** • 1570 60th St [16th Ave]
718-331-9000
Nightlife in Borough Park: this is it, folks.

Nowhere, apart from maybe Israel, do you have so many kosher options. Falafel does a mean, competitive business. Try **Cheskel's Shwarma King** for some of the best. There are some international offerings here too, including **China Glatt** for sloppy Chinese that's been blessed by a Rabbi.

Restaurants

• **A&J Pizzeria** •
4412 Fort Hamilton Pkwy [New Utrecht Ave]
718-871-5745 • $
Extra-crunchy, extra-cheesy pie.

• **Cheskel's Shwarma King** •
3715 13th Ave [37th St]
718-435-7100 • $
Shwarma, salad bar, baba ghanoush.

• **China Glatt** • 4413 13th Ave [44th St]
718-438-2576 • $$
Kosher Chinese. Only in New York. And Israel.

• **Cracovia Deli** • 5511 13th Ave [55th St]
718-851-7357 • $$
Best Polish Deli in Borough Park? Why not? No one's reading this anyway.

• **Crown Deli** • 4909 13th Ave [49th St]
718-853-9000 • $$
Authentic Jewish deli.

• **Donut Man** • 4708 13th Ave [47th St]
718-436-7318 • $$
Authentically retro luncheonette.

• **El Morro** • 4018 14th Ave [40th St]
718-851-8976 • $$
South and Central American.

• **Glatt a la Carte** • 5123 18th Ave [51st St]
718-438-6675 • $$
Fancy pants kosher steakhouse.

• **Kosher Delight Family Restaurant** •
4600 13th Ave [46th St]
718-435-8500 • $$
Kosher fast food.

• **La Asuncion** •
3914 Fort Hamilton Pkwy [39th St]
718-437-0864 • $
Authentic Mexican.

• **Mendel's Pizza** • 4923 18th Ave [49th St]
718-438-8493 • $
Kosher pizza plus blintzes, falafel, and such.

• **World Tong Seafood** •
6202 18th Ave [62nd St]
718-236-8118 • $$
Good dim sum, rest assured, despite chef Joe Ng's departure.

Map 12 · **Borough Park**

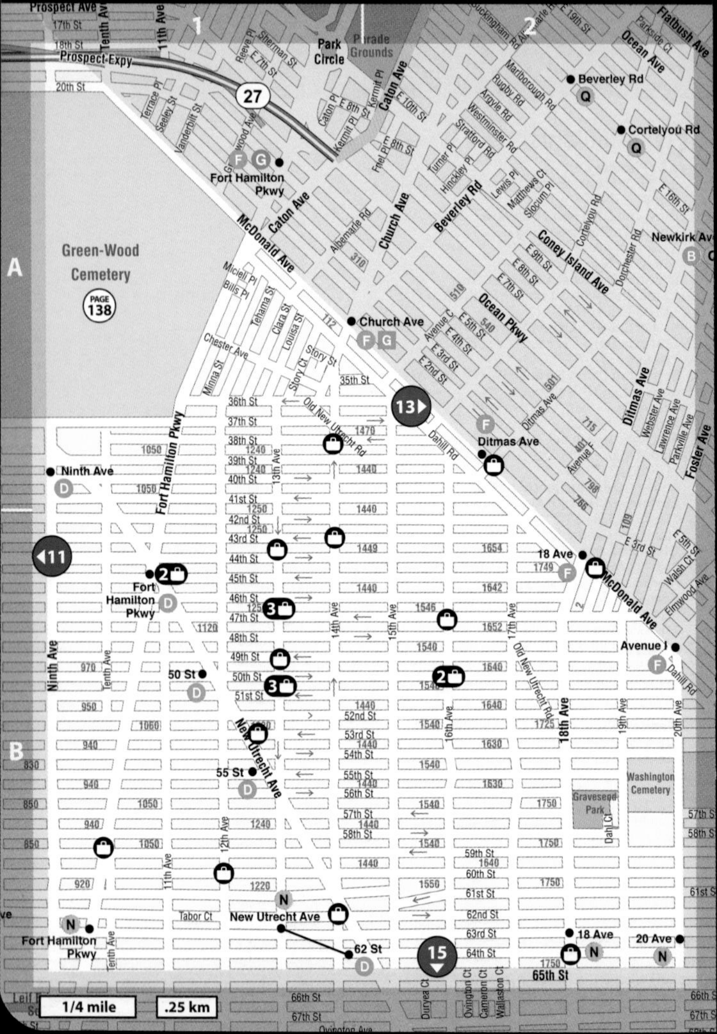

Ⓝ

Prospect Ave
17th St
Tenth Ave
11th St
18th St
Prospect-Expy
20th St

Park Circle
Parade Grounds

Caton Ave
Buckingham Rd
Marlborough Rd
Rugby Rd
Ocean Ave
Parkside Ave
E 19th St

● Beverley Rd Q

Westminster Rd
Argyle Rd
Rugby Rd
E 8th St
● Cortelyou Rd Q

Ⓝ 27

Fort Hamilton Pkwy
Ⓕ Ⓖ ●

Caton Ave
McDonald Ave
Church Ave

Stratford Rd
Westminster Rd
Marlborough Rd
Rugby Rd
E 9th St

Beverley Rd
E 9th St
E 8th St
E 7th St

Coney Island Ave
Newkirk Ave

Green-Wood Cemetery
PAGE 138

Micelli Pl
Bull's Pl
Chester Ave
Minna St
Clara St
Louisa St
Story Ct
Story St
112
Old New Utrecht Rd

Church Ave
Ⓕ Ⓖ ●
35th St

Ocean Pkwy
E 5th St
E 4th St
E 3rd St

Ditmas Ave
Dahill Rd
E 4th St
E 5th St
715

Ⓕ Ditmas Ave

Ditmas Ave
Lawrence Ave
Parkville Ave
Foster Ave

A

Fort Hamilton Pkwy
36th St
37th St
38th St 1470
39th St
40th St
13th Ave
1240
1240

1440
1440

Dahill Rd

13 ►

Ⓕ
Ditmas Ave
⬛
1440

786

E 5th St
E 3rd St

● Ninth Ave
Ⓓ
1050
1050

41st St
42nd St
43rd St
44th St
250
1250
⬛

14th Ave
1440

1443

1654

● 18 Ave
Ⓕ
1749

McDonald Ave

◄ 11

Ⓓ
2 ⬛
Fort Hamilton Pkwy
Ⓓ
1120

45th St
46th St
47th St
3 ⬛
1440

15th Ave
1546

1642

1652

18th Ave

B

Ninth Ave
970
950

Tenth Ave
1060

New Utrecht Ave
12th Ave

50 St
Ⓓ
48th St
49th St
50th St
3 ⬛
51st St
52nd St

Ⓕ
4 ⬛
9 ⬛

1540

1540

2 ⬛
1640

1640

Avenue I ●
Ⓕ
Dahill Rd
19th Ave

940
830
940
1050

55 St
Ⓓ

53rd St
54th St
55th St
56th St
1440
1440
1440

16th Ave
1540

1540

1725

Old New Utrecht Rd

Wash Ct
E 3rd St
Elmwood Ave

650
540
940

11th Ave
1240
1220

57th St
58th St
59th St
60th St
1440
1540

1630

1630

1750
1750

Gravesend Park

Washington Cemetery
57th St
58th St

920
● N
1050

Tabor Ct
61st St
62nd St
1550

1640
1750

● 18 Ave
61st St

Ⓝ ●
Fort Hamilton Pkwy
New Utrecht Ave
Ⓝ
62 St
Ⓓ

63rd St
64th St
65th St

Dunyea Ct
Ovington Ct
Camden Ct
Wallaston Ct

1750
Ⓝ

20 Ave ●

15 ▼

66th St
67th St
Ovington Ave

1/4 mile | .25 km

Apart from God, shopping is the main attraction in Borough Park and Eichler's is the spot to get your Borough Park souvenir. Then, do as the Borough Parkites do—get a challah at **Kaff's Bakery** and a hat at **Kova Quality**. Otherwise, hit **Trainworld** if you're a model train buff or **Bulletproof Comics** if you're, well, a geek.

Shopping

- **A Touch of Spirit Liquors** •
4720 16th Ave [47th St]
718-438-2409
Kosher wine is more than just Manischewitz.
- **Antiques & Decorations** •
4319 14th Ave [43rd St]
718-633-6393
Bubbe's living room, for sale!
- **Bari Pork Store** • 6319 18th Ave [64th St]
718-837-9773
Paradise for pig products.
- **Berkowitz Baby Carriages** •
5314 New Utrecht Ave [53rd St]
718-436-3333
Be fruitful and multiply.
- **Bulletproof Comics** •
4507 Fort Hamilton Pkwy [45th St]
718-854-3367
Comics. If you're into that sort of thing.
- **Circus Fruits** •
5916 Fort Hamilton Pkwy [59th St]
718-436-2100
Fantastic selection and prices; some exotic stuff.
- **Coluccio & Sons** • 1214 60th St [12th Ave]
718-436-6700
Imported Italian specialties.
- **Eichler's** • 5004 13th Ave [50th St]
718-633-1505
Borough Park Judaica superstore.
- **Focus Electronics** • 4509 13th Ave [46th St]
718-436-4646
Local B&H with appliances that go off and on automatically on Shabbos.
- **Jacadi** • 5005 16th Ave [50th St]
718-871-9402
European-style children's boutique.
- **Kaff's Bakery** •
4518 Fort Hamilton Pkwy [45th St]
718-633-2600
Kosher bread-a-plenty.

- **Kosher Candy Man** • 4702 13th Ave [47th St]
718-438-5419
Yummy holiday and gift arrangements.
- **Kova Quality Hatters** •
4317 13th Ave [44th St]
718-871-2944
Men's black fedoras with a variety of brims.
- **Mostly Music** • 4815 13th Ave [49th St]
718-438-2766
Mostly Jewish music.
- **The Peppermill** • 5015 16th Ave [50th St]
718-871-4022
Upscale cookware and bakeware.
- **Polski Sklep** • 8146 18th Ave [81st St]
You'll get stares while finding unique imported eats.
- **Scribbles** • 3720 14th Ave [38th St]
718-435-8711
Classroom supplies and crafts.
- **Strauss Bakery** • 5115 13th Ave [51st St]
718-851-7728
Amazingly fancy cakes.
- **Trainworld** • 751 McDonald Ave [Ditmas Ave]
718-436-7072
Wholesale prices on hundreds of model trains. A choo choo paradise.
- **Underworld Plaza** •
1421 62nd St [New Utrecht Ave]
718-232-6804
Underwear city.
- **United Colors of Benetton** •
4610 13th Ave [46th St]
718-853-3420
Orthodox-approved selection of modest clothes.
- **Weiss Bakery** • 5011 13th Ave [50th St]
718-438-0407
Wedding cakes to party-size challahs.

Map 13 • **Kensington / Ditmas Park**

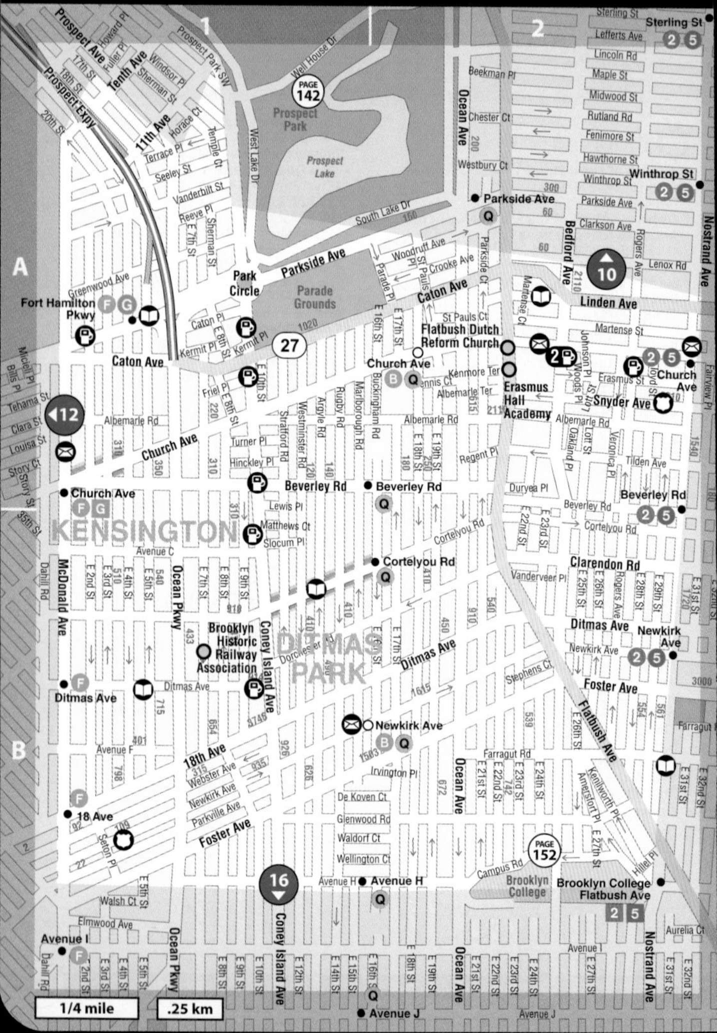

N

Sterling St
Sterling St
Lefferts Ave
Lincoln Rd
Maple St
Midwood St
Rutland Rd
Fenimore St
Hawthorne St
Winthrop St
Winthrop St
Parkside Ave
Clarkson Ave
Bedford Ave
Lenox Rd
Linden Ave

Prospect Ave
Prospect Ave
Howard Pl
Windsor Pl
Prospect Park SW
Sherman St
Tenth Ave
11th Ave
Prospect Expwy
Prospect Park
Prospect Lake
PAGE 142
UJC Horse Dr
Beekman Pl
Chester Ct
Ocean Ave
Westbury Ct
South Lake Dr
Parkside Ave

Terrace Ct
Seeley St
Horace Ct
Temple Ct
Vanderbilt St
Reeve Pl
Sherman St
West Lake Dr
Park Circle
Parkside Ave
Woodruff Ave
Crooke Ave
Caton Ave
St Pauls Ct
Albemarle Ter
Dennis Ct
Kenmore Ter
Albemarle Rd
Martense Ct
Johnson Woods Pl
Linden Ave
Martense St
Erasmus St
Church Ave
Snyder Ave

Parade Grounds
Flatbush Dutch Reform Church
Church Ave
Erasmus Hall Academy

Fort Hamilton Pkwy
Greenwood Ave
Caton Ave
Kermit Pl
Friel Pl
Albemarle Rd
Church Ave
KENSINGTON
Church Ave
Beverley Rd
Beverley Rd
Beverley Rd
Lewis Pl
Matthews Ct
Slocum Pl
Cortelyou Rd
Cortelyou Rd
Clarendon Rd
Vanderveer Pl
Ditmas Ave
Newkirk Ave
Newkirk Ave
Foster Ave
Farragut

McDonald Ave
Ocean Pkwy
Brooklyn Historic Railway Association
DITMAS PARK
Dorchester Rd
Ditmas Ave
Stephens Ct
18th Ave
Webster Ave
Newkirk Ave
Parkville Ave
Foster Ave
Irvington Pl
De Koven Ct
Glenwood Rd
Waldorf Ct
Wellington Ct
Avenue H
Avenue H
Campus Rd
PAGE 152
Brooklyn College Flatbush Ave

Ditmas Ave
Avenue F
18 Ave
Walsh St
Elmwood Ave
Avenue I
Coney Island Ave
Ocean Pkwy
Brooklyn College
Avenue I

Aurelia Ct
Nostrand Ave
Farragut Rd

1/4 mile   .25 km

Avenue J

Parkside Ave
Flatbush Ave
Dorchester Rd
Coney Island Ave

Neighborhood Overview

Map 13

Gigantic turreted Victorian homes, many with surprising and unique architectural details, make Ditmas Park one of the least New York-looking neighborhoods in New York, but also one of the most scenic for a long walk or bike ride. You'll see film crews out here regularly, getting the tree-lined moneyed-suburbia shots they'd otherwise have to drive to Connecticut to find. Most assuredly, you'll find yourself wanting one of these mansions of your very own—and to tide you over until you can make the down payment, the place abounds with inexpensive bed and breakfasts. Cortelyou Road, the main drag, has attracted a few notable bourgeois restaurants that have made a light splash in Grub Street and *The New York Times*, setting off a domino effect down the entire street with trendy, organic and specialized, coffee shops, restaurants, and bars cropping up rapidly. Apart from Cortelyou Road, and, to some extent, Newkirk Avenue, Ditmas Park is pretty sleepy and residential but still refreshingly diverse despite its recent influx of Park Slope rent-refugees. Walk down Foster Avenue and you'll pass by Hasidim, Caribbean-Americans, young married couples with strollers, middle-aged guys passing the time together outside the liquor store, and perhaps a crazy cat lady giving you the eye as she weeds her begonia patch.

Lacking the architectural grandeur and quality dining options of Ditmas Park, adjacent Kensington has little to recommend it to those passing through. Comprised mostly of Polish groceries, Mexican restaurants, and discount stores, it is mainly a residential neighborhood and though it's a little on the boring side, residents find the safety and affordability more than enough to recommend this little slice of Brooklyn tucked just below Prospect Park. The homes here are a bit smaller than in Ditmas Park, but there's still a sense of spaciousness and suburbia here. If the backyards here weren't cause enough to make one wonder if they were still in New York, a parade of horses being groomed in the street on Caton Place by **Kensington Stables** certainly will. With easy park access, the barn offers trail rides through the park, lessons and boarding.

Kensington and Ditmas Park were originally settled by the Dutch in the 1600s, remaining mostly farmland until the early twentieth century. In the late 1970s and '80s, Ditmas Park became the fashionable alternative to Long Island for wealthy Manhattan commuters before briefly falling into disrepair and neglect in some areas. Recent interest in both neighborhoods' low rents and space options have brought the attendant gentrification, though it's happening here at a much slower pace than elsewhere in New York.

Stroll down some of Ditmas Park's side streets—try Malborough, Argyle or Rugby—for an eyeful of some breathtaking mansions. Kensington's **Erasmus Hall Academy**, built in 1786, is one of the oldest high schools in the U.S.; the building was abandoned several years ago though restoration efforts are underway. The **Flatbush Dutch Reform Church**, however, is alive and well. The current building was built in 1783-98 and houses a magnificent pipe organ. Listen for the chimes on the hour.

Map 13 • **Kensington / Ditmas Park**

There isn't much in between the local rummy bar **Shenanigans** and the candlelit date-spot **Sycamore**, but with new places like live jazz venue **Solo** on the rise, you can bet it won't be too much longer until more options abound.

Bars

- **Denny's Steak Pub** •
  106 Beverley Rd [Church Ave]
  718-435-2156
  Attracts nefarious souls with missing teeth in need of liberal pours.
- **Michelle's Cocktail Lounge** •
  2294 Bedford Ave [Albemarle Rd]
  718-284-1185
  Rustic pub.
- **Shenanigans Pub** • 802 Caton Ave [E 8th St]
  718-633-3689
  Tavern-like with a dark tropical feel.
- **Solo Kitchen and Bar** •
  1502 Cortelyou Rd [E 15th St]
  718-826-0920?
  Regular live jazz, darts, food and some of the most viable pick-up options.
- **Sycamore** • 1118 Cortelyou Rd [Stratford Rd]
  347-240-5850
  Flower shop by day, barroom by night.

Map 13 · Kensington / Ditmas Park

Between these two neighborhoods, there's some exquisite, in-the-know type of fooding to be done. Church Avenue is a good place to start adventuring; **Taqueria Los Poblanos** and **In Between Eatry and Pastry** are among the best for cheap take-out. For more upscale chowing, Cortelyou Road's latest addition, Filipino **Purple Yam**, competes with mainstays **Picket Fence** and **Farm on Adderley**.

🍴 Restaurants

- **Bahar** • 984 Coney Island Ave [Ditmas Ave]
  718-434-8088 • $$
  Authentic Afghan cuisine (like we'd know).
- **Cafe Tibet** • 1510 Cortelyou Rd [Marlborough]
  718-941-2725 • $
  Near the train station, perfect for
  people-watching. Excellent momos.
- **Cinco De Mayo Restaurant** •
  1202 Cortelyou Rd [E 12th St]
  718-693-1022 • $
  Great taste, large portions.
- **Dougie's BBQ & Grill** • 4310 18th Ave [E 2nd]
  718-686-8080 • $$
  Kosher barbeque.
- **El Gaucho Glatt Steakhouse** •
  4102 18th Ave [E 4th St]
  718-438-3006 • $$$$
  We'll eat at any kind of steakhouse.
- **Exquisite Delight** • 2847 Church Ave [E 17th]
  718-693-4643 • $
  Jerk chicken for president.
- **The Farm on Adderley** •
  1108 Cortelyou Rd [Stratford Rd]
  718-287-3101 • $$
  An unlikely gem in a reviving 'nabe. Killer
  desserts and a heated garden.
- **George's** • 753 Coney Island Ave [Cortelyou]
  718-282-0152 • $$
  Multi-cuisine—American, Greek, and Italian
  smorgasbord.
- **In Between Eatery and Pastry** •
  1003 Church Ave [E 10th St]
  718-856-1919 • $
  Some of the most delicious roti this side of
  Flatbush.
- **Jhinuk** • 478 McDonald Ave [Church Ave]
  718-871-5355 • $
  Homestyle Bangladeshi food. Utensils optional.
- **Little Bangladesh** •
  483 McDonald Ave [Church Ave]
  718-871-7080 • $$
  Bangladeshi delight.
- **Los Mariachis** •
  805 Coney Island Ave [Dorchester Rd]
  718-826-3388 • $$$
  Muy authentic, especially on weekends with
  live mariachi music.
- **Madina** • 563 Coney Island Ave [Beverley Rd]
  718-469-3535 • $$
  Pakistani goodness open 24 hours.

- **Mimi's Hummus** • 1209 Cortelyou Rd [E 12th]
  718-284-4444 • $$
  Candlelight and a variety of Middle Eastern
  small plates.
- **Mirage Restaurant** •
  2143 Cortelyou Rd [Flatbush Ave]
  718-941-4452 • $
  Tasty traditional Nigerian.
- **NYC Icy** • 905 Church Ave [Coney Island Ave]
  347-789-1849 • $
  Gourmet Italian Ices, Sorbets, and Cream Ices.
- **Old Brick Cafe** • 507 Church Ave [Ocean Pkwy]
  347-425-8391 • $$
  Hairy-chested leering men might scare, but
  the Balkan fare won't.
- **Picket Fence** • 1310 Cortelyou Rd [Argyle Rd]
  718-282-6661 • $$
  Wonderful comfort food.
- **Pomme de Terre** • 1301 Newkirk Ave [Argyle]
  718-284-0005 • $$
  Fanciest French in Flatbush!
- **Purple Yam** • 1314 Cortelyou Rd [E 13th St]
  718-940-8188 • $$
  Filipino Pan Asian cuisine.
- **San Remo Pizza** • 1408 Cortelyou Rd [Rugby]
  718-282-4915 • $$
  Try the fresh mozzarella pie.
- **Strictly Vegetarian Restaurant** •
  2268 Church Ave [Flatbush Ave]
  718-284-2543 • $
  Vegetarian Caribbean with an every changing
  menu.
- **Sybil's** • 2210 Church Ave [Flatbush Ave]
  718-469-9049 • $$
  Delicious Caribbean bakery.
- **Taqueria Los Poblanos** •
  733 Church Ave [E 8th St]
  718-436-5705 • $
  Killer tortas and cemitas, but the festive
  jukebox prevents conversation.
- **Thai Tony's** • 3019 Fort Hamilton Pkwy [E 3rd]
  718-436-6932 • $$
  Nice decor and presentation in Kensington?
  Oh! And, the food's good too.
- **To B Thai** • 126 Beverley Rd [Church Ave]
  718-435-0459 • $
  Inexpensive and tasty. Try the mock duck.
- **Yen Yen** • 404 Church Ave [E 4th St]
  718-633-8711 • $$
  Above-average Szechuan/Hunan cuisine, with
  a pretty sweet bar to boot.

Map 13 • **Kensington / Ditmas Park**

Golden Farm, with its 24 hours of operation and cheap food, is a reason unto itself to move to here, as is the **Flatbush Food Co-Op**. Otherwise, Kensington and Ditmas Park are pretty woefully devoid of shopping. Instead, spend your time at **Shakespeare & Co**, **Golden Farm**, or **Dan's Meats**.

Coffee

• **John's Bakery and Café** •
1322 Cortelyou Rd [Argyle Rd]
718-287-6799
Wheat bread, sandwiches, breakfast.

Shopping

• **Dan's Select Meats** •
250 Church Ave [E 3rd St]
A Polish shop and one of the few places to get meat in Kensington.
• **Flatbush Food Co-op** •
1415 Cortelyou Rd [Argyle Rd]
718-284-9717
The place for all your organic goods.
• **Golden Farm** • 329 Church Ave [E 4th St]
718-871-1009
24 hours and miraculously cheap. A reason to move to Kensington.
• **J & L Landscaping** • 702 Caton Ave [E 7th St]
718-438-3199
Quirky owner dispenses plant and neighborly wisdom.
• **Juice Box Wine & Spirits** •
1289 Prospect Ave [Greenwood Ave]
718-871-1110
Maybe the name appeals to the parents in the area in need of their own juice.

• **MF Discount** • 309 Church Ave [E 3rd St]
718-854-4337
The place to get your keys copied, generic tampons and school supplies.
• **Natural Frontier Market** •
1104 Cortelyou Rd [Stratford Rd]
718-284-3593
Specializing in natural and organic products.
• **Newkirk Plaza** •
Above Newkirk Ave Subway [Foster Ave]
Rumor has it that this was America's first mall.
• **Old Navy Outlet** •
1009 Flatbush Ave [Tilden Ave]
718-693-7507
Cheaper-than-cheap wardrobe basics.
• **One Stop Market** • 626 Caton Ave [E 7th St]
718-436-3410
The cleanest, best-stocked deli in Kensington.
• **Shakespeare & Co** •
150 Campus Rd [Amersfort Pl)]
718-434-5326
Brooklyn outpost of Manhattan mini-chain.
• **TB Ackerson Wine Merchants** •
1205 Cortelyou Rd [E 12th St]
718-826-6600
An unexpected selection. Use your frequent buyer's card and the 13th bottle is free.

Map 14 · **Bay Ridge**

Neighborhood Overview

Map 14

Although Bay Ridge has yet to be pegged as "The Next Williamsburg" (too few coffee shops and velvet blazers), it's come a long way from just "that neighborhood where they filmed Saturday Night Fever." While the extravagant mansions that line Colonial, Narrows, and Shore Road belie the traditionally middle-class roots of the nabe, it's still one of the few havens left for cash-poor renters. Third Avenue's Restaurant Row is the pride of local foodies, and a vibrant shopping scene makes it unnecessary for Ridgeites to hop in their gas guzzling SUV's and souped-up Mustangs (but they do anyway). Add in a finally realized **Farmers Market** and a profusion of greenery in the form of parks, promenades, and (gasp!) lawns, and it seems almost too good to be true...unless you're a Democrat. That's OK—as long as both sides can agree on where to get a good rigatoni bolognese and agree to disagree on most things political, it's pretty much utopia.

Bay Ridge is chock full of historical intrigue (did you know that Vikings discovered America? Check out the **Leif Ericson Runestone** if you don't believe us), to its important role in harbor defense during the Revolutionary War and the War of 1812. **The Barkaloo Cemetery** (smallest cemetery in Brooklyn) is thought to hold the remains of many of these Revolutionary heroes, and real live warriors can still be found at **Fort Hamilton**, the only active military base in NYC. Maybe you'll even spot a soldier at **St. John's Episcopal Church**, originally established to serve the increasing number of Episcopalians on the base. Known as the "Church of the Generals," St. John's has been a house of worship for officers from every conflict since the Mexican War, counting Generals Robert E. Lee and Thomas J. (Stonewall) Jackson as past devotees.

So what's in a name? Turns out, a lot. After discarding the moniker "Yellow Hook" (to avoid any plague-like connotations), the nabe was newly christened after its proximity to New York Bay, and the literal "ridge" in the land left over from the last Ice Age. Prime water views attracted the wealthy, and their extravagant taste in real estate. Notable examples still standing today are **Fontbonne Hall**, former residence of actress Lillian Russell, **The Gingerbread House**, an impressive example of Arts and Crafts architecture (and an occasional resort getaway for Santa's elves), and the **James F Farrell House**, which has been at 125 95th Street since the early twentieth century. Legend has it the house was turned so that its "widow's walk" (a balcony that overlooks the sea so women could watch for their husbands' ships) would no longer face The Narrows.

Water's been playing a key role in the area ever since, from the 69th Street Pier, former ferry pick-up site and key recreation spot for sports fisherman, to the imposing **Verrazano-Narrows Bridge**. Completed in 1964, this once-controversial structure was intended to ease transport between Brooklyn and Staten Island (now was that really necessary?), and held the title for the world's longest suspension bridge for nearly a quarter century. Views of it from various spots around Bay Ridge are stunning. So much for controversy.

Map 14 · **Bay Ridge**

Afternoon sports bars that cater to late-night karaoke lovers abound (**Salty Dog**, **Bean Post**, **Lonestar**), as do pick-up spots for the heavily muscled and spray tanned (**Trace**), yet the neighborhood is finally spreading its wings. **Tat 2 Lounge** offers an acoustic open-mic on Thursday evenings, while **Aloha Grinds** serves as a chilled out respite for the alcohol free... complete with board games and Wi-Fi.

🍸 Bars

- **Aloha Grinds** • 7604 3rd Ave [76th St]
  718-238-0456
  Board games and wi-fi for those in AA.
- **Bean Post** • 7525 5th Ave [Bay Ridge Pkwy]
  718-745-9413
  Popular pub/sports bar.
- **Bullshots** • 8121 5th Ave [81st St]
  718-567-2337
  Low-key pub where the locals gather.
- **Delia's Lounge** • 9224 3rd Ave [93rd St]
  718-745-7999
  When you need to get in the mood.
- **Hall of Fame Billiards** •
  505 Ovington Ave [5th Ave]
  718-921-2694
  Large pool hall with celeb cachet.
- **The Humidor** • 9212 3rd Ave [93rd St]
  718-238-2224
  Chomp a cigar with the (wise) guys.
- **JJ Bubbles** • 7912 3rd Ave [79th St]
  Comfortable dive bar.
- **Kelly's Tavern** • 9259 4th Ave [93rd St]
  718-745-9546
  Classic NY Irish bar.
- **Kitty Kiernan's** • 9715 3rd Ave [97th St]
  718-921-0217
  Another Irish pub.
- **Lonestar** • 8703 5th Ave [87th St]
  718-833-5180
  Burger and a brew for under $10? We're sold!
- **Salty Dog** • 7509 3rd Ave [Bay Ridge Pkwy]
  718-238-0030
  Good food and boisterous dancing. (Don't tell Bloomberg.)
- **Tat 2 Lounge** • 8011 3rd Ave [80th St]
  718-836-4515
  Get some ink with your drink.
- **Trace Restaurant** • 8814 3rd Ave [88th St]
  718-921-9500
  Lounge/restaurant serving modern Mexican bites.
- **Wicked Monk** • 8415 5th Ave [84th St]
  718-921-0601
  Intimate Gothic pub.

🎱 Billiards

- **Hall of Fame Billiards** •
  505 Ovington Ave [5th Ave]
  718-921-2694
  Large pool hall with celeb cachet.
- **Status Billiards** • 8218 3rd Ave [82nd St]
  718-836-0805
  Because billiards is a posh game, after all.

Restaurants

Map 14

Middle Eastern powerhouse **Tanoreen** has become a destination stop for visitors, but it's hardly the only place worth braving the R train for. Try **Tuscany Grill** for Italian or **Nouvelle** for Japanese. **Petit Oven** has drawn raves for their market-driven fare, and their 3-course, $25 prix fixe on Wednesdays can't be beat.

Restaurants

- **Agnanti Meze** • 7802 5th Ave [78th St]
718-833-7033 • $$
Local outpost of the Astoria favorite. Try rooster!
- **Anopoli** •
6920 3rd Ave [Bay Ridge Ave]
718-748-3863 • $
No artisinal BS here, just a classic diner with ice cream.
- **Arirang Hibachi Steakhouse** •
8812 4th Ave [88th St]
718-238-9880 • $$$$
Japanese hibachi with a free show.
- **Bridgeview Diner** • 9011 3rd Ave [90th St]
718-680-9818 • $$
Bay Ridge's best diner.
- **Cebu Bar & Bistro** • 8801 3rd Ave [88th St]
718-492-5095 • $$$
Where locals do brunch.
- **Chadwicks** • 8822 3rd Ave [88th St]
718-833-9855 • $$$
More on the upscale side of Bay Ridge.
- **Chianti** • 8530 3rd Ave [85th St]
718-921-6300 • $$$
High-quality rustic Italian; nearly everything made in house.
- **Elia** • 8611 3rd Ave [87th St]
718-748-9891 • $$$
Michelin recommended, upscale Greek.
- **Embers** • 9519 3rd Ave [95th St]
718-745-3700 • $$$
Massive steaks—try the potato potpie.
- **Gino's** • 7414 5th Ave [74th St]
718-748-1698 • $$
Classic Brooklyn Italian.
- **Grand Sichuan House** •
8701 5th Ave [87th St]
718-680-8887 • $
Food critics love this authentic Sichuan house.
- **Greenhouse Café** • 7717 3rd Ave [77th St]
718-833-8200 • $$$$
An elegant favorite for that special night.
- **Hinsch's Confectionery** •
8518 5th Ave [85th St]
718-748-2854 • $$
Timeless ice cream parlor.
- **Karam** • 8519 4th Ave [85th St]
718-745-5227 • $
Best of the growing Mid-Eastern.

- **Mezcals** • 7508 3rd Ave [Bay Ridge Pkwy]
718-748-7007 • $$
Fine Mexican fare, but we came for the tequila.
- **Mr Tang** • 7523 3rd Ave [Bay Ridge Pkwy]
718-748-0400 • $$$
Upscale Chinese Institution.
- **MyThai Café** • 7803 3rd Ave [78th St]
718-833-1700 • $$
Slammin' Pan-Asian eats.
- **Nouvelle** • 8716 3rd Ave [88th St]
718-238-8250 • $$$$
Brooklyn's answer to Nobu; creative sushi/Asian fusion.
- **The Pearl Room** • 8201 3rd Ave [82nd St]
718-833-6666 • $$$
Hip and modern seafood.
- **Peppino's** • 7708 3rd Ave [77th St]
718-833-3364 • $$
Brick oven goodness.
- **Petit Oven** • 276 Bay Ridge Ave [3rd Ave]
718-833-3443 • $$$
Cozy affordable French/American.
- **Pho Hoai** • 8616 4th Ave [87th St]
718-745-1640 • $
Fee Fi Pho Yum.
- **Piattini** • 9824 4th Ave [99th St]
718-759-0009 • $$$
Best in Brooklyn gelato, from the famous Gino Cammarata.
- **Polonica** • 7214 3rd Ave [73rd St]
718-630-5805 • $$
Cheese-stuffed, bacon-wrapped kielbasa, anyone?
- **Saint Germain** • 8303 3rd Ave [83rd St]
718-745-8899 • $$$
Frenchy brunch in Bay Ridge.
- **Schnitzel Haus** • 7319 5th Ave [73rd St]
718-836-5600 • $$
A multitude of meats and beers you can't pronounce.
- **Skinflints** • 7902 5th Ave [79th St]
718-745-1116 • $$
Get the burger with bleu cheese.
- **Tanoreen** • 7523 3rd Ave [76th St]
718-748-5600 • $$
Small Middle Eastern with big flavors.
- **Tuscany Grill** • 8620 3rd Ave [86th St]
718-921-5633 • $$$
Worth going to/staying in Bay Ridge for; get the steak.

Map 14 • **Bay Ridge**

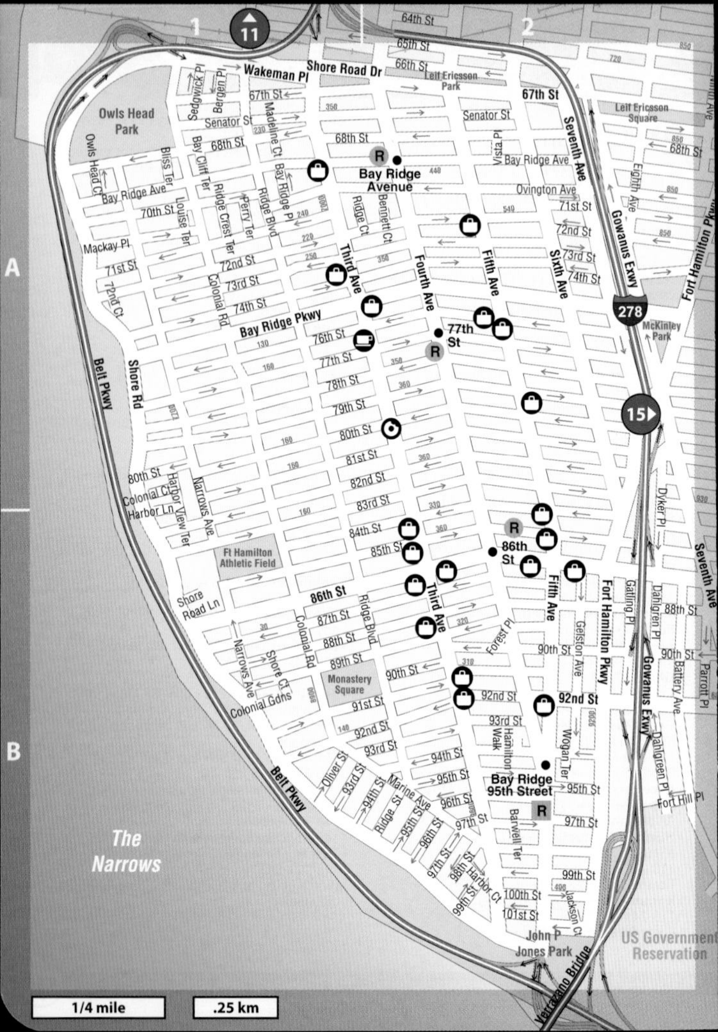

N

1   **11**   **2**

64th St
65th St
66th St
Wakeman Pl
Shore Road Dr
Leif Ericsson Park
67th St
Shore Road Dr
720

Owls Head Park
Colwick Pl
Barwell Pl
Madeline Ct
67th St
Senator St
68th St
Bay Ridge Avenue
Senator St
Vista Pl
Bay Ridge Ave
67th St
Leif Ericsson Square
68th St

Owls Head Ct
Bliss Ter
Bay Cliff Ter
Ridge Crest Ter
Perry Ter
Ridge Blvd
Ridge Pl
Element Ct
Ridge Ct
Third Ave
Fourth Ave
Fifth Ave
Sixth Ave
Seventh Ave
Eighth Ave
Gowanus Pkwy

Bay Ridge Ave
70th St
Louise Ter
71st St
72nd St
Mackay Pl
73rd St
71st St
72nd Ct
Colonial Rd
74th St
Bay Ridge Pkwy
130

Ovington Ave
71st St
72nd St
73rd St
74th St
540

A

77th St
77th St
78th St
79th St
80th St

R 77th St
360
360

Harbor View Ter
Narrows Ave
80th St
Colonial Rd
Harbor Ter
81st St
82nd St
83rd St
84th St
85th St
Ridge Blvd
Third Ave
86th St
87th St
88th St
89th St

Fort Hamilton Athletic Field

Shore Rd
Belt Pkwy
Shore Road Ln

R 86th St
Fifth Ave
Fort Hamilton Pkwy
Forest Pl
Gatling Pl
Dahlgren Pl
88th St
Dyker Pl
90th St
Battery Ave
Seventh Ave

278
McKinley Park

15

Monastery Square
90th St
91st St
92nd St
93rd St
94th St

Bay Ridge 95th Street
R

92nd St
93rd St
Hamilton Walk
Wogan Ter
95th St
Gelston Ave
Colonial Gdns
Oliver St
93rd St
Marine Ave
Ridge Blvd
95th St
96th St
97th St
98th St
99th St
100th St
101st St

Barwell Ter
Fort Hill Pl

Belt Pkwy
Shore Ct
Narrows Ave
Colonial Rd

The Narrows

B

John P Jones Park
Verrazano Bridge

US Government Reservation

1/4 mile   .25 km

Brand-name stores reign supreme on 86th Street (**Century 21, The Gap**, etc), but there are plenty of opportunities to support small business on Third and Fifth avenues. **HOM** is a neighborhood original, peddling home accents and high tea, while **Frank and Eddie's Meat Market** provides a touch of old school in a modern age. Watch out for elbows, the local elderly are serious about their prosciutto and ham cappy!

Bagels

- **Bagel Boy** • 8002 3rd Ave [80th St]
718-748-0366
Bay Ridge's most popular bagelry.

Coffee

- **Aloha Grinds** • 7604 3rd Ave [76th St]
718-238-0456
A real, live coffee shop with Hawaiian flair! In Bay Ridge!

Shopping

- **Aida Spa** • 7318 3rd Ave [74th St]
718-833-1250
Aida delivers low-cost, high-quality cuts. In stiletto heels.
- **Arayssi Bakery** • 7216 5th Ave [72nd St]
718-745-2115
Popular Lebanese bakery.
- **The Bookmark Shoppe** •
8415 3rd Ave [84th St]
718-833-5115
Mostly bestsellers and children's.
- **Celtic Rose** • 89-05 3rd Ave [85th St]
718-238-2582
Cead Mille Failte! Bits and pieces direct from the Emerald Isle.
- **Century 21** • 472 86th St [4th Ave]
718-748-3266
Discounted apparel, housewares, and linen—everything!
- **Chef with Sole** • 8618 3rd Ave [87th St]
718-680-7653
Fresh fish shack in the middle of suburbia.
- **Choc-Oh!-Lot Plus** • 7911 5th Ave [80th St]
718-748-2100
Happy fun times with bulk candy and cake decorating supplies.
- **Frank & Eddies Meat Market** •
302 86th St [3rd Ave]
718-836-5784
Bay Ridge butcher—an institution.

- **Frank & Eddies Meat Market** •
7502 3rd Ave [Bay Ridge Pkwy]
718-836-4168
One of the few real butcher stores left in Brooklyn.
- **Havin' a Party** • 8414 5th Ave [84th St]
718-836-3701
Party supplies and novelties.
- **HOM** • 8806 3rd Ave [88th St]
718-238-4466
Antiques Shopping + Homemade Cupcakes + Big Gay Sal = Fabulous!
- **Jean Danet Pastry** • 7526 5th Ave [76th St]
718-836-7566
40-year-old den of calorie-laden iniquity.
- **Leske's Bakery** • 7612 5th Ave [76th St]
718-680-2323
There's only one Babka left…watch out for elbows!
- **Little Cupcake Bakeshop** •
9102 3rd Ave [91st St]
718-680-4465
Now, who doesn't just love a good cupcake?
- **Modell's** • 531 86th St [Fifth Ave]
718-745-7900
Sports. Sports. Sports. Get your Cyclones stuff here!
- **Nordic Delicacies** •
6909 3rd Ave [Bay Ridge Ave]
718-748-1874
Norwegian carryout and grocery store.
- **Panda Sport** • 9213 5th Ave [92nd St]
718-238-4919
Full line of ski equipment. Ask about ski trips!
- **Paneantico Bakery and Café** •
9124 3rd Ave [92nd St]
718-680-2347
Killer paninis made with just-baked Crown Bakery bread.

Map 13 • **Dyker Heights / Bensonhurst** N

Fort Hamilton
Pkwy

Tabor Ct   New Utrecht Ave

Leif Ericsson
Square

Fort Hamilton Pkwy

65th St
66th St
67th St
Ovington Ave

70th St
71st St
72nd St
73rd St
74th St

Bay Ridge Pkwy

76th St
77th St
78th St
79th St
80th St
81st St
82nd St
83rd St
84th St
85th St
86th St

DYKER
HEIGHTS

BENSONHURST

62 St

71 St

79 St

18 Ave
63rd St
64th St
20 Ave

65th St
66th St
67th St
68th St

19th Ave

20th Ave

18th Ave

Benson Ave

Rutherford Pl

Cropsey Ave

Dyker Beach
Golf Course

PAGE
151

Seventh Ave

Poly Pl

US Government
Reservation

General Lee Ave

Fort
Hamilton

Dyker Beach
Park

Independence Ave

Shore Rd

Shore Pkwy (Leif Ericsson Dr)

Gravesend
Bay

Bath Ave

20th Dr
19th Ln

20th Ln

21st Dr

1/4 mile   .25 km

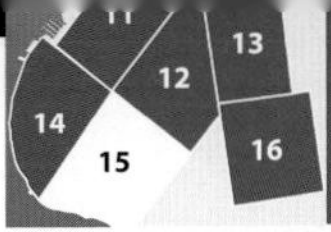

Map 15

Nothing big ever happens in the Dyker Heights/Bensonhurst part of Brooklyn, but then again, that's how the mostly laid-back residents here like it. Walk east across noisy New Utrecht Avenue, however, and you've stumbled upon the full-on Eastern European area of Bensonhurst. You're in for the cold shoulder treatment here because if you can't speak at least three non-English languages fluently, they can tell you're just a "new" Brooklynite. Even if you don't look like a hipster. But these areas have plenty to offer, especially for the gourmet shopper and adventuresome eater.

Historically, this area of Brooklyn was created as an upscale housing development and was built as such in the late 1800s. Though much has been torn down, several of these large homes are still standing today and make for a nice walk while you're not gorging yourself at the many bakeries and bagelries around town. While you're in this part of Brooklyn, you might as well play a round of golf at one of the world's oldest courses, the **Dyker Beach Golf Course**. The world's busiest golf course in the mid-'50s, today the attached Dyker Beach Park has added facilities for tennis, handball, and bocce, as well as the usual American team sports.

Did you know that there's an amusement park in town not named Coney Island? That's right; the **Adventurers Family Entertainment Center** (formerly Nelly Bly Amusement Park) has enough thrills, chills, and spills for anyone under the age of 10. It's a cute park good for a family treat, but not exactly a rival to Six Flags. Though if it's cold outside and around Christmastime, why not hop on over to 84th Street between 11th and 13th Avenues, otherwise known as the epicenter for the famous **Dyker Heights Christmas Lights** spectacular? Join locals and tourists from all over the U.S. as they amble along the suburban-ish streets admiring these amazingly overdecorated mini-mansions.

Also go food shopping, and we don't mean at your run-of-the-mill supermarket. We're talking your Hungarian marts, your ravioli outposts, and your local fresh rabbit vendors. No joke. Try **Great Wall Supermarket** to find probably the cheapest and best place in all of the city to buy Asian groceries. Stop by **B&A Pork Store** and other bakeries on 13th Avenue for great eats and a semi-local specialty called Pizza Rustica. This thick, savory pie is stuffed with prosciutto, ham, egg, cheese, and more to produce a delicious dish that's not related to pizza in the least. Meanwhile, most of 18th Avenue is a food lover's paradise, from Asian noodle soup (**Hand Pull Noodle and Dumpling House**) to fresh spices and sausages (**Frank and Sal Prime Meats**) and more.

Finally, find jewelry galore on East 86th Street or 18th Avenue. Go clothing shopping on 86th Street. Enjoy taking a stroll along Leif Ericson Park (66th & Fort Hamilton Pkwy), or step out right near the water's edge with a walk along the ocean. Sure, the highway's right on the other side of you, but at least you can feel that salty breeze.

Map 43 Dyker Heights/Bensonhurst   N

Fort Hamilton Pkwy
N
Tabor Ct
New Utrecht Ave
N
62 St
D
12

62nd
63rd
18 Ave
N
64th St
20 Ave
N

Leif Ericson Square
68th St

Tenth Ave
1060
961
950

65th St
66th St
67th St
Ovington Ave

1250
1250
1250
1430

13th Ave

Duryea Ct
16th Ave
Ovington Ct
Cameron Ct
Wallaston Ct

66th St

17th Ave

67th St
68th St

1650

1760

19th Ave

20th Ave

Fort Hamilton Pkwy
1060
1060
1020
1050
940
950

70th St
71st St
72nd St
73rd St
74th St

1250

Bay Ridge Ave
1430
1440

71 St
D

1650

1670

1750

1250
1440

920

11th Ave

12th Ave

Bay Ridge Pkwy
1250

1540

15th Ave

16th Ave

New Utrecht Ave

1750

18th Ave

19th Ave

McKinley Pkwy
A

14

DYKER
HEIGHTS

76th St
77th St
78th St
79th St
80th St
81st St
82nd St
83rd St
84th St
85th St
86th St

1250
1250

BENSONHURST

79 St
D

1760

1670

1760

82nd St
83rd St
84th St

1910

1910

Dyker Pl
1050
1050
930
1040

18 Ave
D

1570
1670

1910

88th St
90th St
92nd St

Dyker Pl
Fort Pl
682

20 Ave
D

14th Ave

Benson Ave
580
9760
9752
8691

Bay 7th St
Bay 8th St
Bay 10th St
Bay 11th St
Bay 13th St
Bay 14th St

20
20
9669
8691

Rutherford Pl

Bay 16th St

Bay 17th St
Bay 19th St
Bay 20th St

20 Ave

Bay 22nd St
Bay 23rd St

Bay 25th St
Bay 26th St

Bath Ave

Battery Ave
Dahlgren Pl
Fort Hill Pl

Dyker Beach
Golf Course
PAGE
151

Seventh Ave

Cropsey Ave
17th Ct

O

20th Dr
19th Ln

21st
20th Ln

Poly Pl

Independence Ave

Shore Rd

Fort Hamilton Pkwy

White Ave

Verrazano-
Narrows
Bridge

General Lee Ave

US Government
Reservation

Fort
Hamilton

Dyker
Beach
Park

Shore Pkwy (Leif Ericson Dr)

B

Gravesend
Bay

1/4 mile   .25 km

Map 15

The number of bars you won't pass here is staggering. Walk around all you like, but we challenge you to find a good club, bar, or nightlife locale in these parts. Try an espresso bar instead. What's the verdict? Hang here by day but go pretty much ANYWHERE else at night.

⑧ Billiards

• Lucky Cue Billiards •
1741 Bath Ave [Bay 17th St]
718-236-3623
Shoot pool near the water.

Map 15 • Dyker Heights / Bensonhurst

N

Fort Hamilton Pkwy
N

Tabor Ct
New Utrecht Ave
N

62 St
D
12

18 Ave
N

62nd St
63rd St
20 Ave
N

64th St

Leif Ericson Square
68th St

Tenth Ave
1060
1960
1250
1250
65th St
66th St
67th St
Ovington Ave

13th Ave

1430
1250

66th St
67th St
68th St

950
1020
940
1050
950
1040
920

950

1050
1050
1050
1050

1020
1430
1440
1440
1540
1670

70th St
71st St
72nd St
73rd St
74th St

Bay Ridge Ave
Bay Ridge Pkwy
75th St
76th St
77th St
78th St
79th St
80th St
81st St
82nd St
83rd St
84th St
85th St
86th St

11th Ave
12th Ave

15th Ave

16th Ave

New Utrecht Ave

Duryea Ct
16th Ave
Ovington Ct
Cameron Ct
Wallaston Ct

17th Ave

1650
1650
1670

71 St
D

1760
1750
1750

2

67th St
68th St

1670
1670
1570
1670

79 St
D
1760

18th Ave

1910
1910
1910

19th Ave

20th Ave

82nd St
83rd St
84th St
18 Ave
D

2

20 Ave
D

DYKER HEIGHTS
BENSONHURST

14

930

1040

Dyker Pl

Seventh Ave

Gatling Pl

Fort Hamilton Pkwy

88th St
90th St
92nd St

Parrott Pl
626

Dahlgren Pl

Bakery Ave
Fort Hill Pl

Dyker Beach Golf Course
PAGE 151

14th Ave
Benson Ave

Bay 7th St
Bay 8th St
Bay 10th St
Bay 11th St
Bay 13th St
Bay 14th St

8740
8752
8691

215

Bay 16th St
Bay 17th St
Bay 19th St
Bay 20th St

Rutherford Pl

Bay 22nd St
Bay 23rd St
Bay 25th St
Bay 26th St
Bath Ave

Cropsey Ave

17th Ct
19th Ln

Shore Rd

20th Dr
21st Dr
20th Ln

Independence Ave
Shore Pkwy (Leif Ericson Dr)

White Ave
General Lee Ave

Poly Pl

Dyker Beach Park

US Government Reservation

Fort Hamilton

Verrazano Narrows Bridge

Gravesend Bay

1/4 mile   .25 km

Map 1

Who cares if the menu's not in English around here? Go for hibachi at **Shiki**, souvlaki at **Meze**, or pizza and upscale Italian at **Ristorante Viccaro**, where you can still get a slice to go at the walk-up window.

Restaurants

- **Casa Calamari** • 1801 Bath Ave [18th Ave]
  718-234-7060 • $$
  Italian seafood…just ask the locals.
- **Columbus Restaurant & Deli** •
  6610 18th Ave [66th St]
  718-236-8623 • $
  Club sandwiches to die for.
- **Gino's Focacceria** • 7118 18th Ave [71st St]
  718-232-9073 • $
  Great Sicilian sandwiches and snacks. Try any of the Gino's Specialities.
- **Hand Pull Noodle and Dumpling House** •
  7201 18th Ave [72nd St]
  718-232-6191 • $
  The most entertaining noodles you've probably ever had.
- **Hanna Vermicelli** •
  7524 18th Ave [Bay Ridge Pkwy]
  718-331-9259 • $
  Fab Vietnamese selection.
- **Il Colosseo** • 7704 18th Ave [77th St]
  718-234-3663 • $$
  Hands-down the best pizza in the 'hood.
- **Meze** • 6601 13th Ave [66th St]
  718-234-6393 • $$
  Get your souvlaki on.

- **Outback Steakhouse** •
  1475 86th St [Bay 8th St]
  718-837-7200 • $$$
  A little taste of suburbia.
- **Ristorante Vaccaro** •
  6716 Fort Hamilton Pkwy [67th St]
  718-238-9447 • $$$
  Good, simple Italian.
- **Shiki** • 1863 86th St [Bay 20th St]
  718-837-1586 • $$
  Hibachi-style Japanese.
- **Tenzan** • 7116 18th Ave [71st St]
  718-621-3238 • $$
  Japanese on pretty pillows.
- **Tommaso's** • 1464 86th St [Bay 8th St]
  718-236-9883 • $$$
  Good enough for the Godfather.
- **Villa Paradiso** • 1969 Bath Ave [Bay 23rd St]
  718-837-2696 • $$
  Yup. More Italian in Brooklyn.
- **Vstrecha Restaurant** • 8421 20th Ave [84th St]
  718-266-4817 • $$$
  You might get a waiter who speaks some English.

This area isn't exactly Fifth Avenue, but you can find some amazing bargains here. Stay east of 17th Avenue for clothing bargains at **Kings** and **Telco**, and keep your eyes peeled for little bakeries or ethnic shops. If you can avoid the dozens of 99 cent stores, that is.

🅑 Bagels

- **New Millenium Bagels** • 6424 20th Ave [65th]
  718-236-4447
  A lot of bagels and more in a spacy store.

🛍 Shopping

- **Arcobaleno Italiano** • 7306 18th Ave [73rd St]
  718-259-7951
  For all your Fellini needs.
- **B&A Pork Store** • 7818 13th Ave [78th St]
  718-833-9661
  Friendly service along with tasty dishes and homemade sausages.
- **Cristoforo Colombo Bakery** •
  6916 18th Ave [70th St]
  718- 256-3973
  Delicious smells must mean good baking.
- **Frank and Sal Prime Meats** •
  8008 18th Ave [80th St]
  718-331-8100
  A true Italian market with fresh and imported everything.
- **Gourmet Brands., Inc.** • 7017 20th Ave [70th]
  718-331-7325
  Fancy-schmancy good gourmet grub.
- **Great Wall Supermarket** •
  6722 Fort Hamilton Pkwy [67th St]
  718-680-2889
  Probably the best Asian grocery you've ever stepped foot in.
- **Im Mondello Fish Market** •
  6824 18th Ave [Bay Ridge Ave]
  718-236-3930
  You can stand the smell of this really fresh fish.
- **Lioni Latticini** • 7819 15th Ave [78th St]
  718-232-7852
  Lots and lots of mighty fine mozzarella.
- **Maggio Music Center** •
  8403 18th Ave [New Utrecht Ave]
  718-259-4468
  Sheet music and lessons at this friendly neighborhood noisemaker.
- **Meats Supreme** • 1949 86th St [20th Ave]
  718-373-7045
  Safe for vegetarians too, a great neighborhood gourmet market.
- **Mona Lisa Bakery** • 7717 13th Ave [78th St]
  718-256-7706
  Mini pastries, giant breads, many choices.

- **New Star Cheese Co.** • 7305 20th Ave [73rd]
  718-259-2982
  Peculiar location, but someone's gotta eat all that cheese.
- **Pastosa Ravioli** •
  7425 New Utrecht Ave [74th St]
  718-236-9615
  Pasta heaven.
- **Perez Records** • 7818 20th Ave [78th St]
  718-256-3989
  An eclectic collection of DVDs, CDs, records, T-shirts, and more.
- **Queen Ann Ravioli** •
  7205 18th Ave [72nd St]
  718-256-1061
  18 varieties of ravioli—totally awesome.
- **Ravioli Fair** • 1484 86th St [15th Ave]
  718-256-5288
  You might find some ravioli among these gourmet goods.
- **Sal & Jerry's Bakery, Inc.** •
  6817 20th Ave [68th St]
  718-232-9358
  Famous for their prosciutto bread but loved for their cookies.
- **SAS Italian Records** • 7113 18th Ave [71st St]
  718-331-0539
  Italian music, games, beauty products, and soccer paraphernalia.
- **Sea Breeze** • 8500 18th Ave [85th St]
  718-259-9693
  Fresh fish at great prices.
- **Telco Discount Stores Inc** •
  6628 18th Ave [67th St]
  718-232-8811
  Suspiciously cheap everything for you and your home.
- **Three Guys from Brooklyn** •
  6502 Fort Hamilton Pkwy [65th St]
  718-748-8340
  Fresh produce from nice guys.
- **Villabate Alba** • 7001 18th Ave [70th St]
  718-331-8430
  This place is da bomb!!! Don't go on an empty stomach.

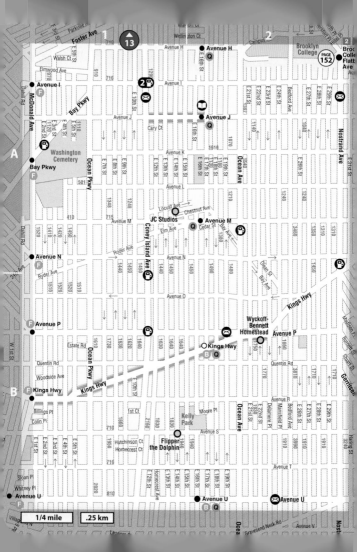

If you want Kosher Sushi, award-winning pizza, 100 grams of Vodka (roughly a shot) and, heck why not, let's throw in an overstuffed but delicious gyro, then you've got to come down to Midwood. About a 45-minute ride from Midtown Manhattan, it's certainly worth your while to check out the neighborhood that Orthodox Jews, Russians & Ukrainians, Turks, among others (and New Yorkers thought the F train was diverse) call home, and where you can find some seriously good food and good shopping. But don't expect to rock the night away here; Midwood conservatively shuts down come sundown Friday in observance of the Shabbos.

There's more to Midwood than its bakeries, Yeshivas, abundant shoe stores, synagogues, decadent homes, and fun, sleek airy cafe-style hangouts—really there's more! Midwood offers two distinct landmarks that'll have the history buffs nodding in approval in their discreet, golf clap-like way. Midwood had its hand in the entertainment industry and helped produce and launch great television shows. Just ask NBC who owned two large studios right in the heart of Midwood, NBC Brooklyn Studio 1 and NBC Color Studio 2. NBC sold the studios and now the landmark is known as **JC Studios**. Movies, TV shows such as Saturday Night Live (very briefly), As the World Turns, The Cosby Show, and the Sammy Davis Jr. Show, among many others were produced right here, in Midwood! This place was like a mini-me Hollywood—heck even Don Rickles taped here. Betcha didn't know that little factoid.

In addition to its ritzy Hollywood past, Midwood offers another impressive landmark: On a quiet street there sits a quaint house that to a passerby might seem like any other house on that street, though that is the beauty of exceptional design (and once again the Dutch have outdone themselves). Pay closer attention because this house is actually a landmark due to the fact that it was built during the American Revolution, it is the **Wyckoff House**. Currently it's privately owned (rest assured, the City is trying to "fix" that), so do not plan on having some kind of museum-like experience and touring the house while snapping pictures with outdated but albeit historical houseware that you could post on your favorite social networking site.

Potential visitors to Midwood will delight in its many shopping opportunities, primarily on Kings Highway. Come to the neighborhood in the early afternoon and visit the many shoe stores that house great quality Italian and other European imported shoes. Also chic clothing boutiques that carry formal gowns, feminine dresses, designer jeans, jackets, and handbags can all be found here. Finish off your afternoon/early evening with a primarily healthy and almost always kosher cuisine that's priced very fair. Don't forget to visit the delicious bakeries and other dessert hotspots, also very reasonably priced. L' Chaim.

Midwood doesn't really offer a nightlife, unless you love dive bars like **Nitecaps.** You can step inside a lounge or two on the outskirts of the neighborhood, but don't expect a bar-hopping, club-hitting kind of scene, because there just aren't any. Instead, opt for a Russian or Japanese restaurant. Let the vodka flow and voilá.

Bars

• **Nitecaps** • 1164 Coney Island Ave [Avenue H]
718-434-9685
Dive bar not for beginners.

🎱 Billiards

• **Playboy Billiards & Table Tennis** •
1814 Coney Island Ave [Ave O]
718-645-0074
Because shooting pool is what playboys do.

😀 Movie Theaters

• **Kent Triplex** • 1170 Coney Island Ave [Ave H]
718-338-3371
Moron blockbuster destination.

Lotsa food, so little time: Vist **DiFara** for award-winning pizza or for home-style Russian food with a shot of cold vodka, hit up **Obzhora**. Pop into **Ostrovitsky Bakery** for kosher pastries that you'll smell from a block away. For all things shish-kebab get to **Sahara**, pronto. Want unique sushi? Try **Nagoya**.

Restaurants

- **Adelman's Kosher Deli** •
1906 Kings Hwy [E 19th St]
718-336-4915 • $
Pastrami piled high.
- **Anna's Luncheonette** •
2925 Ave I [Nostrand Ave]
718-951-7617 • $
Counter service.
- **Buckley's** • 2926 Ave S [Nostrand Ave]
718-998-4222 • $$
Neighborhood tavern & steakhouse with great Sunday brunch
- **Burgers Bar** • 1906 Coney Island Ave [Ave P]
718-998-3200 • $$
Local fav imported from Israel. No cheeseburgers allowed.
- **Carlos and Gabby's Glatt Kosher Mexican Grill** • 1376 Coney Island Ave [Ave J] • $
A kosher Mexican restaurant. Juan Epstein would be proud.
- **DiFara** • 1424 Ave J [E 14th St]
718-258-1367 • $
Top NYC pizza; well worth the wait. Say hi to Dom.
- **Essex on Coney** •
1359 Coney Island Ave [Ave J]
718-253-1002 • $
Glatt kosher deli.
- **Estihana** • 1217 Ave J [E 15th St]
718-677-1515 • $$
Kosher Asian bistro restaurant.
- **La Villita** • 1249 Ave U [Homecrest Ave]
718-998-0222 • $
Authentic, hearty Mexican.
- **Mabat** • 1809 E 7th St [Kings Hwy]
718-339-3300 • $$
Hole-in-the-wall with tasty Moroccan dishes.
- **Michael's** • 2929 Ave R [Nostrand Ave]
718-998-7851 • $$$$
Sprawling menu…everything from rack of lamb to pasta.

- **Napoli Pizza** • 2270 Nostrand Ave [Ave I]
718-338-0328 • $$
If you can't get over to DiFara's.
- **Olympic Pita** • 1419 Coney Island Ave [Ave K]
718-258-6222 • $
Heaven in a pita. Fantastic sauces—try the zhoug.
- **Pizza Time** • 1324 Ave J [E 13th St]
718-252-8801 • $
Kosher Italian.
- **Salud** • 1308 Ave H [Argyle Rd]
347-295-1191 • $
Beautifully designed serving organic Mexican tortas, soups, and smoothies.
- **Schnitzi** • 1299 Coney Island Ave [Ave J]
718-338-4015 • $$
Lots and lots of schnizel.
- **Sunflower Café** • 1223 Quentin Rd [E 12th St]
718-336-1340 • $
Surprising selection of foo-foo Kosher, including pizza.
- **Sushi Tokyo** •
1360 Coney Island Ave [Ave O]
718-434-2444 • $$
Rabbi approved sushi? Now that's kosher. Better for take-out.
- **Taci's Beyti** • 1955 Coney Island Ave [Ave P]
718-627-5750 • $$
Really fresh, really tasty Turkish cuisine.
- **Tblisi** • 811 Kings Hwy [E 8th St]
718-382-6485 • $$
Good Georgian food—we're not talking pecan pie, we're talking former Soviet chicken hearts.
- **Tea for Two** • 547 Kings Hwy [E 4th St]
718-998-0020 • $$
Kosher. Slammin' seafood.
- **Turkish Café Restaurant** •
1618 E 16th St [Ave P]
718-375-9237 • $
24-hour gyro haunt that is mind-blowing and dirt cheap.

Map 16 · **Midwood**

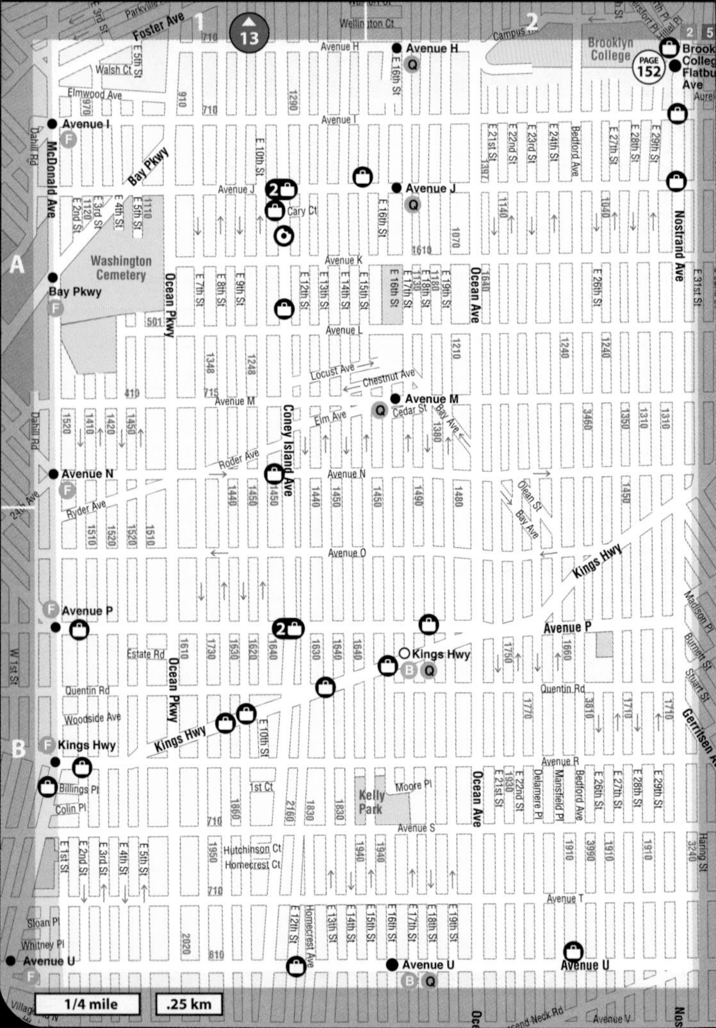

N

Foster Ave

Wellington Ct

1

13

2

2 **5**

Campus Rd

Brook
College
Flatbu
Ave

PAGE
152

Avenue H.

E 4th St

Q

Walsh Ct

Elmwood Ave

E 21st St
E 22nd St
E 23rd St

Bedford Ave

E 26th St
E 27th St
E 28th St

E 29th St

Avenue I

910
710

1290

Avenue I

Avenue H

1640

McDonald Ave

Bay Pkwy

E 10th St

E 16th St

Dahill Rd

2

Cary Ct

Avenue J

Q

Nostrand Ave

E 31st St

Avenue J

1382
1140

Avenue J

1070

1610

A

E 2nd St
E 3rd St

1110
1120

Avenue K

E 7th St
E 9th St

E 12th St
E 13th St
E 14th St
E 15th St

E 16th St

E 18th St
E 19th St

1640

Ocean Ave

E 26th St

501

Bay Pkwy

Washington
Cemetery

Ocean Pkwy

E 5th St

1248

Avenue L

1210

1240
1240

1310

F

410

715
1348

Locust Ave

Chestnut Ave

Cedar St

Bay Ave

1350
1350

Dahill Rd

1520
1410
1450

Avenue M

Elm Ave

Q

Avenue M

1380

3460

1310

1490

1490

Ryder Ave

Coney Island Ave

2

1450
1440

Avenue N

1450
1440

1450

Ocean St

Bay Ave

F

Avenue N

1510

1520

1440

1450

Kings Hwy

Avenue O

Estate Rd

2

E 10th St

1640
1640

Avenue P

F

Avenue P

1610
1620
1730
1640

1830

1750
1660

Mansfield Pl
Bonnet Pl
Stuart St

1710

Quentin Rd

Quentin Rd

1770

3810

Woodside Ave

E 5th St

Ocean Pkwy

Kings Hwy

Kings Hwy

B

Kings Hwy

Kings Hwy

B

Q

Germison A

F

Billings Pl

Colin Pl

Ocean Ave

Avenue R

E 21st St
E 22nd St

Delamere Pl
Mansfield Pl

Bedford Ave

E 26th St
E 27th St

E 29th St

Haring St

1st Ct

Moore Pl

1830
1930
1940

1910

1910

3240

E 1st St
E 2nd St
E 3rd St
E 4th St
E 5th St

1660

Kelly
Park

Ocean Ave

B

2160

1830

Avenue S

Hutchinson Ct
Homecrest Ct

1990

E 12th St

1940
1940

3990

Sloan Pl

710

810

Homecrest Ave
E 14th St
E 15th St
E 16th St

E 18th St
E 19th St

Avenue T

Whitney Pl

2020

Avenue U

B Q

Avenue U

E 17th St

1910

Village

F

Neck Rd

Ocea

Avenue V

1/4 mile   .25 km

Bagels, Coffee, & Shopping

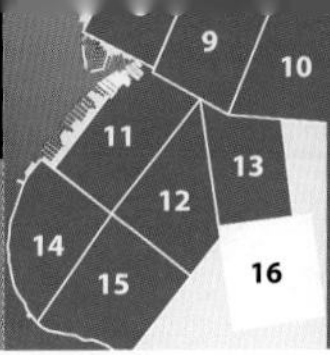

Shop **Fox's** for designer gear with a considerable discount. Visit the many shoe stores to get your casual sneakers, stylish office pumps and those weekend Va-va-voom heels (**Tsakiris Mallas**). You'll also find evening gowns, sexy dresses, and chic street wear at the many neighborhood boutiques on Kings Highway.

Map 16

Bagels

• **Kosher Bagel Hole** •
1431 Coney Island Ave [Ave K]
718-377-9700
They know bagels.

Shopping

• **Canal Jean Company** •
2236 Nostrand Ave [Ave H]
718-421-7590
Not as good as Manhattan locales, but still has nice deals.
• **Chiffon Bakery** • 430 Ave P [E 2nd St]
718-258-8822
Holla at the challah, kid.
• **Chuckies** • 1304 Kings Hwy [E 13th St]
718-376-1003
Possibly the best shoe store in Brooklyn. We're talking Manolos and Jimmy Choos.
• **Downtown** • 2502 Ave U [Bedford Ave]
718-934-8280
Trendy in a junior high sorta way. But (holla!) they do midnight madness sales.
• **Eichler's** • 1401 Coney Island Ave [Ave J]
718-258-7643
"The World's Judaica Store" brings joy, also "oy!"
• **Fish Expo** • 2370 Nostrand Ave [Ave J]
718-253-6400
Tropicals for your viewing pleasure.
• **Floral Kingdom** •
1444 Coney Island Ave [Ave K]
718-677-9797
You have NOT seen flowers 'till you've been here.
• **Fox's** • 923 Kings Hwy [E 10th St]
718-645-3620
Brand-name everything, discounted sweetly. Century 21's arch enemy.
• **Here's a Book Store** •
1964 Coney Island Ave [Ave P]
718-645-6675
Quaint and impressive, rare finds, new and used, knowledgeable staff.

• **Kiev Bakery** • 1611 Kings Hwy [E 17th St]
718-627-5438
Elegant pastries and indulgent cakes. A Russian staple in NY.
• **Manhattan Lights** •
1941 Coney Island Ave [Ave P]
718-998-1111
Any lighting you've ever dreamt up, is located here—seriously.
• **Mansoura** • 515 Kings Hwy [E 3rd St]
718-645-7977
Amazing bakery with Jewish specialties. Best baklava on the planet.
• **Oh Nuts!** • 1503 Ave J [E 15th St]
718-530-9255
If there were a kosher Willy Wonka, he would live here.
• **Ostrovitsky Bakery** •
1124 Ave J [E 12th St]
718-951-7924?
You can smell the deliciousness before you open the door.
• **Pickle Guys** •
1364 Coney Island Ave [Ave J]
718-677-0639
Pickled pickles, tomatoes, carrots, everything pickled, everything yummy!
• **Pomegranate** • 1507 Coney Island Ave [Ave L]
718-951-7112
Glitzy kosher supermarket. Be prepared, you won't leave empty-handed.
• **Studio 19 Salon & Spa** •
1610 E 19th St [Kings Hwy]
718-336-7373
A spa, a salon, a favorite for many years, darling.
• **Tsakiris Mallas** • 1206 Kings Hwy [E 13th St]
718-998-3090
Beautiful European shoes that'll make you a real woman.
• **Wig Showcase** • 820 Kings Hwy [E 8th St]
718-339-8300
Lots of oddly coiffed mannequin heads.
• **Zelda's Art World** • 2291 Nostrand Ave [Ave I]
718-377-7779
Art supplies. F. Scott rarely around.

Parks & Places · **Eastern Brooklyn**

Overview

Nearly every community of Eastern Brooklyn is surrounded by water, and while you wouldn't exactly get an "Aye, matey" vibe from its inhabitants, this section of the borough is home to over a dozen boating and yacht clubs. In the summer, inlets along Sheepshead Bay, Plum Beach, and Paerdegat Basin become packed with jet skiers, windsurfers, and the occasional million-dollar schooner. Some neighborhoods such as Canarsie and Marine Park exude an almost suburban tranquility, while seriously affluent areas like Mill Basin and Manhattan Beach cater to an exclusive crowd that includes State Senator Carl Kruger. Densely populated East New York and Brownsville are packed with drab public housing, though remnants of a former Art Deco glory can be found along Pitkin Avenue. The population is a mixed bag, and with Brooklyn's seaside real estate once again on the rise, the nabe can only improve with time.

Transportation

Although the subway extends all the way out to East New York (🇯 🇿 🇦 🇨 🇨) and Canarsie (🇱), there are many neighborhoods that can be accessed only by bus or car (notably Marine Park, Mill Basin, Bergen Beach, parts of East Flatbush, and the Flatlands). If you need to travel to any of these areas, consult the Brooklyn bus map on the foldout—there are a number of bus routes that will deliver you exactly where you need to go.

Communities

Brooklyn is a borough of individual neighborhoods. The main communities that make up Eastern Brooklyn are:

Bergen Beach (pop. 12,500)
Flatlands (pop. 59,500)
Brownsville (pop. 82,900)
Gerritsen Beach (pop. 6,900)
Canarsie (pop. 89,500)
Gravesend (pop. 93,600)
Cypress Hills (pop. 56,000)
Marine Park (pop. 20,100)
East Flatbush (pop. 181,300)
Mill Basin (pop. 11,800)
East New York (pop. 117,000)
Sheepshead Bay (pop. 127,800)

*Figures based on the 2000 US Census.

Nature

What Eastern Brooklyn lacks in trendiness, it makes up for in scenery. The Eastern Brooklyn shore is lined with more than 3,000 acres of amazing parks that offer a plethora of activities: Nature trails, golf courses, horseback riding, camping, fishing, bird watching, boating, and organized athletics. When you need a break from it all, **Marine Park**, **Floyd Bennett Field**, the **Jamaica Riding Academy**, and **Canarsie Beach Park** provide a nice diversion from city life.

🅞 Landmarks

- **Lady Moody House** •
27 Gravesend Neck Rd [McDonald Ave]
- **Old Gravesend Cemetery** • McDonald Ave & Gravesend Neck Rd [McDonald Ave]

Nightlife

- **The Wrong Number** • 168 Ave T [W 6th St]

Restaurants

- **Del'Rio Diner** • 166 Kings Hwy [W 12th St]
- **El Greco Diner** • 1821 Emmons Ave [Sheepshead Bay]
- **Frank's Pizza** • 2134 Flatbush Ave, Flatlands [Quentin]
- **Joe's of Avenue U** • 287 Ave U [McDonald Ave]
- **John's Deli** • 2033 Stillwell Ave [Bay 50th St]
- **Jordan's Lobster Dock** •
2771 Knapp St, Sheepshead Bay [Harkness Ave]
- **King's Buffet** • 2637 86th St [Ave U]
- **L&B Spumoni Gardens** • 2725 86th St [W 10th St]
- **La Palina** • 159 Ave O [W 5th St]
- **Liman** • 2710 Emmons Ave [E 27th St]
- **Mill Basin Kosher Delicatessen** •
5823 Ave T, Mill Basin [E 58th St]
- **Peter Pizza** • 2358 80th St [Ave U]
- **Randazzo's** •
2017 Emmons Ave, Sheepshead Bay [Ocean Ave]
- **Roll-n-Roaster** •
2901 Emmons Ave, Sheepshead Bay [E 29th St]
- **Sahara** • 2337 Coney Island Ave [Ave T]
- **Sweik** • 2027 Emmons Ave, Sheepshead Bay [Ocean]
- **XO Creperie** • 2027 Emmons Ave [Ocean Ave]

🅞 Shopping

- **Calligaris Shop by AKO** • 2184 McDonald Ave [Ave T]
- **Dairy Maid Ravioli** • 216 Ave U [W 5th St]
- **Enterprize** • 1601 Sheepshead Bay Rd [E 16th St]
- **Le Monti** • 2074 McDonald Ave [Ave S]
- **Leohmann's** • 2807 E 21st St [Shore Pkwy]
- **Mini Centro** •
1659 Sheepshead Bay Rd, Sheepshead Bay [Voorhies]
- **Nuts & Candy** • 2079 86th St [Bay 26th St]
- **Omni Health** • 265 Ave U [Lake St]
- **Pisa Pork Store** • 306 Kings Hwy [W 6th St]
- **Sheepshead Bay Gourmet** • 1518 Ave Z [E 15th St]

135

Ahhh, but remember that the city is a funny place
Something like a circus or a sewer…
Coney Island baby
Man, I'd swear, I'd give the whole thing up for you
—Lou Reed, "Coney Island Baby"

Coney Island

No matter what the crowd is like, there is an undeniable nostalgia involved every time you step onto the boardwalk. Whether you're with your kids or trying to reenact your favorite scenes from *The Warriors*, Coney Island is a blast for everyone. Featuring two amusement parks, the **New York Aquarium**, **Sideshows by the Seashore**, the **Coney Island Museum**, **Nathan's Famous** hot dog stand, and **MCU Park**—unless you hate fun, you'll find something here to your liking. The winter of 2009 saw the final and much-feared transformation of Coney Island after being bought by the Astroland developer, but the noticeable changes are few. The Cyclone and all the other essential rides still exist at the same eye-gouging prices as before.

Getting there:
Subway: take the **D F** or **N Q** train to Coney Island/ Stillwell Ave. For the Aquarium, take the **F** or **Q** to W 8th Street/NY Aquarium.
Buses: B36 B68 and B74 all go to Coney Island.

Coney Island, USA

Address:	1208 Surf Ave (near W 12th St)
Phone:	718-372-5159
Website:	www.coneyisland.com

Coney Island, USA is the not-for-profit arts organization responsible for maintaining the Coney Island Museum, producing Sideshows by the Seashore, and organizing the annual Mermaid Parade.

The **Coney Island Museum** is open weekends from noon to 5 pm and is free for members but 99 cents for everyone else. Try the distortion mirrors and view other artifacts from the sideshow heyday. The gift shop has capitalized on pretty much every exploitable image available and it's a great spot to pick up some jumbo postcards.

Sideshows by the Seashore remains the only 10-in-1 circus sideshow in the USA. Eak the geek and Insectavora are highlights, and we recommend sipping a cold beer at the Freak Bar in the lobby. From Memorial Day to Labor Day, performances run 2 pm–8 pm on Fridays and 1 pm–11 pm on Saturdays and Sundays, depending on demand. Performances also run (albeit with a reduced cast) on Wednesdays and Thursdays 2 pm–8 pm. Tickets cost $5 for adults and $3 for kids, though "periodic specials" are announced outside if audiences begin to dwindle.

The annual **Mermaid Parade** takes place on the first Saturday after the Summer Solstice. Rain or shine, more freaks than you knew existed strut their stuff down the main drag dressed as… mermaids! Seeing is believing and this is a don't-miss event.

For some of the best thin-crust pizza in Brooklyn go to **Totonno Pizzeria Napolitano**, 1524 Neptune Ave, 718-372-8606.

New York Aquarium

Address:	Surf Ave & W 8th St
Phone:	718-265-FISH
Website:	www.nyaquarium.com

In sobering contrast to the natural environs just footsteps away, the New York Aquarium has a colorful collection of sea life swimming happily in clean tanks. The exhibits strike a nice balance between interesting and educational. The aquarium is open every day of the year from 10 am until 6 pm (Memorial Day–Labor Day) or 4:30 pm (September–May) and

remains open for 45 minutes after the last ticket is sold. Entry is $12 for adults and $8 for seniors and children 12 and under. Children under 2 are free.

MCU Park/Brooklyn Cyclones

Location: Surf Ave b/w W 16th St & W 19th St
Phone: 718-449-8497
Website: www.brooklyncyclones.com

After a 44-year absence, professional baseball returned to Brooklyn in 2001 in the shape of the class-A minor league Brooklyn Cyclones (affiliate of the NY Mets). MCU's location couldn't be better, allowing any trip to the ballpark to double as a day at the beach or a great first date screaming your brains out and clutching hands on the Cyclones' namesake. On top of that, the team is actually pretty good. Field box seats will only set you back $14 and bleacher seats are $6. You can purchase tickets either on their website or by calling 718-507-TIXX. Go 'Clones!). As a bonus, MCU has also started moonlighting as a concert venue, and Daft Punk's laser-enhanced performance was one of NYC's most talked about summer shows.

Luna Park

Address: 1000 Surf Ave
Phone: 718-373-5862
Website: www.lunaparknyc.com

Keep your mind off impending doom while in line for the Cyclone by contemplating the historical ride you are about to take. One of the last remaining wooden roller coasters in existence, the Cyclone is the place to be at Luna Park. An all-day wristband costs $26 Monday through Thursday only. On other days you can purchase a Luna Credit Card, where of course the more you buy, the more you save. Open every day during the summer and on weekends through the cooler months. Keep in mind, there isn't any high-tech DisneyWorld

or Six Flags fare here…these are the original rides (with perhaps some of the original carnies still attached). The next day you may feel like you were in a bar fight, but the memories are worth it.

Deno's Wonder Wheel Park

Address: 3059 Denos Vourderis Pl (W 12th St)
Phone: 718-372-2592 or 718-449-8836
Website: www.wonderwheel.com

A slightly sticky quality adds a touch of authenticity to this 85-year-old amusement park. The Wheel of Wonder is still the major draw and offers a romantic moment well worth the $5 each for the stationary cars. Those looking to have their lives flash before their eyes can wait in a separate line for the "moving cars" and believe us, those things really move. Admission to the park is free and $18 buys 10 kid rides or 5 adult rides.

Brighton Beach

Slightly less frenetic than the Coney Island beach and boardwalk (but only slightly) is nearby Brighton Beach. Named for a resort town on the English Channel, this area is now often referred to as "little Odessa." Russian food, Russian vodka, and Russian-style bathing suits are the name of the game on this sandy stretch. The restaurants on the boardwalk are WAY over-priced—pack a lunch and skip the hassle. And a word to the wise—despite shirtless vendors parading up and down the beach hocking ice cold Coronas with lime—there are also cops on ATV's ready to hand out open container violations, so drink at your own risk! Bear in mind however that this is no white-sandy national park, but still probably your best beach bet by subway. Had enough sun? After the beach, head to the famed restaurant and cabaret, **National** (273 Brighton Beach Ave, 718-646-1225) whose doors whisk you off the street and into Moscow. To access Brighton Beach by subway, take the 🅱 or the 🆀 to the Brighton Beach stop.

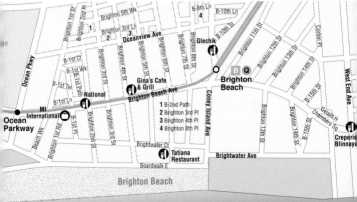

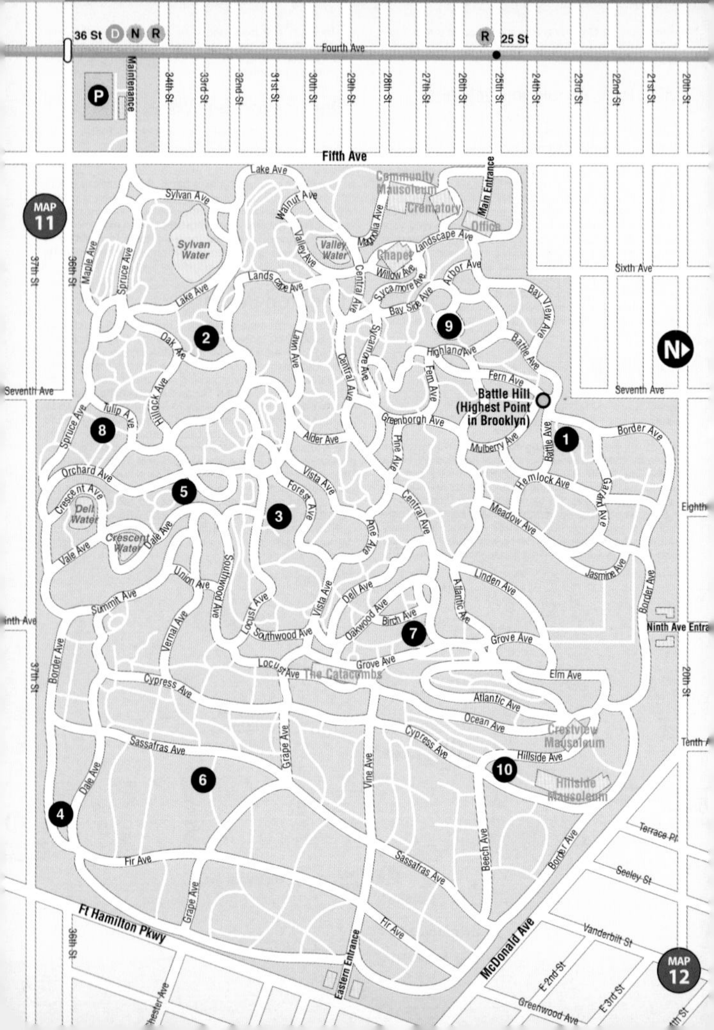

36 St D N R   R   25 St

Fourth Ave

34th St · 33rd St · 32nd St · 31st St · 30th St · 29th St · 28th St · 27th St · 26th St · 25th St · 24th St · 23rd St · 22nd St · 21st St · 20th St

P · Maintenance

Fifth Ave

MAP 11

Lake Ave

Sylvan Ave

Community Mausoleum /Crematory

Sixth Ave

36th St · Maple Ave · Spruce Ave

Sylvan Water

Walnut Ave

Valley Ave

Valley Water

Magnolia Ave

Office

Main Entrance

37th St

Oak Ave

Lake Ave

Landscape Ave

Chapel

Willow Ave

Landscape Ave

Sycamore Ave

Bay Side Ave

Bay View Ave

Battle Ave

2

Holly Ave

Lawn Ave

Central Ave

Highland Ave

9

Seventh Ave

Tulip Ave

Spruce Ave

Alder Ave

Border Ave

Seventh Ave

Greenbough Ave

Fern Ave

Battle Hill (Highest Point in Brooklyn)

Fern Ave

Mulberry Ave

8

Orchard Ave

Crescent Ave

Dell Water

5

Vale Ave

Dale Ave

Forest Ave

Vista Ave

Pine Ave

Central Ave

Hemlock Ave

1

Bay Grove Ave

Eighth Ave

Crescent Water

Crescent Ave

3

Meadow Ave

Summit Ave

Union Ave

Southwood Ave

Locust Ave

Linden Ave

Jasmine Ave

Ninth Ave

Border Ave

Varian Ave

Locust Ave

Southwood Ave

Vista Ave

Call Ave

Oakwood Ave

Atlantic Ave

Birch Ave

7

Grove Ave

Ninth Ave Entra

37th St

Cypress Ave

Ivy Ave

Locust Ave

Grove Ave

Elm Ave

The Catacombs

26th St

Sassafras Ave

Dale Ave

Ivy Ave

Vine Ave

Cypress Ave

Atlantic Ave

Ocean Ave

Crestview Mausoleum

6

Hillside Ave

10

Tenth Ave

4

Fir Ave

Sassafras Ave

Beech Ave

Border Ave

Hillside Mausoleum

Terrace Pl.

Seeley St.

36th St

Ft Hamilton Pkwy

Fir Ave

Eastern Entrance

McDonald Ave

Vanderbilt St.

E. 2nd St.

E. 3rd St.

Greenwood Ave

MAP 12

General Information

NFT Maps: 11 & 12
Main Entrance: Fifth Ave & 25th St
Phone: 718-768-7300
Website: www.green-wood.com
Subway: **R** to 25th St; **D** to Ninth Ave;
               F to Ft Hamilton Pkwy

Overview

When Green-Wood Cemetery opened in 1838, it was the largest outdoor park in all of New York City. With its winding paths, rolling hills, Victorian sculpture, and manmade lakes, this lush 478-acre cemetery inspired a contest to create a park in Manhattan—Central Park. The winning design, by Frederick Law Olmstead and Calvert Vaux, was based on Green-Wood. Today the picturesque grounds are dotted with the mausoleums and tombstones of nearly 600,000 people and counting, including several famous figures (see below). As a member of the Audubon Cooperative, this cemetery is a wildlife sanctuary and a haven for bird-watching. Green-Wood is also home to 220-foot Battle Hill, the highest point in all of Brooklyn. During the Revolutionary War, 400 Maryland soldiers held off the British Army here, allowing the rest of George Washington's troops to survive and fight another day. There are memorials to Revolutionary and Civil War dead at the summit that afford incredible views of lower Manhattan and New York Harbor. If you're craving some peace and solitude in the outdoors, this is the perfect retreat. The creepy beauty of the cemetery is now starting to be noticed by film crews and hipsters; check out Pitchfork's "Cemetery Gates" series to get a sneak-preview of the stained glass magic of the cemetery's chapel.

Visiting

The administrative offices are open Monday through Saturday 8 am–5 pm. The cemetery itself is open to the public every day and can be accessed from three different points:

• Main Entrance (Fifth Avenue & 25th Street): Open everyday 8 am–5 pm (7 am–7 pm in the summer).
• Ninth Avenue Entrance (Ninth Avenue & 20th Street): Open 8 am–4 pm on weekends only.
• Eastern Entrance (Fort Hamilton Parkway & Chester Avenue): Open 8 am–4 pm on weekends only.

For the most impressive entry into the cemetery, we recommend walking through the main entrance gate. Designed by Richard Upjohn in 1860, this brownstone Gothic revival gate is embellished with four carved panels portraying scenes of death and resurrection—a great way to kick off your grim excursion.

Walking Tours

Three distinct walking tour routes provide unique commentary on the history of the cemetery and its interred. Check the website for schedules. Tours usually last about 2½ hours and cost $10 per person. We highly recommend the Special Halloween Tour, which includes local ghost stories and tales of murder for $15. These popular tours (scheduled around Halloween), are first-come, first-served, so arrive early.

Famous Graves

1. **Leonard Bernstein** – composer, conductor.
2. **Horace Greeley** – founder of the *New Yorker* and the *New York Tribune*.
3. **"Boss" Tweed** – corrupt politician.
4. **Susan Smith McKinney-Steward** – first black female doctor in New York
5. **Samuel F.B. Morse** – inventor of the telegraph.
6. **John Michel Basquiat** – graffiti artist and painter.
7. **Peter Cooper** – founder of Cooper Union; inventor of Jell-O.
8. **Joey "Crazy Joe" Gallo** – mobster killed in Umberto's Clam House.
9. **DeWitt Clinton** – politician; brain behind the Erie Canal.
10. **Henry Ward Beecher** – abolitionist.

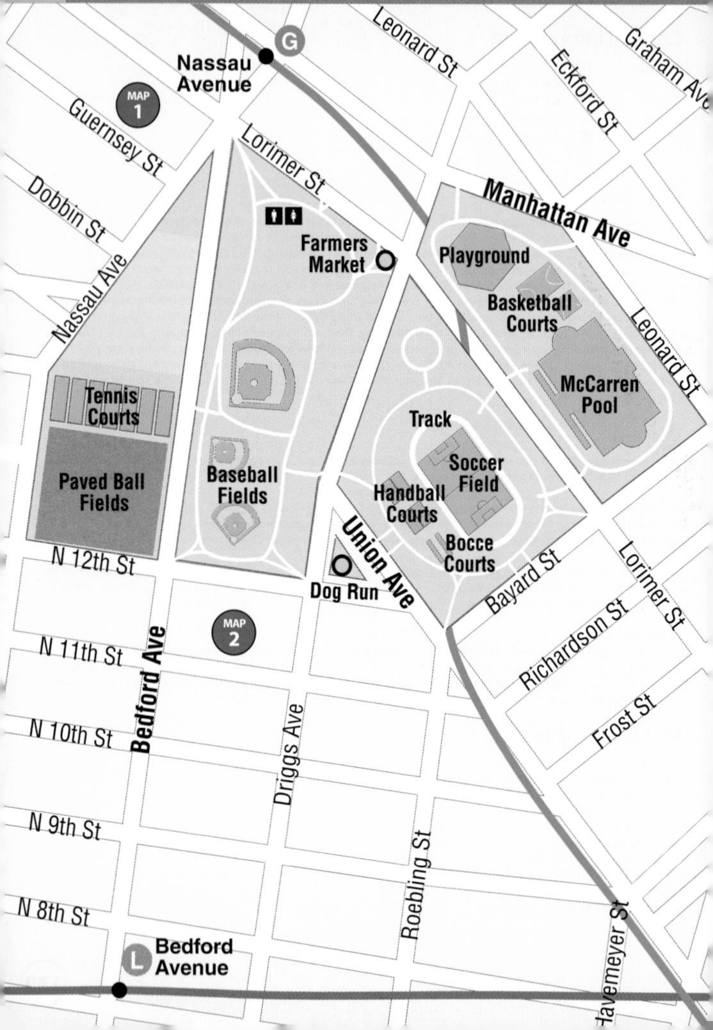

Leonard St

Graham Ave

Eckford St

MAP 1

Nassau Avenue

G

Guernsey St

Lorimer St

Dobbin St

Nassau Ave

Manhattan Ave

Farmers Market

Playground

Basketball Courts

Leonard St

Tennis Courts

McCarren Pool

Paved Ball Fields

Baseball Fields

Track

Soccer Field

N 12th St

Handball Courts

Bocce Courts

Bayard St

Richardson St

Lorimer St

Frost St

Dog Run

Union Ave

MAP 2

Bedford Ave

N 11th St

N 10th St

Driggs Ave

N 9th St

Roebling St

N 8th St

Bedford Avenue

L

Havemeyer St

Overview

McCarren Park is not easy on the eyes, but it's getting easier. Serving Greenpoint and Williamsburg, this 35-acre park reflects both the industrial and increasingly condo-ified surroundings of the neighborhood The grass is brown or even nonexistent in many patches, the graffiti-laden McCarren Pool has been re-imagined as a performance venue, and cars race through the park on three streets. However, McCarren Park is all about *function*, not form. When the sun is shining, the park is packed with a wide cross-section of people enjoying this rare open space. It is a much-needed sports and social hub in a part of Brooklyn that has very little parkland. Besides, where else can you play kickball in the shadow of the Empire State Building while still being within walking distance of the local dive bar selling cheap beer in styrofoam cups?

How to Get There

The easiest way to access the park is by walking, biking, or taking the subway. Take the Ⓛ train to the Bedford Avenue stop or the Ⓖ train to the Nassau Avenue stop. The 62 Bus also runs right through the park along Bedford Avenue. Parking can usually be found fairly easily in the surrounding blocks.

Activities

Public space is a limited commodity for folks in Greenpoint and Williamsburg, so the locals take full advantage of McCarren Park. There are several facilities for sports, including seven tennis courts, a soccer field, five ball fields (although two "fields" are made of asphalt), and a running track. There are also handball, basketball, and two nice bocce courts. The Vincent V. Abate Playground is a great place to take the kids and includes animal-shaped fountains for summer cooling. Other activities include sunbathing, picnicking, and people-watching from the numerous benches. On Sunday afternoons you'll find Billyburg hipsters in ironically designed uniforms hanging out and playing kickball. There is a decent year-round farmers market at the corner of Driggs Avenue and Lorimer Street every Saturday from 8 am to 3 pm. The park stays open until 1 am, and it is a fine place to check out the view of the Manhattan skyline on a summer evening.

The McCarren Pool

The McCarren Pool is a dilapidated yet beautiful Art Deco landmark on the rebound. There is an excellent view of the interior of the pool from the Vincent V. Abate Playground. Opened in 1936, the pool accommodated an astounding 6,800 swimmers. It quickly became a popular destination for all of Brooklyn. It closed in the 1980s after a long decline. Various ideas have been proposed to restore the pool, but none have advanced past the preliminary planning stages. However, there is hope. Noemi LaFrance's dance company held a successful performance in the summer of 2005 that opened the space to the public for the first time in many years. The Jelly NYC "Pool Parties" were forced to move to the Williamsburg Waterfront in 2009 when long-debated plans to renovate the pool to make it—gasp!—a pool finally got underway. The new pool, which will include multiple recreation spaces and convert to a skating rink in the winter, is scheduled to open in summer 2012. But stay tuned for more announcements before you grab your 80s-shades and Aquasocks.

General Information

NFT Maps:	9, 10, 13
Address:	95 Prospect Park W
Phone:	718-965-8951
Events:	718-965-8999
Website:	www.prospectpark.org

Overview

Visit Prospect Park on a sunny Saturday and you'll witness thousands of people barbecuing, biking, fishing, sunbathing, flying kites, and playing ball games. Designed by famed landscape architects Frederick Law Olmstead and Calvert Vaux (better known as the team behind Central Park in Manhattan), the park is the 585-acre home to Long Meadow, Brooklyn's only forest, and the relatively enormous Prospect Lake. In winter, smart locals know to eschew Manhattan's overcrowded and overpriced Rockefeller Center and ice skate at Wollman Rink for less than half the price. Prospect Park is also proud to have the first urban Audubon Center, housed in a brand-new building that opened in 2002.

Getting There:

Depending on where in the park you're visiting, subway lines ②
③ ④ ⑤ ⑧ ⑩ ⑫ and ⑬ stop around the perimeter. If you drive, there is limited parking available in the park at the Wollman Center (use the Parkside/Ocean Avenue entrance), Bartel-Pritchard Circle, and Litchfield Villa (enter at 3rd Street).

1. Prospect Park Zoo/Wildlife Center

Address:	450 Flatbush Ave
Phone:	718-399-7339
Website:	ww.prospectparkzoo.com
Subway:	⑧ ⑩ ⑤ to Prospect Park

The Prospect Park Zoo boasts more than 80 different species of animals in environments mirroring their natural habitats. Open 365 days a year, the zoo opens at 10 am and closes at 5 pm on weekdays, 5:30 pm on weekends from April to October. November to March, the Zoo is open from 10 am to 4:30 pm daily. Admission is $6 for adults, $2 for children aged 3–12, and $2.25 for seniors. Free parking is available on Flatbush Avenue and the park is handicapped accessible. Eating options are limited to vending machines, but there are plenty of outdoor picnic tables for those who take their own lunch. Purchases at the gift shop contribute to the maintenance of the zoo.

2. Picnic House

After a year-long renovation, the Picnic House reopened in 2005 and is now better than ever. To reach it, enter the park at 3rd Street and Prospect Park West and head southeast towards the Long Meadow. The Picnic House is available for rent to the public (718-287-6215) and, in addition to its magnificent view of the Long Meadow, features an open interior of 3600 square-feet, a raised stage, fireplace, piano, and restrooms.

3. Long Meadow and Nethermead

The two largest open areas of the park, Long Meadow and Nethermead, play host to group picnics, ball-playing, frisbee-throwing, kite-flying, strolling, lazing about, and everything else people do in big green spaces.

4. Wollman Center and Rink

Located near the Lincoln Road entrance, the Wollman Center and Rink offers ice skating from late November to March and pedal boating from mid-May to mid-October. It costs adults $5 to skate, $3 for seniors and children under 14, and $5.50 for skate rentals. Pedal boating will set you back $15 per hour, plus a $10 refundable deposit.

5. Lefferts Historic House

Lefferts Historic House is located on Flatbush, near Empire Boulevard between the zoo and the Carousel (open April to October, $1.50 per ride). The house is used primarily as a children's museum and aims to impart knowledge about America's history through crafts, workshops, storytelling, displays, and a variety of hands-on activities, like candle-making and butter-churning. The house is open to the public April-November, Thursday through Sunday 12 pm–5 pm, December–March 12 pm–4 pm on weekends and school holidays only, and admission is always free.

6. Prospect Lake

In addition to pedal boat rides, the Lake also accommodates anglers, but don't expect to catch your evening's dinner—there is a "catch and release" rule that helps to ensure the healthiness of the fish population. Macy's holds a fishing contest every July for kids 14 and under at the rustic shelter located near the Wollman Rink.

7. The Bandshell

Each summer, the Bandshell hosts the Celebrate Brooklyn! Performing Arts Festival, which organizes performances in music, dance, film, and spoken word from June through August. For a $3 suggested donation, this is an inexpensive way to enjoy the Brooklyn arts in the summer months. Check the website for performance details at www.brooklynx.org/celebrate.

8. The Boathouse and Camperdown Elm

One of New York's first landmarks, this majestic building houses the nation's first urban Audubon Center. In addition to exhibits, hands-on activities, and an environmental reference library, the Audubon Center also provides nature trail maps so you can take a self-guided tour of some of the most beautiful areas of the park. The space is also available for rental (718-287-6215).

If you decide against the self-guided tour, at least check out the Camperdown Elm (the result of grafting a Scotch Elm onto an American Elm), a prime example of the exquisite European trees in Prospect Park. You can find it on the southeast side of the Boathouse.

9. Drum Circle

Totally cool, and regularly scheduled—every Sunday from 2 pm to dusk, April–October. Bring your bongos!

10. Parade Grounds

Across Parkside Avenue on the southeast corner of the park, the Parade Grounds offer playing fields and a year-round tennis center, complete with pro shop, clubhouse, locker rooms, a café, and even tennis lessons. The tennis center (718-436-2500) is open daily from 7 am until midnight.

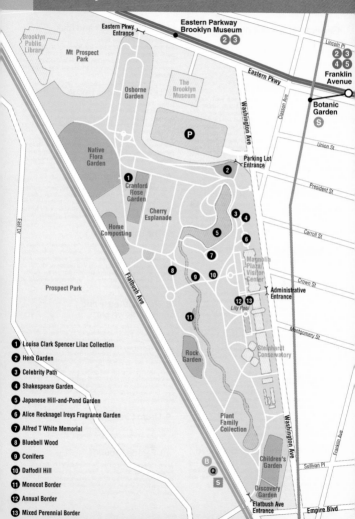

Brooklyn Museum & Botanic Garden

Eastern Pkwy Entrance

Eastern Parkway
Brooklyn Museum 2 3

Brooklyn Public Library

Mt Prospect Park

Osborne Garden

The Brooklyn Museum

Lincoln Pl
2 3
4 5

Franklin Avenue

Botanic Garden S

Native Flora Garden

P

Parking Lot Entrance

Union St

1 Cranford Rose Garden

2

President St

Cherry Esplanade

3 4

5

6

Carroll St

Home Composting

7

8 9 10

Magnolia Plaza/ Visitor Center

Crown St

Prospect Park

Flatbush Ave

12 13

Administrative Entrance

Lily Pool

11

Montgomery St

Rock Garden

Steinhardt Conservatory

Plant Family Collection

Washington Ave

1 Louisa Clark Spencer Lilac Collection

2 Herb Garden

3 Celebrity Path

4 Shakespeare Garden

5 Japanese Hill-and-Pond Garden

6 Alice Recknagel Ireys Fragrance Garden

7 Alfred T White Memorial

8 Bluebell Wood

9 Conifers

10 Daffodil Hill

11 Monocot Border

12 Annual Border

13 Mixed Perennial Border

B
Q
S

Children's Garden

Sullivan Pl

Discovery Garden

Flatbush Ave Entrance

Empire Blvd

Franklin Ave

East Dr

Washington Ave

Classon Ave

Brooklyn Botanic Garden

NFT Maps:	9 & 10
Address:	1000 Washington Ave
Phone:	718-623-7200
Website:	www.bbg.org
Subway:	B Q to Prospect Park; 2 3 to Eastern Pkwy/Brooklyn Museum

Literally rising from the ashes (it was built on the site of a late 1800s ash dump), the Brooklyn Botanic Garden houses a number of diverse gardens, including the Plant Family Collection, Japanese Hill-and-Pond Garden, the Cranford Rose Garden, the Native Flora Garden, as well as the extraordinary Steinhardt Conservatory. Special events include the lovely Sakura Matsuri (Cherry Blossom Festival) in the spring, a lush, Asian flower market and indoor festival celebrating the Lunar New Year, plus plant sales, lectures, and changing exhibits. There is also a charming Children's Garden, offering tours and events just for kids. A welcome oasis in the bustling city, the garden is open to the public Tuesday to Friday, from 8 am on weekdays and 10 am on weekends. The gardens close at 4:30 pm from November to March, and at 6 pm from April to October.

Admission is free on Saturdays 10 am to 12 noon and on weekdays from mid-November to the end of February. Otherwise, entrance fees are $8 per adult, 44 for seniors and students (seniors are free on Fridays, and zilch if you're under 12 years of age. If you visit a lot, you can pick yourself up a "Frequent Visitor Pass," which allows unlimited entry for a year and costs $20 for individuals and $30 for two adults.

While you're there, be sure to check out the Terrace Cafe, serving gourmet lunches and drinks outdoors in the warmer months and in the Conservatory in the winter months.

Brooklyn Museum

NFT Map:	9
Address:	200 Eastern Pkwy
Phone:	718-638-5000
Website:	www.brooklynmuseum.org
Subway:	2 3 to Eastern Pkwy/Brooklyn Museum

In an effort to triple its annual attendance, the Brooklyn Museum recently underwent a $63 million face lift. The renovations include a new ultramodern glass entrance, complete with minimalist water fountains and a sleek new name and logo. (The "of Art" was officially dropped in 2004.) The museum, which anywhere else would be considered a must-see, has always struggled to lure visitors from Manhattan. Maybe the shiny new galleries and innovative exhibits will help. Recent highlights have included the hyper-realist sculptures of Ron Mueck, Brooklyn landscapes by Francis Guy, and other borough-centric shows; the museum's permanent collection of Egyptian artifacts is one of world's most extensive. The second largest art museum in New York City, the space boasts an outdoor sculpture garden, an appealing mix of wares in its museum shop, and a newly revamped café serving gourmet snacks.

Admission is an $8 contribution for adults, $4 for students, seniors, and Metrocard carriers, and free for members and children under 12. The museum, café, and shops are closed on Monday and Tuesday, open Wednesday to Friday 10 am–5 pm, and weekends 11 am–6 pm. Museum libraries and archives are open by appointment only. If you're up for a double dose of culture and nature, you can buy a combination "Art & Garden Ticket" for the museum and Botanic Garden. Tickets can be purchased only at the museum and cost $11 for adults and $6 for "older adults" and students. Parking at the museum will cost you $3 for the first hour, and $2 each additional hour.

The "First Saturday" series is a popular program of free art and entertainment held during the evening of the first Saturday of every month. These Target-sponsored events feature live music, performance art, lectures, and dance parties set in the elegant Beaux-Arts Court with a cash bar and café. On "First Saturdays," there is $4 flat rate parking starting at 5 pm, and the museum closes at 11 pm. The museum also offers free "Arty Facts" workshops and activities for kids ages 4–7, every weekend from October to June. The Gallery/Studio program provides a variety of cool art classes for children and adults, including free work-study courses for teens.

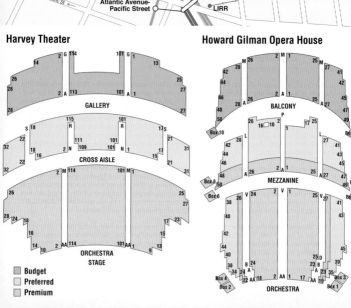

Harvey Theater

GALLERY

STAGE

CROSS AISLE

ORCHESTRA
STAGE

Howard Gilman Opera House

BALCONY

MEZZANINE

ORCHESTRA

Budget
Preferred
Premium

General Information

NFT Map:	6
Gilman Opera House:	30 Lafayette Ave
Harvey Theater:	651 Fulton St
Box Office Phone:	718-636-4100
Box Office Hours:	by phone, Mon-Fri: 10 am-6 pm, Sat: 12 noon-6 pm
	in person, Mon-Sat: 12 noon-6 pm
Website:	www.bam.org
Subway to Opera House:	**2 3 4 5 Q D N R** to Atlantic Avenue
Subway to Harvey Theater:	**2 3 4 5** to Nevins Street

Overview

Historic Fort Greene is home to the world-famous Brooklyn Academy of Music, better known to locals as BAM. A brilliant, thriving urban arts center, BAM brings domestic and international performing arts and film to Brooklyn by way of two theaters (the Harvey Theater and classic Howard Gilman Opera House), the BAM Rose Cinemas, and the BAMcafé. For theater and dance buffs, BAM presents two main seasons annually—the *Spring Season* and the *Next Wave Festival*—both of which are three-month celebrations of cutting-edge dance, theater, music, and opera. Live performances at the BAMcafé happen year-round, as do BAMcinématek presentations at the BAM Rose Cinemas. Visit the BAM website for a comprehensive calendar of events and ticket information. A word of warning: If you're buying tickets for performances at the Harvey, be prepared to either spend a little extra on decent seats, or take a cushion with you to prevent fanny fatigue in the cheap seats (something akin to Jeremy Irons' various "medical instruments" in *Dead Ringers*).

In recent years, BAM has increased its film profile by hosting several festivals throughout the year, most notably the Brooklyn version of the Sundance Film Festival, but also including the African Diaspora Film Festival, the BAMkids Film Festival, and many others.

Seeing Stuff at BAM

With BAM, "hit or miss" is taken to a new level—ridiculously god-awful Shakespeare adaptations are presented right after the most exquisitely beautiful dance performances. However, it's rarely just boring at BAM—so we definitely recommend going at least a few times to check out the scene. One great way to get your feet wet is at the BAMcinématek series, where showings of first-run films and classic screenings are $10—or just $7 for Cinema Club Members. Another good bargain is the subscription option—you buy at least four different performances from either the Spring Season or the Next Wave and get a good discount for each in the process. The public spaces are cool and the stripped-down Harvey Theater is a must-see (though we reiterate: Pay extra for the good seats!).

Here are the main spaces of BAM:
The Howard Gilman Opera House—The main space. A beautiful setting for music, dance, and just about anything else. Recommended.
The Harvey Theater—As we mentioned, horrific seating upstairs, but a great stripped-to-the-bones renovation makes it look utterly cool. The site of many of BAM's theater performances.
The BAM Rose Cinemas—Great first-run movies, excellent documentaries, revivals, and festivals, good seating, and munchies like everywhere else. A recent partnership with Sundance has made BAM an even more popular destination for film. Not quite Park City, but with Sundance premiere films, documentaries, readings, and shorts, it's not too shabby.
BAMcafé—More than just for noshing, the café now hosts the "Dinner and a Reading" series and has free music on many nights.
The Mark Morris Dance Center—It's not officially part of BAM, but it's right across the street and looks cool. Sign up for a class and release your inner Twyla (or Mark, in this case).

How to Get Tickets

Buy individual tickets through the BAM website or by calling the box office. BAM Subscription packages offer a 20% discount when you purchase the same number of tickets for four or more BAM performances. Friend of BAM memberships are also available. Packages start at $75 and benefits include priority notice of upcoming shows and events, no handling fees on ticket purchases, invitations to working rehearsals, reservation privileges at the BAMcafé, and access to the exclusive Natman Room member lounge.

General Information

NFT Map: 5
Address: 12 MetroTech Ctr/330 Jay St
Website: www.metrotechbid.org
Subway: (A) (C) (F) (R) to Jay St MetroTech;
                (2) (3) to Hoyt Street

Overview

The MetroTech Center is a 16-acre commercial/governmental/educational/cultural/yuppie pedestrian entity adjacent to Borough Hall in Downtown Brooklyn. Built on what was one of the earliest settled ambits in Brooklyn, the factories, frame houses, and shops that used to occupy the ten-block neighborhood were leveled to make way for the MetroTech project in the '70s. Envisioned as a center of research and technology to rival California's Silicon Valley, New York's Polytechnic University signed on as the project's sponsor and remains an integral focus of MetroTech's continued expansion. Needless to say, it is but a faint shadow of Silicon Valley.

Today, the MetroTech Commons—located between Jay Street and Duffield Street—provides the area with a necessary verdant refuge from the surrounding cement, exhibiting proof of the urban center's successful development. The compound is home to such prestigious blue-chip companies as Bear Stearns & Company, KeySpan Energy, JP Morgan Chase, and Chase Manhattan Bank. The public tenants that also reside within the hyper-sterile universe include the New York City Fire Department's central data processing center, the MTA, and the city's Department of Information and Telecommunications Technology, as well as the New York State Supreme Court and Kings County Family Court.

Several scholastic institutions including Polytechnic University, the New York City College of Technology, Brooklyn Friends School, St. Joseph High School, and the Helen Keller Services for the Blind are all located within the campus. There's even a hotel (New York Marriott Brooklyn Hotel) and a church (St. Boniface Church). Empire Blue Cross and Blue Shield is housed at 9 MetroTech Center South, a 19-story edifice that was the first commercial office building constructed in New York City after September 11th, 2001.

In 1990, four historic houses were moved from their Johnson Street homes to now-permanent residences on nearby Duffield Street. Along with Brooklyn's Old Fire Department Headquarters on Jay Street, Poly's Student Center (a renovated Episcopal Church originally built in 1847) right on the Commons, and the beautiful Old American Telegraph & Telephone building on Willoughby Street, the transplanted buildings are part of MetroTech's effort to preserve the community's historic architecture.

In an effort to support local emerging artists, the Commons features rotating outdoor art exhibitions as part of the Public Art Fund. Participants are encouraged to respond to the exhibition space and the surrounding downtown area in their work. The Commons also hosts to several cultural events throughout the year, including the Festival of Traditional Music and the BAM Rhythm & Blues Festival.

Perhaps our favorite little-known fact about MetroTech Center is the presence of one of the city's three TKTS booths, right on Jay Street between Tech Place and Willoughby. You should still get there early (15 minutes before it opens at 11 am is perfect), but it's better than fighting the crowds in Times Square, hands-down.

Schools

Brooklyn Friends School · 375 Pearl St · 718-852-1029
George Westinghouse Information Technology High School · 105 Tech Pl · 718-625-6130
Helen Keller Services for the Blind · 57 Willoughby St · 718-522-2122
Institute of Design & Construction · 141 Willoughby St · 718-855-3661
New York City College of Technology · 300 Jay St · 718-260-5500
Polytechnic Institute of New York University · 6 Metrotech Ctr · 718-260-3600
St Joseph High School · 80 Willoughby St · 718-624-3618

Big Business

Bear, Stearns & Company · 1 MetroTech Ctr · 212-272-1000
Brooklyn Renaissance Plaza · 333-335 Adams St · 718-263-3800
Chase Manhattan Bank · 4 MetroTech Ctr · 718-935-9935
Empire Blue Cross and Blue Shield · 9 Metrotech Ctr · 718-510-8015
JP Morgan Chase & Co · 3 MetroTech Ctr · 718-858-9593
KeySpan Energy · 1 MetroTech Ctr · 718-403-1000
New York Marriott at the Brooklyn Bridge · 333 Adams St · 718-246-7000
Verizon · 7 & 8 MetroTech Ctr · 718-890-1550

1. Brooklyn Bridge

NFT Map: 5
At the time of its construction in 1883, this was the world's longest suspension bridge. Today, it is still widely celebrated for its structural functionality and beauty, and crossing the Brooklyn Bridge remains a quintessential New York experience. We recommend you stroll across by foot from Manhattan and reward yourself with lunch at Patsy Grimaldi's upon arrival.

2. Brooklyn Heights Promenade

NFT Map: 5
This 1,826-foot promenade undoubtedly boasts the best views of lower Manhattan (unless you live in one of the houses behind it). In addition to the skyline, the path offers spectacular vistas of the Statue of Liberty, the Brooklyn Bridge, and the boat traffic in New York Harbor. There are also plenty of benches on which to rest your weary bones and take it all in. The serenity of the path is an engineering triumph considering it's right above the BQE.

3. Dyker Beach Golf Course

NFT Foldout: G1
Okay, so it's not the best course you've ever played, but considering its location and price, the DBGC is an attractive choice for urban golfers. The course has a good mix of difficult and easy holes and great views of the Verrazano Bridge. For more information, call 718-836-9722.

4. Empire-Fulton Ferry State Park

NFT Map: 5
This little hideaway is nestled between the Brooklyn and Manhattan Bridges and offers dramatic views of lower Manhattan and the underbellies of both bridges. This is also one of the only parks in which you can see the river lapping an actual shore. Every summer, the park is the site of an outdoor sculpture gallery. And, for Brooklynites in love, this is the choice destination to pitch your wedding tent. No pets, bikes, or alcohol allowed.

5. Floyd Bennett Field

NFT Foldout: G6
Formerly marshland, this plot of land has been used for a variety of purposes: Garbage dump, glue factory, municipal airport, and naval base. Today Floyd Bennett Field is part of the Gateway National Recreation Area. At 1,500 acres, this park is hardly ever crowded and contains nature trails, two public campgrounds, a wildlife refuge and grassland

bioreserve, and breathtaking views of the bay. FBF is quite expansive, so be sure to take some form of wheels to explore the grounds.

6. Marine Park

NFT Foldout: G5
Marine Park, connected to Floyd Bennett Field, is another great getaway in Eastern Brooklyn. This 798-acre park offers nature trails through the salt marshes, fishing, a running track, the Marine Park Golf Course (the largest in Brooklyn), and organized athletics (most notably baseball). Marine Park is also a haven for bird-watching enthusiasts—over one hundred species of birds have been spotted in this area.

7. Fort Greene Park

NFT Map: 6
The oldest park in Brooklyn, this hilly Olmsted and Vaux park (the same duo that designed Central Park) is a sanctuary for the residents of Fort Greene. During the summer, Fort Greene Park hosts a series of outdoor films and free concerts. The park also offers a farmers market every Saturday on the corner of Washington Park and DeKalb Avenue. www.fortgreenepark.org.

8. Brooklyn Brewery

NFT Map: 2
Since 1987 this independent brewery has been cranking out top-notch beers. Free tours of the brewery's Williamsburg digs happen on Saturdays, every hour on the hour 1 pm–4 pm. And did we mention the free samples at tour's end? The brewery also offers a happy hour every Friday night 6 pm–11 pm (take your own eats!) and organizes the annual Brooklyn Beerfest every September. 718-486-7422; www.brooklynbrewery.com.

9. Piers in Red Hook

NFT Map: 8
Two points of interest here. For gawking purposes only—head over to Red Hook's Brooklyn Cruise Terminal to catch *The Queen Mary 2*, the largest ocean liner doing the transatlantic run these days. If "The Mary" is there, you don't really need an address, you'll see 'er. Secondly, and worth more than just a stare—check out Louis Valentino Jr. Park and Pier, located at the western end of Coffey Street in Red Hook. This pier is great to check out at dusk for a romantic stroll. And if it ever does actually happen, this will be THE place to see The Statue of Liberty come alive and attack Manhattan (i.e. great views).

Brooklyn College at CUNY

NFT Maps:	13 & 16
Address:	2900 Bedford Ave
Phone:	718-951-5000
Website:	www.brooklyn.cuny.edu
Subway:	② ⑤ to Brooklyn College/ Flatbush Ave

Brooklyn College is a part of the City University of New York, the nation's leading public urban university. CUNY comprises eleven senior colleges, six community colleges, a graduate school, a law school, and a medical school. BC was recently ranked by the *Princeton Review* as the third "best value" college in the US based on its quality academics and low tuitions.

Brooklyn Law School

NFT Map:	5
Address:	250 Joralemon St
Phone:	718-625-2200
Website:	www.brooklaw.edu
Subway:	② ③ ④ ⑤ to Borough Hall; ℝ to Court St; Ⓐ Ⓒ Ⓕ to Jay St

Brooklyn Law School first opened its doors in 1901 with 18 students. Today, the school has an enrollment of over 1,400. It is headquartered at 250 Joralemon Street and One Boerum Place, the intersection of the landmark Brooklyn Heights Historic District, the Brooklyn Civic Center, and Downtown Brooklyn.

Long Island University - Brooklyn Campus

NFT Map:	5
Address:	1 University Plz
Phone:	718-488-1011
Website:	www.brooklyn.liu.edu
Subway:	② ③ ④ ⑤ to Nevins St; ℝ to DeKalb Ave; Ⓐ Ⓒ Ⓖ to Hoyt-Schermerhorn

LIU offers more than 160 programs of study to undergraduate and graduate students within the Conolly College of Arts and Sciences, School of Business, Public Administration and Information Sciences, School of Education, School of Health Professions, School of Nursing, and the Arnold & Marie Schwartz College of Pharmacy and Health Sciences.

Polytechnic Institute of New York University

NFT Map:	5
Address:	6 MetroTech Ctr
Phone:	718-260-3600
Website:	www.poly.edu
Subway:	Ⓐ Ⓒ Ⓕ ℝ to Jay St MetroTech; ② ③ ④ ⑤ to Borough Hall; Ⓑ Ⓠ to DeKalb Ave

Polytechnic University is New York City's leading educational resource in science and technology education and research. A private, co-educational institution, Polytechnic offers degrees in electrical engineering, polymer chemistry, aerospace, and microwave engineering. Currently, it is a leader in telecommunications, information science, and technology management.

Pratt Institute

NFT Map:	6
Address:	200 Willoughby Ave
Phone:	718-636-3600
Website:	www.pratt.edu
Subway:	Ⓖ to Clinton-Washington

Pratt Institute is an undergraduate and graduate institution that includes the School of Architecture, School of Art and Design, School of Information and Library Science, School of Liberal Arts and Sciences, and Center for Continuing Education and Professional Studies. Pratt's grounds are endlessly fascinating and beautifully landscaped, featuring a burgeoning collection of outdoor sculpture. Improvements to the campus are all an effort to help garner more contributions to elevate the school's infrastructure and educational programs to the same high level.

SUNY Downstate Medical Center

NFT Map:	10
Address:	450 Clarkson Ave
Phone:	718-270-1000
Website:	www.downstate.edu
Subway:	② ⑤ to Winthrop St

Formally known as The State University of New York Health Science Center at Brooklyn, the center is better known to locals as SUNY Downstate Medical Center. The original school of medicine was founded as the Long Island College Hospital in 1860, one of the first institutions to recognize that medical students should be trained in the field as well as in university lecture halls. SUNY Downstate encompasses a College of Medicine, College of Health Related Professions, College of Nursing, School of Graduate Studies, and University Hospital of Brooklyn.

General Info

Prospect Park Horseback Riding:	www.prospectpark.org/acti/main.cfm?target=horse
Gowanus Dredgers Canoe Club:	www.waterfrontmuseum.org/dredgers
Brooklyn Kickball League:	www.brooklynkickball.com
NYC Park Facilities:	www.nycgovparks.org/sub_things_to_do/facilities.php
NYC Marathon:	www.nycmarathon.org

Nothing beats a summer evening at a Cyclones game on Coney Island. But if you'd rather participate than watch, from dark billiard halls to transcendent yoga studios, Brooklyn has it all. Some highlights include horseback riding in Prospect Park, bocce tournaments in Marine Park in summer or Union Hall in winter, or for the truly adventurous, kayaking the Gowanus Canal. Until McCarren pool is filled with water instead of drugged-out hipsters, the **Metropolitan Pool (Map 2)** in Williamsburg is a steal at $75 per year. If you have a need to relive your childhood, join the Brooklyn Kickball League. For all you Anglophiles, Brooklyn even has three cricket fields. Don't miss the NYC Marathon every November, which runs right through the heart of Brooklyn. Brooklynites stumble out of bed to heartily cheer on runners from around the globe. Finally, don't forget to save your money for season tickets to the Brooklyn Nets, who are tentatively scheduled to move into a controversial new arena (named after a British banking conglomerate, of course) by 2010 at the earliest. Until then, cheer on the Cyclones and show some Brooklyn spirit.

Golf

Driving Range	Address	Phone	Fees	Map
Brooklyn Golf Center	3200 Flatbush Ave	718-253-6816	$10 for 150 balls, $12 for 285 balls	p134

Golf Courses	Address	Phone	Fees	Map
Dyker Beach Golf Course	86th St & Seventh Ave	718-836-9722	Weekend fees $17/early, twilight/$38 morning and afternoon; weekday fees $16–$27, non-residents add $8	15

Swimming

Metropolitan Rec Center	261 Bedford Ave	718-599-5707	Year-round	Indoor	2
Bushwick Houses	Flushing Ave & Humboldt St	718-452-2116	June–Labor Day	Outdoor	3
Commodore Barry Swimming Pool	Park Ave & Navy St	718-243-2593	June–Labor Day	Outdoor	5
Douglass and Degraw	Third Ave & Nevins St	718-625-3268	June–Labor Day	Outdoor	6
PS 20 Playground	225 Adelphi St	718-625-6101	June–Labor Day	Outdoor	6
JHS 57/ HS 26	117 Stuyvesant Ave	718-452-0519	June–Labor Day	Outdoor	7
Kosciusko	Kosciusko b/w Marcy & DeKalb	718-622-5271	June–Labor Day	Outdoor	7
Red Hook Pool	155 Bay St	718-722-3211	June–Labor Day	Outdoor	8
Sunset Swimming Pool	Seventh Ave & 43rd St	718-965-6578	July–Labor Day	Outdoor	11

General Information

• Website: www.nycgovparks.org
Permit Locations: The Arsenal, 830 5th Ave @ 64th St; Paragon Sporting Goods Store, 867 Broadway & 18th St

Overview

There are a decent number of courts in Brooklyn, but they vary greatly in quality. If you're anal (like us), always carry some rope with you so you can strap down the center of the net to a reasonable height—it's usually the first thing to go (with the actual net itself being second) on non-maintained courts. Juxtaposed with all this is one of the crown jewels of NYC tennis, the **Prospect Park Tennis Center (Map 13)**, on the corner of Parkside Avenue and Coney Island Avenue in the Parade Grounds just across the street from Prospect Park itself. The center has a bunch of well-maintained Har-Tru (green clay for you bashers) courts as well as two hard courts. You can reserve courts in advance with a credit card, take lessons, play competitively, and chill out at the café. In winter the center puts a bubble over the courts so you can play year-round—and permits aren't required for the winter season, so just bring your credit card. Check out www.prospectpark.org for more information on rates, lessons, etc.

Getting a Permit

The tennis season, according to the NYC Parks Department, lasts from April 7 to November 18. Permits are good for use until the end of the season at all public courts in all boroughs, and are good for one hour of singles or two hours of doubles play. Fees are:

Juniors (17 yrs and under) $10	Adults (18–61 yrs) $200	
Senior Citizens (62 yrs and over) $20	Single-play tickets $15	

Tennis

	Address	Phone	Type—Fees	Map
McCarren Park	N 13th St & Bedford Ave	718-963-0830	Outdoor, 7 courts, hard surface, lessons offered	2
Ft Greene Park	DeKalb Ave & S Portland Ave	718-722-3218	Outdoor, 6 courts, hard surface	6
Decatur Playground	Decatur St b/w Marcus Garvey Blvd & Lewis Ave	718-493-7612	Outdoor, 1 court, hard surface	7
Jackie Robinson	Malcolm X Blvd & Chauncey St	718-439-4298	Outdoor, 4 courts, hard surface	7
One Van Voohrhes Park	Pacific St & Hicks St	718-722-3213	Outdoor, 2 courts, hard surface	8
Gravesend Playground	18th Ave & 56th St	718-965-6502	Outdoor, 8 courts, hard surface	12
Prospect Park Tennis Center	95 Prospect Park W Marcus Garvey Blvd & Lewis Ave	718-436-2500	Indoor, lessons offered $30–$66 per hour per court	13
Ft Hamilton High School Playground	Colonial Rd & 83rd St	718-439-4295	Outdoor, 4 courts, hard surface	14
JJ Carty	95th St & Ft Hamilton Pkwy	718-439-4298	Outdoor, 10 courts, hard surface, lessons offered	14
Leif Ericsson Park	Eighth Ave & 66th St	718-259-4016	Outdoor, 9 courts, hard surface, lessons offered	14
McKinley Park	Seventh Ave & 75th St	718-259-4016	Outdoor, 8 courts, hard surface, lessons offered	14
Shore Road Playground	Shore Rd & 95th St	718-259-4016	Outdoor, 8 courts, hard surface	14
Lucille Ferrier-Bay	Bay 8th St & Cropsey Ave	718-259-4016	Outdoor, 9 courts, hard surface, lessons offered	15
Friends Field	Ave L & E 4th St	718-965-6502	Outdoor, 2 courts, hard surface	16
Kelly Playground	Ave S & E 14th St	718-946-1373	Outdoor, 4 courts, hard surface	16
McDonald Avenue Playground	McDonald Ave & Ave S	718-946-1373	Outdoor, 7 courts, hard surface	16

Bowling

A North Brooklyn bowling duel was set off in 2009 with the grand opening of **Brooklyn Bowl (Map 2)**, the first LEED-certified bowling facility complete with 16 lanes and fancy bar food from Blue Ribbon. It's smaller, slightly older rival **The Gutter (Map 2)** is a vintage style bowling alley with great brews and vintage fixtures so retro you don't even mind when they mess up your score. **Melody Lanes (Map 11)** will provide everything you could hope for in an old-school bowling experience. Another bowling hot spot is the much larger, much flashier **Maple Lanes (Map 12)**. On Fridays and Saturdays, Maple Lanes features a live DJ, raffles, and a phenomenal Cosmic Bowl—complete with disco balls and dance club lighting. There are 48 lanes, so if the Cosmic Bowl is too wild, standard bowling is available for the tamer set. With a full bar and specials like Sunday Dollar Mania (9:30 pm–close; $6 cover and $1 for each game) and International Bowling Karaoke Superstar (the name says it all), Maple Lanes is definitely worth a night out. They have a slick website to boot: www.bowlmaple.com.

Bowling	Address	Phone	Fees	Map
Brooklyn Bowl	61 N Wythe Ave	718-963-3369	$40 per lane per hour, $4.00 for shoe rental	2
The Gutter	200 N 14th St	718-387-3585	$6.00–$7.00 per game, $2.00 for shoe rental	2
Melody Lanes	461 37th St	718-832-2695	$5.50–$7.00 per game, $3.50 for shoe rental	11
Maple Lanes	1570 60th St	718-331-9000	$4.50–$6.50 per game, $4.25 for shoe rental	12
Gil Hodges Lanes	6161 Strickland Ave	718-763-3333	$6.00–$8.00 per game, $4.25 for shoe rental	p134
Shell Lanes	1 Bouck Ct	718-336-6700	$3.25–$5.25 per game, $3.50 for shoe rental	p134

Yoga

Yoga	Address	Phone	URL	Map
Bikram Yoga Williamsburg	108 N 7th St	718-218-9556	www.bikramyogawilliamsburg.com	2
Go Yoga	112 N 6th St	718-486-5602	www.goyoga.ws	2
Greenhouse Holistic	445 Grand St	718-599-3113	www.greenhouseholistic.com	2
Greenhouse Holistic & Wellness Center	88 Roebling St	718-599-3113	www.greenhouseholistic.com	2
Sangha Yoga Shala	107 N 3rd St	718-384-2097	www.sanghayoganyc.com	2
The Well	25 Broadway	718-387-7570	www.thewellwilliamsburgh.com	2
Sapere Studio	222 Varet St	347-987-1478	www.saperestudio.com	3
Bikram Yoga Brooklyn Heights	106 Montague St, 2nd Fl	718-797-2100	www.bikramyogabrooklyn.com	5
Dahn Yoga Brooklyn Heights	130 Clinton St	718-254-8833	www.dahnyoga.com	5
White Wave Dance Studio	25 Jay St	718-855-8822	www.whitewavedance.com	5
Yoga People Brooklyn Heights	160 Montague St	718-522-9642	www.yoga-people.com	5
Bija	412 Waverly Ave	718-483-4795	www.bijakids.com	6
Lucky Lotus Yoga	184 DeKalb Ave	718-522-7119	www.luckylotusyoga.com	6
Area Yoga	320 Court St	718-797-3699	www.areabrooklyn.com	8
Area Yoga & Baby	320 Court St	718-246-9453	www.areabrooklyn.com	8
Bija	162 Court St	718-483-4795	www.bijakids.com	8
Bija	532 Court St	718-483-4795	www.bijakids.com	8
Prema Yoga	236 Carroll St	718-340-3607	www.premayoganyc.com	8
Vayu Yoga Center	259 Columbia St	718-403-0305	www.vayuyoga.com	8
Yogasana Center for Yoga	118 3rd Ave	718-789-7255	www.yogasanacenter.com	8
Bend and Bloom Yoga	708 Sackett St	347-987-3162	www.bendandbloom.com	9
Bija	237 Park Pl	718-483-4795	www.bijakids.com	9
Bikram Yoga Park Slope	289 Flatbush Ave	718-399-3369	bikramyogaparkslope.com	9
BodyTonic	150 5th Ave	718-622-6222	www.body-tonic.com	9
Bikram Yoga South Slope	555 5th Ave	718-788-3688	www.bikramyogasouthslope.com	9
Indigo Pilates Studio	1304 8th Ave	718-832-3464	www.indigo-pilates.com	9
Jaya Yoga & Wellness Center	1626 Eighth Ave	718-788-8788	www.jayayogacenter.com	9
Kundalini Yoga	473 13th St	718-832-1446	www.kundaliniyogaparkslope.com	9
Park Slope Yoga Center	792 Union St, 2nd Fl	718-789-2288	www.parkslopeyoga.com	9
Park Slope Yoga Devi	837 Union St	718-789-2288	www.parkslopeyoga.com	9
Pilates Garage	291 8th St	718-768-1235	www.pilatesgarage.com	9
Shambhala Yoga & Dance Center	348 St Marks Ave	718-622-9956	www.shambhalayogadance.com	9
Spoke the Hub	748 Union St	718-408-3234	www.spokethehub.org	9
Namaste Yoga of Kensington	482 Coney Island Ave	347-533-6226	www.mynamasteyoga.com	13
Dahn Yoga Bay Ridge	8206 Third Ave	718-765-0099	www.dahnyoga.com	14
Body and Soul Central	1123 McDonald Ave	718-421-5766	www.body-and-soul-central.com	16
Yoga Spot	1957 Coney Island Ave	718-339-6425	www.yogaspotny.com	16

Gyms

Gyms	Address	Phone	Map
Aay Fitness	283 Ave O	718-627-4442	16
Absolute Power	750 Grand St	718-387-4711	3
Bally's	2163 Tilden Ave	718-703-6700	13
Bally's	1921 86th St	718-266-6300	15
Bally's	2032 Coney Island Ave	718-376-9444	16
Body Elite	348 Court St	718-935-0088	8
Body Reserve	207 Fifth Ave	718-789-7009	9
Church Avenue Fitness	2228 Church Ave	718-941-1200	13
CKO Boxing	562 Court St	718-222-1822	8
Cobble Hill Fitness Collective	278 Court St	718-643-1109	8
Crunch	691 Fulton St	718-797-9464	6
Crunch	330 Flatbush Ave	718-783-5152	9
Curves (women only)	128 Norman Ave	718-383-0838	1
Curves (women only)	580 Grand St	718-218-8981	2
Curves (women only)	1707 Broadway	718-443-6666	4
Curves (women only)	52 Court St	718-237-9394	5
Curves (women only)	1542 Fulton St	718-771-0097	7
Curves (women only)	317 Flatbush Ave	718-230-9777	9
Curves (women only)	375 9th St	718-788-0003	9
Curves (women only)	6215 Fifth Ave	718-492-7121	11
Curves (women only)	4416 Ft Hamilton Pkwy	718-853-6173	12
Curves (women only)	7409 Third Ave	718-238-4523	14
Curves (women only)	9801 Fourth Ave	718-680-7975	14
Curves (women only)	7203 20th Ave	718-232-6306	15
Curves (women only)	7304 13th Ave	718-833-4222	15
Curves (women only)	1127 McDonald Ave	718-377-3290	16
Curves (women only)	2645 Nostrand Ave	718-692-2950	16
Curves (women only)	2724 Ave U	718-743-1632	16
Dolphin Fitness Club	316 Bay Ridge Pkwy	718-491-2200	14
Dolphin Fitness Club	8701 Fourth Ave	718-680-5500	14
Dolphin Fitness Club	1645 86th St	718-236-5999	15
Eastern Athletic Club	333 Adams St	718-330-0007	5
Eastern Athletic Club	43 Clark St	718-625-0500	5
Eastern Athletic Club	17 Eastern Pkwy	718-789-4600	9
Empire Fitness Clubs	2825 Nostrand Ave	718-677-1400	16
Equinox Fitness Clubs	194 Joralemon St	718-522-7533	5
Exodus Fitness	510 Metropolitan Ave	718-599-1073	2
Frenchie's Gymnasium	303 Broadway	718-384-9461	2
Gold's Gym	85 Livingston St	718-596-4653	5
Green Fitness Studio	232 Varet St	347-599-0663	3
Harbor Fitness	191 15th St	718-965-6200	9
Harbor Fitness	9215 Fourth Ave	718-238-9400	14
Hollywood Fitness (women only)	7414 13th Ave	718-238-1700	15
Kensington Aerobics & Fitness	202 Caton Ave	718-854-8300	13
Kosher Gym	1800 Coney Island Ave	718-376-3535	16
Lucille Roberts Health Club (women only)	540 Fulton St	718-624-4300	5
Lucille Roberts Health Club (women only)	927 Flatbush Ave	718-469-7272	13
Lucille Roberts Health Club (women only)	430 89th St	718-680-8200	14
Lucille Roberts Health Club (women only)	925 Kings Hwy	718-339-0990	16
Maxim Health and Fitness	193 N 9th St	718-486-0630	2
Metropolitan Pool Recreation Center	261 Bedford Ave	718-599-5707	2
New York Sports Club	179 Remsen St	718-246-0600	5
New York Sports Club	110 Boerum Pl	718-643-4400	8
New York Sports Club	324 9th St	718-768-0880	9
New York Sports Club	7118 Third Ave	718-921-5300	14
New York Sports Club	1630 E 15th St	718-375-0026	16
Otom Fitness Center	169 Calyer St	718-383-2800	1
Pilates Boutique	102 1st Pl	718-858-0205	8
Richie's Gym	6 Stanwix St	718-666-4485	3
Richie's Gym	5119 Fourth Ave	718-567-7387	11
The Slope	808 Union St	718-783-4343	9
YMCA	125 Humboldt St	718-782-3000	3
YMCA	1121 Bedford Ave	718-789-1497	7
YMCA	225 Atlantic Ave	718-625-3136	8
YMCA	357 9th St	718-768-7100	9
YMCA	1401 Flatbush Ave	718-469-8100	13
YMCA Greenpoint	99 Meserole Ave	718-912-2260	1
YWCA (women only)	30 Third Ave	718-875-1190	6

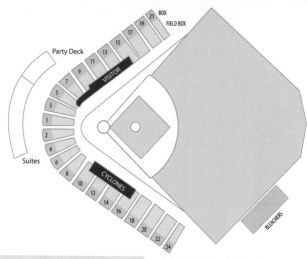

General Information

Website: www.brooklyncyclones.com
Location: 1904 Surf Ave
Phone: 718-449-8497

Overview

Since 2001, MCU Park has been the home of the Brooklyn Cyclones, a Class-A minor league affiliate of the New York Mets. With tickets for games as low as $5, you can take your whole family, stuff them full of hot dogs, beer, and pretzels, and still pay less than half of what you'd pay at Shea or Yankee Stadium. The crowd at MCU (given its location) couldn't be anything but colorful, and the 'Clones keep things lively and competitive, having clinched four division championships since their inception. Mascots Sandy the Seagull and PeeWee (the Seagull) will keep kids and adults alike enamored with their crazy antics. Imagine the crack of the bat, the roar of the crowd, the holy toots of the calliope mixed with screams from the Cyclone's namesake a mere block away, all this cowering in the shadow of the Parachute Drop. This is American baseball—enough to make Ken Burns weep or bring to mind the immortal words of Roy Hobbs: "My dad…I love baseball."

MCU moonlights as a concert venue, and big-name shows have packed crowds onto the field, including Wilco and the Flaming Lips. The Park also hosts the two-day "Across the Narrows" concerts in conjunction with Richmond County Ballpark in Staten Island. Dig it!

How To Get There—Driving

The Belt Parkway to Ocean Parkway S is the quickest route. Stay on Ocean Parkway to Surf Avenue. The stadium is on the south side of Surf Avenue between W 17th and W 19th streets. Parking for all Cyclones games is available in a lot right next to the park. If you're allergic to the Belt, you can take Ocean Avenue from the Prospect Park Expressway all the way to Surf Avenue, but we guarantee it won't be quicker, just different.

How To Get There—Mass Transit

Take the D, N, F, or Q train down to the Coney Island/Stillwell Avenue stop, or ride the B, B, or B bus, or the Coney Island–bound B bus to Stillwell Avenue and Surf Avenue. MCU Park is just a few blocks west along Surf Avenue using either one.

How To Get Tickets

You can order individual or season tickets for Cyclones games online through the website, in person at the box office, or over the phone.

Today, bicycling is booming in Brooklyn. Whether they are atop vintage Schwinns, fancy mountain bikes, fold-up bikes, toy bikes, custom-made stainless-steel bikes, or six–foot tall mutant bikes, thousands of Brooklynites now rely on bikes as their main mode of transport. Just be careful weaving in and out of traffic going the wrong way on a one-way street coming home from a bar at 3 am. If you are going to partake in these kinds of adventures, please at least adhere to some biking laws. Notably, don't ride on the sidewalks and make sure you have a white headlight and a red tail light for evening riding. Also, put aside your vanity and wear a helmet. Your skull and brain will thank you. And don't forget to buy the biggest bike chain you can find—if you park your bike on the street, someone will mess with it at some point. You can see the evidence strewn across Brooklyn in the form of single tires and rusted cut chains clinging to trees and poles. That being said, there are plenty of great bike rides in the BK. Zipping around Prospect Park is always fun. From there you can take the path along Olmsted-designed Ocean Parkway to the Coney Island boardwalk. Biking the famous boardwalk is highly recommended; just make sure you go between 5 am and 10 am to avoid the chance of being ticketed. There is a beautiful ride along the Shore Parkway Greenway on a dedicated bike path. On parts of this trip, you will hardly realize that you are still in Brooklyn. There are also some excellent annual bike events that take place in Brooklyn, including the Tour de Brooklyn, sponsored by Transportation Alternatives. For those of you with a more underground biking inclination, follow the tell-tale markings for Critical Mass spray-painted along the Williamsburg Bridge or surf the web to find some bike jousting events under the BQE. There are many bike shops scattered throughout Brooklyn that offer repair and sales services. If you need to rent a bike, take advantage of the reasonable rates at Spokes and Strings in Williamsburg.

Biking around Brooklyn will give you a deeper affection for this great borough. It will also make you truly appreciate the deliveryman's harrowing journeys to get your pizza to your apartment. If it arrives with the cheese still intact, make sure to tip extra next time.

General Information

Bicycle Defense Fund:
   www.bicycledefensefund.org
Brooklyn Greenway Initiative:
   www.brooklyngreenway.org
Five Borough Bicycle Club:
   www.5bbc.org
NYC Parks:
   www.nycgovparks.org
NYC City Bike Network Development:
   www.nyc.gov/html/dcp/html/bike
NYC DOT:
   www.nyc.gov/html/dot/html/bikeped/
   bikemain.html
NYBC—New York Bicycling Coalition:
   www.nybc.net
Right of Way:
   www.rightofway.org
Time's Up:
   www.times-up.org
Transportation Alternatives:
   www.transalt.org

A Few Bike Shops…

Bespoke Bicycles:
   64 Lafayette Ave, 718-643-6816
Bravo's Bike Repair:
   187 Wilson Ave, 718-602-5150
Dixon's Bike Shop:
   792 Union St, 718-636-0067
Lit Fuse Cyclery:
   409 Willoughby Ave, 347-442-1672
Recycle-A-Bicycle:
   35 Pearl St, 718-858-2972
Velo Brooklyn Bushwick Bike Shop:
   1342 Dekalb Ave, 347-405-7966

A Henry Hudson Bridge
B Spuyten Duyvil Bridge

THE BRONX

Palisades Interstate Pkwy

Henry Hudson Bridge

Bronx & Pelham Pkwy

Bronx River Pkwy

Shore Rd

95

New England Thwy

4

80

Cross Bronx Expy

95

87

895

278

Throgs Neck Bridge

George Washington Bridge

Bruckner Expy

Bronx-Whitestone Bridge

295

Francis Lewis Blvd

Throgs Neck Bridge

9A

Third Ave

RFK Bridge

East River

495

Union Tpke

Cross Island Pkwy

Merrick Blvd

NEW JERSEY

NJ Tpke

95

Hudson River

Queensboro Bridge

Northern Blvd

Queens Blvd

Lincoln Tunnel

3

34th St

Grand Central Pkwy

Astoria Blvd

Hillside Ave

Queens Midtown Tunnel

MANHATTAN

Holland Tunnel

Canal St

Williamsburg Bridge

QUEENS

278

Metropolitan Ave

La Guardia Airport

678

Nassau Expy

JFK Airport

Pulaski Skwy

To Newark

139

78

Manhattan Bridge

Broadway

Brooklyn-Battery Tunnel

Brooklyn Bridge

Atlantic Ave

Linden Blvd

Van Wyck Expy

Jackie Robinson Pkwy

BROOKLYN

278

Prospect Expy

Gowanus Expy

Cross Island Pkwy

Flatbush Ave

Belt Pkwy

Cross Bay Veterans Memorial Bridge

Turnpike

95

Kennedy Blvd

Upper New York Bay

Shore Pkwy

Belt Pkwy

Marine Pkwy

Bayonne Bridge

Goethals Bridge

Staten Island Expy

278

Verrazano-Narrows Bridge

Marine Parkway Gil Hodges Memorial Bridge

W Shore Expy

STATEN ISLAND

Richmond Pkwy

Lower New York Bay

Jamaica Bay

Beach Channel Dr

...terbridge ...ossing

By Foot or Bike

Each day, nearly 4,000 cyclists cross the Brooklyn, Manhattan, and Williamsburg bridges. There's really no more convenient or scenic way to commute to work (or colder, in winter). Each bridge is distinct, with its own unique structure, aesthetic, and even passengers.

• **Brooklyn Bridge**
The most famous of them all, and the most easily recognizable, it is New York's Golden Gate. Separate bicycle and pedestrian lanes run down the center, with the bicycle lane on the north side and the pedestrian lane on the south. Because of the bridge's landmark appeal, both lanes are often clogged with picture-taking tourists, so cyclists need to stay alert. Rollerbladers and skateboarders must watch themselves over some of the bumpy wooden planks. For the most part, the bridge is level, and the ride is smooth and enjoyable.

Brooklyn Access: Ramp at Adams St & Tillary St or
                      stairs at Cadman Plz E & Prospect St
                      in DUMBO
Manhattan Access: Chambers St & Centre St

• **Manhattan Bridge**
The last of the three bridges to have bike and pedestrian paths installed. The bicycle lane is on the north side of the bridge, and the pedestrian lane is on the south side. The enforced separation allows cyclists to pedal worry-free, with no dawdling walkers in sight. Pedestrians, in return, don't have to stress about getting run over. One annoyance, which affects only those on foot, is the entrance on the Brooklyn side. To access this, one must climb a steep set of stairs, which is particularly hard on those with strollers or suitcases. Bikers, however, have no stairs to contend with, and can enter and leave Brooklyn without a care.

Brooklyn Access: Jay St & Sands St
Manhattan Access: Bike Lane – Canal St & Forsyth St
Pedestrian Lane – Bowery, just
south of Canal St

• **Williamsburg Bridge**
The bridge of the chosen people (Jews and well-off hipsters), with the biggest bike/pedestrian path of all three. The northern lane is 12 feet wide and the southern lane is 8 feet wide, and both are shared by cyclists and pedestrians. Usually, only one of the paths is open at any given time. When entering or exiting the bridge on both sides, the gradient is quite steep. Going up can be a workout, and going down, depending on how "extreme" you are, can either be exhilarating or scary.

Brooklyn Access: North Entrance – Driggs Ave,
right by the Washington Plz
South Entrance – Bedford Ave
b/w S 5th & S 6th Sts
Manhattan Access: Delancey St & Clinton St/Suf-
folk St

Driving Across the Bridges

Rush-hour traffic is notoriously awful on all of these bridges. Listen to 1010 WINS or Newsradio 880 for the latest updates.

• **Brooklyn Bridge**
No commercial vehicles are allowed (including your U-Haul rental van, newbie!). With the fewest amount of traffic lanes (6), delays are sometimes unavoidable. If you're coming into Manhattan, you've got easy access to the FDR Drive north, but reaching the BQE on the reverse route is a pain in the ass. Currently the NYPD thinks it's interesting to block one lane of traffic in either direction during rush hour for "security" reasons.

• **Manhattan Bridge**
Commercial vehicles are permitted. Seven lanes of traffic allow for a reasonable commute. The newly reconstructed lower roadway provides three extra lanes into Manhattan and back into Brooklyn between 5 am and 3 pm. A lane for high-occupancy vehicles (it pays to bring a friend!) has been established for upper roadway drivers between 6 and 10 am on weekdays. The bridge places you directly onto major streets in Manhattan (Canal) and Brooklyn (Flatbush). However, connecting to speedier thoroughfares on both sides, including the FDR and BQE, is far from convenient.

• **Williamsburg Bridge**
Commercial vehicles are permitted across the Williamsburg Bridge, and the eight traffic lanes are generally fast-flowing. Reaching the Queens-bound BQE on the Brooklyn side is butter. On the Manhattan side, you'll end up on the traffic mess that is Delancey Street. Good luck.

• **Brooklyn-Battery Tunnel**
Gridlock can be intense, and you have to pay a toll ($4.50), but isn't it worth it to use the longest underwater vehicular tunnel in North America? It's also damn convenient. On the Manhattan side you'll end up directly on the West Side Highway (with an option to immediately make a left so you can loop under Battery Park and be on the FDR in seconds), and on the Brooklyn side you'll find yourself smack dab on the BQE. Take the tunnel if you need to go to Coney Island, the Verrazano Bridge, JFK, or the ever-popular Home Depot.

• **Verrazano Bridge**
Giovanni da Verrazano, the first European to enter New York Harbor, would probably turn over in his grave if he knew his name was associated with a bridge that's best known for its traffic and for charging a fee ($9) to enter Staten Island (it's at least free going back to Brooklyn). But the efficiency factor is high, especially if you're looking to head to the Jersey Shore, Washington DC, Colonial Williamsburg, and other points south.

Getting to Brooklyn

It is a decision fraught with peril: Manhattan Bridge vs. Brooklyn Bridge? Brooklyn Bridge vs. Brooklyn-Battery Tunnel? Verrazano Bridge vs. well, nothing?

Consequently, listening to traffic updates (such as 1010 WINS) is the way to go. Because traffic is usually fairly heavy, stations are lax about mentioning buildup on the East River crossings. But if there's a major accident or bridge closure and you tune in, you can be sailing over an alternate bridge with a big smile on your face.

Most of the time, we do think it's worth the $4.50 (unless you're driving back and forth four times a day) to take the Brooklyn-Battery Tunnel. The tunnel gives you instant access to both the West Side Highway and FDR Drive in Manhattan, or the Gowanus Expressway and the Carroll Gardens/Park Slope/Sunset Park area in Brooklyn.

As for the bridges, the Williamsburg to Brooklyn will only give you direct access to the BQE heading towards Queens—for south Brooklyn-bound access to the BQE, you'll encounter some annoying traffic lights. The same southbound BQE access problem exists from both the Manhattan and Brooklyn bridges.

Getting Around Brooklyn

With no highway that actually runs *through* Brooklyn, you've simply got to suck it up if you're heading to Canarsie or the Rockaways. Pick your poison: The Belt Parkway, a route with innumerable slowdowns that takes you 15 miles out of your way but avoids surface roads with traffic lights, or Flatbush Avenue, a direct line from the Manhattan Bridge with one lane for traffic and one lane for double-parked cars and many, many traffic lights.

The same dilemma exists for getting out to eastern Brooklyn and southern Nassau County. The alternative to the Belt Parkway is Atlantic Avenue, which moves more fluidly than Flatbush, especially once you get out past Utica Avenue. You'll experience slowdowns on the Belt Parkway around the Verrazano Bridge, Coney Island, JFK, and other random locations, but it is still vastly the fastest, albeit longest, route.

For trips to northwestern Brooklyn, the best options are the BQE north to Williamsburg or Greenpoint or the "coastal route" of Flushing to Kent to Franklin.

The route you choose will depend on your desire to avoid traffic and look at Hasidim standing on street corners (corner of Kent & Flushing), or get the nice city views while waiting in traffic (BQE just south of Kosciuszko Bridge).

The strange thing is that even with the hassle of driving in Brooklyn, it's often much easier than trying to train or bus it when traveling throughout the borough. A straphanger from the Slope has to take an Odyssean journey into the city and back again just to get to Williamsburg a mere 5 miles away—so if you have access to a car, it's probably worth it. Remember that driving in Brooklyn is all about attitude. Keep your wits about you, look out for unparking cars and psychotic livery drivers, and rediscover the true use of your horn—as an additional appendage.

A Few Tips

Most of these tips are probably not worth a damn, but they seem to work for us…

• For northwestern Brooklyn, Kent Street is a good way to save time if you don't want to deal with the BQE.
• Fourth Avenue is a good alternative north/south between Bay Ridge and Park Slope/Carroll Gardens/Atlantic Avenue.
• 9th Street is a quick through-street east over the Gowanus Canal from Carroll Gardens to Park Slope.
• Don't ask us to choose between McDonald Avenue, Ocean Parkway, Coney Island Avenue, and Ocean Avenue when traveling north/south between Prospect Park and Coney Island/Brighton Beach—they can all suck.
• Metropolitan Avenue is a wonderfully scenic way to get to central Queens if you're not in a hurry.
• Traffic on the Gowanus heading towards the Brooklyn-Battery Tunnel always looks like a nightmare, but most of it is not tunnel traffic—get in the far left lane as early as possible to avoid BQE traffic.
• The Pulaski Bridge is a much better way to cross between Queens and Brooklyn than the Kosciusko Bridge, but where does that get you?

Parking in Brooklyn is pretty straightforward—most folks just park on the street, unless they're lucky enough to have their own garage. Street parking is relatively easy in places like Clinton Hill and Greenpoint, and maddening in more densely populated areas like Park Slope, where the only solution is to become one of those parallel-parking ninjas who can shrink their cars to fit any available spot. Here's a tip: When leaving your car overnight, try to avoid parking alongside a park, as these secluded areas seem to invite break-ins (of course, that's why you can usually find a spot there).

The chief nemesis of street parking is street cleaning: The city will tow your car or slap you with a nasty ticket if you're in the wrong place at the wrong time. Posted signs will alert you to street cleaning times. During these times, the alternate side parking rules dictate that you may double park along the opposite side of the street (e.g. If there is no parking on the north side of the street 11–2 on Thursdays, then during that time it is permissible to double park along the south side of that same street). You'll get the hang of this slightly confusing yet strangely graceful system soon if you haven't already. But just in case, you can always check www.nyc.gov/html/dot/html/motorist/scrintro.html for rules, exceptions, and suspensions. The best tip we can give you is to always have a few dollars' worth of quarters with you—you can usually find commercial spots in Brooklyn, but the parking meter nazis are never far away.

The only area where parking is truly a grind is downtown. Unofficially, you can try the lot at the Brooklyn Bridge Marriott, which charges $14 a day and sometimes accommodates non-guests. Below is a list of some of the key parking lots/garages in the downtown area:

Downtown Parking Lots / Garages

- **Adams Parking** · 66 Adams St
- **Albee Square Parking** · 420 Albee Sq
- **Central Parking** · 9 Metrotech Center
- **Central Parking** · 15 Hoyt St
- **Central Parking** · 71 Schermerhorn St
- **Central Parking** · 75 Henry St
- **Central Parking** · 85 Livingston St
- **Central Parking** · 333 Adams St
- **Central Parking** · 351 Jay St
- **College Place Enterprises** · 48 Love Ln
- **Edison Parkfast** · 71 Smith St
- **Edison Parkfast** · 160 Livingston St
- **Edison Parkfast** · 203 Jay St
- **Flatbridge Car Park** · 120 Concord St
- **One Pierrepont Plaza Garage** · 300 Cadman Plaza W
- **Willoughby Street Parking** · 120 Willoughby St

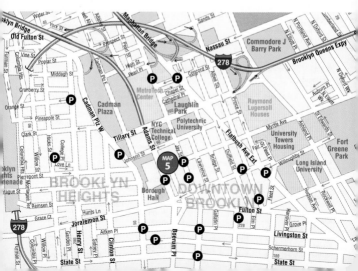

Transit • JFK Airport

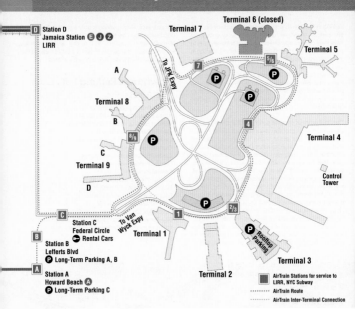

Airline	Terminal
Aer Lingus	4
Aeroflot	1
Aerolineas Argentinas	4
Aero Gal	4
Aero Mexico	1
Aerosvit Ukrainian	4
Air Berlin	8
Air Canada	7
Air China	1
Air Europa	4
Air France	1
Air India	4
Air Jamaica	4
AirPlus Comet	4
Air Tahiti Nui	4
Alitalia	1
Allegro (seasonal)	4
American	8
American Eagle	8
ANA	7
Asiana	4
Austrian Airlines	1

Airline	Terminal
Avianca	4
Azteca	4
Biman Bangladesh	4
British Airways	7
Caribbean	4
Cathay Pacific	7
Cayman Airways	1
China Airlines	1
China Eastern	1
Comair	3
Copa Airlines	4
Czech Airlines	4
Delta	3
Egypt Air	4
El Al	4
Emirates	4
Etihad	4
Eurofly	4
Finnair	8
Flyglobespan	4
Iberia	7
Icelandair	7

Airline	Terminal
Japan Airlines	1
Jet Airways	8
Jetblue(San Juan)	4
JetBlue Airways	5
KLM	4
Korean Air	1
Kuwait Airways	4
Lacsa	4
Lan Chile	4
Lan Ecuador	4
Lan Peru	4
LOT	4
Lufthansa	1
Malev Hungarian	8
Mexicana	8
Miami Air (charter)	4
North American	4
Northwest	4
Olympic	1
Pakistan	4
Qantas	7
Qatar	4

Airline	Terminal
Royal Air Maroc	1
Royal Jordanian	4
Saudi Arabian Airlines	1
Singapore	4
South African	4
SN Brussels Airlines	8
Sun Country	4
Swiss International	4
TACA International	4
TAM	4
Travel Span	4
Turkish	1
United Airlines	7
US Airways/ America West	7
US Helicopter	3
Uzbekistan	4
Virgin American	4
Virgin Atlantic	4
XL Airways	4

General Information

Address:	JFK Expy Jamaica, NY 11430
Phone:	718-244-4444
Lost & Found:	718-244-4225
Website:	www.kennedyairport.com
AirTrain:	www.airtrainjfk.com
AirTrain Phone:	718-570-1048
Long Island Rail Road:	www.mta.info/lirr

Overview

JFK, once known as Idlewild Airport, is the international air passenger gateway to the United States. It's long been an onus to Knickerbockers due to the fact that it's the farthest of the three airports from the city. However, for Brooklyners it's convenient (because it's close) and a good reason to take a short trip to Queens (as if you haven't already got a good reason). For Brooklyn's international jetsetters, JFK is their pivot since Newark is two boroughs and a pallid state away, and LaGuardia paves tarmac for flights over our land of liberty, alone. With the addition of the AirTrain, taking the subway to JFK has become a breeze if you have a stale two hours to kill.

JetBlue's new Terminal 5 rises just behind the landmark TWA building, which you should check out if you have time to kill after getting up an hour earlier. Its bubbilicious curves make this 1950s gem a glam spaceship aptly prepared to handle any swanky NY soiree. Top that, Newark.

Rental Cars (On-Airport)

The rental car offices are all located along the Van Wyck Expressway near the entrance to the airport. Just follow the signs.
Avis · 718-244-5406 or 800-230-4898
Budget · 718-656-6011 or 800-527-0700
Dollar · 718-656-2401 or 800-800-4000
Enterprise · 718-659-1200 or 800-260-0196
Hertz · 718-656-7600 or 800-654-3131
National · 718-632-8300 or 800-CAR-RENT

Hotels

Best Western JFK Airport · 144-25 153rd Lane · 718-977-2100
Comfort Inn JFK · 144-36 153rd Ln · 718-977-0001
Courtyard by Marriott JFK Airport · 145-11 North Conduit Ave · 718-848-2121
Days Inn · **144-26 153rd Court** · 718-527-9025
Doubletree Hotel at JFK · 135-30 140th St · 718-276-2188
Fairfield Inn by Marriott · 156-08 Rockaway Blvd · 718-977-3300
Hampton Inn · 144-10 135th Ave · 718-322-7500
Hilton Garden Inn · 148-18 134th St · 718-322-4448
Holiday Inn Express Kennedy Airport · 153-70 South Conduit Ave · 718-977-3100
Holiday Inn JFK Airport · 144-02 135th Ave · 718-659-0200
Howard Johnson Express Inn at JFK Airport · 153-95 Rockaway Blvd · 718-723-6700
JFK Inn · 154-10 South Conduit Ave · 718-723-5100
Ramada Plaza Hotel · Van Wyck Expy · 718-995-9000
Sheraton JFK Airport Hotel · 132-26 South Conduit Ave · 718-322-7190

Car Services & Taxis

Taxis in Brooklyn to and from the airport do not cost a flat fee like they do to Manhattan. The meter is turned on and you pray that the driver knows the shortest and quickest route (usually Atlantic Avenue to Conduit Boulevard). As a result, the fare can and shall vary greatly depending on where your trip originates in Brooklyn. However, catching a yellow cab in Brooklyn can be tricky, and the majority of Brooklyners rely on car services. Most car services charge around $30 to $35 for a ride from Brooklyn to JFK. But there are some deals out there, so calling around may save you some hard-earned cash. Be SURE to agree on a price ahead of time.

For a listing of Brooklyn car services see page 171.

How to Get There—Driving

You can take the corroded pave of the Belt Parkway or the Van Wyck. Stay at home if 'round rush hour—you'll be squandering hours of your life. If the brake-wearing bliss of stop-and-go highway traffic irks you, you might entertain an alternate route using local roads, like Atlantic Avenue in Brooklyn, and drive east until you hit Conduit Avenue. Follow this straight to JFK—it's direct and fairly simple. JFK also has two AM frequencies solely devoted to keeping you versed in all of the airport's endeavors that may affect traffic. Tune into 1630AM for general airport information and 1700AM for construction updates en route to your next flight. It may aid in alleviating the headache you're bound to acquire, anyway.

How to Get There—Mass Transit

The subway + AirTrain, while not the best, is really the cheapest option for patient and attentive Brooklyners. You avoid traffic, save a bouquet of bills, and get to spend some time catching up on your favorite book. The trip will only set you back $7.25 and there is no one to tip. However, do make sure to check the MTA website or station posters ahead of time for service delays. The Far Rockaway Ⓐ train connects to the AirTrain at the Howard Beach/JFK stop (be certain to board the correct A; there are two; NOT toward Ozone Park). Remain alert when nearing. The Ⓙ Ⓩ line also conveniently connects to the AirTrain at the Sutphin Blvd-Archer Ave stop. Another, though lesser practiced for obvious reasons, subway option is to take the Ⓩ train to New Lots Ave and catch the Ⓑ bus to JFK. This saves a few bucks, but requires the intangible cost of spending well-being as well as requiring you to haul your own luggage onto the bus. Finally, you might choose to take the LIRR—doing so will ensure your trip will progress a lot quicker. Do beware, not all trains stop at Jamaica, so double check the LIRR schedule before departing.

Parking

Daily rates for the Central Terminal Area lots cost $3 for the first half-hour, $6 for up to one hour, $3 for every hour after that, up to $33 per day. Long-term parking costs $18 for the first 24-hours, then $6 in each 8-hour increment thereafter. Be warned, though—many of the ongoing construction projects at JFK affect both their short-term and long-term lots, so be sure to allow extra time for any unpleasant surprises. For updated parking availability, call 718-244-4080.

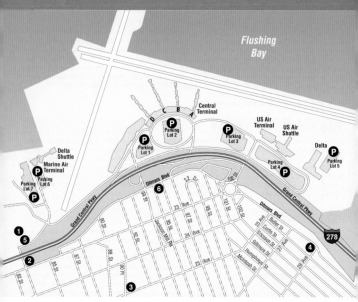

Airline	Terminal
Air Canada	A
Air Tran Airways	B
American	D
American Eagle	C
Colgan	US Airways
Comair	Delta
Continental	A
Continental Express	A
Delta	Delta
Delta Connection	Delta
Delta Shuttle	Marine
Frontier Airlines	B
jetBlue Airways	B
Midwest	B
Northwest	Delta
Southwest	B
Spirit	B
United	C
United Express	C
US Airways	US Airways
US Airways Express	US Airways
US Airways Shuttle	US Airways Shuttle

General Information

Address:	LaGuardia Airport
	Flushing, NY 11371
Recorded Information:	718-533-3400
Lost & Found:	718-533-3988
Police:	718-533-3900
Website:	www.laguardiaairport.com

Overview

Welcome to Queens' other airport. It is so tiny compared to JFK, it feels like a glorified bus station. The best thing we can say about LaGuardia is that it's named for a most excellent former New York City mayor, Fiorello LaGuardia. Although LaGuardia has improved in recent years, it still has a long way to go before it can hold its own against the nation's other airports. Although LaGuardia remains inconvenient to public transportation, especially from Brooklyn, it's still closer than Newark and much easier to navigate than JFK.

How to Get There—Driving

If it is not jammed, take the BQE to Grand Central Parkway right to the airport. Alternatively, you can take the BQE to Exit 38/Northern Blvd, then follow Northern Boulevard to 94th Street, where you take a left. This will lead directly to the airport.

How to Get There—Mass Transit

For those Brooklynites dependent on their Metrocard, getting to LaGuardia is a long haul. Thanks to poor urban planning, there is no direct subway connection to LaGuardia. That leaves the illustrious 🔟 bus as the airport's public transportation lifeline. You can hook up with the 🔟 in upper Manhattan on the 🔟 ② ③ ④ ⑤ ⑥ and ⑩ lines. You can also catch it by taking the ⑩ train to Astoria Blvd in Queens. The one small benefit is that it will take you right to your terminal—not a bad deal for $2. If it is the evening (9 pm–5:30 am) or weekends, a more creative way to get there is to take the lovely ⑥ train to Jackson Heights-Roosevelt Avenue in Queens, where you can connect to the 🔟 and 🔟 buses operated by Triboro Coach. The ⑥ train and bus schedule can be erratic and do not stop at all terminals, so check their website, www.triborocoach. com, for appropriate information. Or better yet, just see the next section.

How to Get There—Really

Two words: Car service. Call them, they'll pick you up at your door and drop you at the terminal. If you have the extra cash, it is certainly worth it. Most trips from Brooklyn are in the $25 to $35 range. See page 170 for car service listings.

Parking

Daily parking rates at LaGuardia cost $3 for the first half-hour, $6 for up to one hour, $3 for every hour thereafter, and up to $33 per day. Long-term parking is $18 for the first 24-hours, then $6 in each 8-hour increment thereafter. (though only in Lot 3). You can use cash, credit card, or E-Z Pass to pay. Another option is independent parking lots, such as The Crowne Plaza (104-04 Ditmars Blvd, 718-457-6300 x295), Clarion Airport Parking (Ditmars Blvd & 94th St, 718-335-6713) and AviStar (23rd Ave & 90th St, 800-621-PARK). They run their own shuttle buses from their lots, and they usually charge $14–$17 per day. If all the parking garages onsite are full, follow the "P" signs to the airport exit and park in one of the off-airport locations.

Rental Cars

1. **Avis** · LGA · 800-230-4898 or 718-507-3600
2. **Budget** · 83-34 23rd Ave · 800-527-0700 or 718-639-6400
3. **Dollar** · 90-05 25th Ave · 718-779-5600 or 800-800-4000
4. **Enterprise** · 104-04 Ditmars Blvd · 718-457-2900 or 800-736-8222
5. **Hertz** · LGA · 800-654-3131 or 718-478-5300
6. **National** · Ditmars Blvd & 95th St · 800-227-7368 or 718-429-5893

Hotels

Airway Inn · 82-20 Astoria Blvd · 718-565-5100
Airway Inn · 82-20 Astoria Blvd · 718-565-5100
Best Western · 113-10 Corona Ave · 718-699-4500
Clarion · 9400 Ditmars Blvd · 718-335-1200
Courtyard · 90-10 Grand Central Pkwy · 718-446-4800
Crowne Plaza · 104-04 Ditmars Blvd · 718-457-6300
Holiday Inn · 37-10 114th St · 718-651-2100
Howard Johnson · 135-33 38th Ave · 718-461-3888
LaGuardia Airport Hotel · 100-15 Ditmars Blvd · 888-307-7555
Lexington Marco LaGuardia Hotel · 137-07 Northern Blvd · 718-445-3300
Marriott · 102-05 Ditmars Blvd · 718-565-8900
Sheraton · 135-20 39th Ave · 718-460-6666
Skyway Motel at LaGuardia · 102-10 Ditmars Blvd · 718-899-6900
Wyndham Garden · 100-15 Ditmars Blvd · 718-426-1500

Map 1 · Greenpoint

America United	718-349-5900
Java Car Service	718-383-5600
Malone Car Service	718-383-1500
McGuinness Car Service	718-383-6556

Map 2 · Williamsburg

Brooklyn Car Service	718-384-7070
Metro-Line Car Service	718-388-1800
Mobil Car Service	718-349-7111
The New Brooklyn Car Service	718-388-2828
Northside Car Service	718-387-2222

Map 3 · East Williamsburg

#1 Mexicali Car Service	718-456-4444
Bushwick Car Service	718-386-5002
New Eastern Car & Limousine Service	718-387-0222

Map 4 · Bushwick

Freedom Limousine & Car Service	718-452-5400
New Ridgewood Car Service	718-456-0777
New York Limo & Car Service	718-455-1010

Map 5 · Brooklyn Heights / DUMBO / Downtown

Cadman Express	718-858-7771
Clinton Car & Limo Service	718-522-4474
Promenade Car Service PCS Limousine	718-858-6666
Prominent Car & Limo Service	718-855-7900
River Car & Limousine Service	718-852-3333

Map 6 · Fort Greene / Clinton Hill

New Bell Car Service	718-230-4499
Pratt Car Service	718-789-4900

Map 7 · Bedford-Stuyvesant

Brown & Brown	718-574-4900
United Express Car & Limo Service	718-452-4000

Map 8 · BoCoCa / Red Hook

Cobble Hill Car Service	718-643-1113
Court Express	718-237-8888
Golden Express Car Service	718-797-0777
Jerusalem Car Service	718-522-2111
Trans Union Car Service	718-858-8889

Map 9 · Park Slope / Prospect Heights / Windsor Terrace

11th Street Car Service	718-499-3800
Arecibo Car Service	718-783-6465
Castle Car Service	718-499-9333
Continental Car Service	718-499-0909
Eastern Car Service	718-499-6227
Evelyn Car Service	718-230-7800
Family Car Service	718-596-0664
International Car Service	718-230-0808
Legends Car & Limousine Service	718-643-6635
Monaco Car Service	718-230-0202
Pacific Express Car Service	718-488-0000
Seventh Avenue Car Service	718-965-4242

Map 10 · Prospect-Lefferts Gardens / Crown Heights

Bedstar Car Service	718-771-2299
Econo Express Car Service	718-493-1133
Transportation Unlimited Car Service	718-363-1000

Map 11 · Sunset Park / Green-Wood Heights

Bell Car Service	718-833-2929
Elegant Car Service	718-833-6262
Mega Car Service Corporation	718-633-2020
Puebla Express Car Service	718-633-4400

Map 12 • Borough Park

Aemunah Car Service	718-633-3135
American Car Service	718-238-4558
Aviv-Express Car & Limousine Service	718-338-8888
Church Avenue Car Service	718-633-4444
Empire Car and Limousine Service	718-972-7212
Golden Express Car Service	718-972-6666
Haimish Car Service	718-972-5151
Jay's Car Service	718-236-5900
Keshet Car Service	718-854-8200
Khageirekh Car Service	718-438-5400
Munkacs Car Service	718-854-4700
New Mazel Car Messenger Service	718-871-9000

Map 13 • Kensington / Ditmas Park

California Car Service	718-282-4444
Five Star Car Service	718-940-0044
Hummingbird Car Service	718-856-6155
Marlboro Car Service	718-434-4141
Mex Express Car Service	718-941-5200
New American Car & Limousine Service	718-972-7979
On Your Way Car Service	718-675-3333
Ontime Car Service	718-891-2600
Rachel's Car Service	718-972-2223
US Express Car & Limousine Service	718-633-4800

Map 14 • Bay Ridge

Alexandria Limo & Car Service	718-491-3111
Apple Express	718-836-8200
Bridgeview Car Service	718-833-3015
Dyker Car Service	718-745-0900
Harbor View Car Service	718-680-2500
Marine Limousine & Car Service	718-680-0003
Max Car & Limousine Service	718-921-3399
Ridge Car Service	718-748-4444
Sam's Car Services & Limo	718-238-8888
Your Car Service	718-680-2900

Map 15 • Dyker Heights / Bensonhurst

18th Avenue Private Car Service	718-256-2190
AR Car & Limo	718-236-8881
Car Service 69	718-234-6666
L&Y Car & Limousine Service	718-837-6464
My Way Car Service	718-232-2435
Strictly Car Service	718-256-4225
Tripp Car Service	718-256-2190

Map 16 • Midwood

Best Way Car Service	718-252-6363
ELAT Car & Limousine Service	718-339-5111
Jaffa Car Service	718-376-6400
Jilly's Car Service	718-859-8300
Monte's Car Service	718-258-2880
Rechev Car Service	718-338-2003
TOV (Too) Car & Limousine Service	718-375-8877

Month	Event	Information
January	New Year's Fireworks	*Prospect Park* B-side fireworks in the park.
January	New Year's Day Dip	*Coney Island* The Polar Bears come out and play.
February	Chinese New Year Celebration	*Sunset Park* An annual celebration featuring singing, dancing, and fireworks.
March	Brooklyn Irish-American Parade	*Prospect Park* Irish Pride. www.brooklynirishamericanparade.com
March	Opening Day in Prospect Park	*Prospect Park* Lefferts Historic House and the 1912 carousel open for the season
March–April	Central Brooklyn Jazz Festival	*various locations* Event is hosted by the Central Brooklyn Jazz Consortium and musicians from all over the country attend. 718-875-1016
April	Earth Day Weekend Celebration	*Prospect Park* Various events in Prospect Park honoring Baby Blue.
May	BayFest/Blessing of the Fleet	*Sheepshead Bay* Celebrating the working fishing village of the neighborhood.
May	Brooklyn Bridge Day Parade	*Brooklyn Bridge* Commemorates the bridge's anniversary.
May	Brooklyn Designs	*DUMBO* Furniture designers show off their creations.
May	Haitian-American Independence	*Nostrand Avenue, Empire Blvd – Foster Ave* Haitian Pride Day Parade.
May	Norwegian-American Parade	*Bay Ridge* Even the Vikings get their own parade. www.may17paradeny.com/
May	SONYA Art Studio Stroll	*various locations* The South of the Navy Yard Artists hold an annual event to show artist studios. www.sonyaonline.org
May–June	BWAC Pier Show	*Red Hook* Contemporary art exhibit featuring work by Brooklyn artists. www.bwac.org
Summer	Celebrate Brooklyn	*Prospect Park* Brooklyn's long-running, outdoor, summer-long performing arts festival. www.celebratebrooklyn.org
Summer	Rooftop Films	*Various Locations* Snuggle up on the romantic rooftops of Brooklyn.
June	Brooklyn Cyclones Opening Day	*MCU Park* Brooklyn's own start another season.
June	Brooklyn Pride Parade & Festival	*Park Slope* Celebrate gay pride. www.brooklynpride.org
June	Mermaid Parade	*Coney Island* Slap on your fins and celebrate summer. www.coneyisland.com
June	Smith Street Fun Day	*Carroll Gardens* Smith Street vendors sell their wares at reduced rates.
June	Brooklyn International Film Festival	*Brooklyn Museum* International, competitive festival for and by independent film makers. www.wbff.org
July 4th wknd	International African Arts Festival	*Commodore Barry Park* Outdoor cultural festival with live performances, marketplace, and kids events. www.internationalafricanartsfestival.com
July 4th wknd	Fulton Art Fair	*Fulton Park* Public viewing of fine arts and crafts, dance, comedy, drama, and music performances. www.fultonartfair.com
July 4th	Nathan's Hot Dog Eating Contest	*Coney Island* The one and only.
July	The Feast of Giglio	*Williamsburg* Italian festival with parades and food.
July	Siren Festival	*Coney Island* Great live music for free.
July/August	Martin Luther King Jr. Concert Series	*Wingate Field* R&B, Gospel, and Carribean music.
July/August	Seaside Summer Concert Series	*Coney Island* Classic Rock, Oldies, and "Salsa by the Sea".
August	Brighton Jubilee	*Brighton Beach* A sea of crafts and food.
September	Brooklyn BeerFest	*Williamsburg* Brooklyn's answer to Octoberfest.
September	Brooklyn Book Festival	*Borough Hall* Look for the NFT table. www.brooklynbookfestival.org
September	Conflux Festival	*Various locations* Exploring urban public space with art and technology.

Month	Event	Information
September	Harvest Fair	*Botanic Gardens* Celebrate the start of autumn with live music and square dancing.
September	Santa Rosalia Festival	*Bensonhurst* Celebration of Italian food (rivals San Gennaro).
September	West Indian Day Parade	*Eastern Parkway* Labor Day weekend, West Indian parade. Lots of good food.
October	Atlantic Antic	*Atlantic Avenue* Huge, totally awesome street fair.
October	DUMBO Art Center Festival	*DUMBO* Art all over the place.
October	Gowanus Open Studio Tour	*Carroll Gardens* Check out lots of cool art for free.
October	Brooklyn Eats	*Brooklyn Marriott Hotel* Annual tasting event featuring food, beer, wine, and beverages from Brooklyn. www.brooklyneats.com
October	Halloween Tours	*Greenwood Cemetery* Get spooked.
October	Ragamuffin Parade	*Bay Ridge* Watch the kiddies parade in their costumes.

Don't let it ever be said that Brooklyn lets a festival go unnoticed. Borough Of Brooklyn: http://www.visitbrooklyn.org/calendar.html. Check out their full calendar if you yearn for more!

Brooklyn Timeline

1609: Henry Hudson explores Coney Island.
1646: Town of Breuckelen chartered by Dutch West India Company.
1776: The Battle of Brooklyn results in British victory.
1814: Steamboat service begins from DUMBO to Manhattan.
1834: City of Brooklyn is chartered.
1849: The Great Cholera Epidemic begins and Brooklyn Borough Hall opens.
1855: Walt Whitman publishes *Leaves of Grass*.
1868: Prospect Park completed.
1871: East River freezes and thousands stream across to Manhattan for the day.
1883: Brooklyn Bridge opens with a one-cent toll.
1887: Peter Luger launches New York's best steakhouse.
1890: Brooklyn candy store owner invents the egg cream, which contains neither egg nor cream.
1896: The borough's first free library begins service at Pratt Institute, with an interior designed by Tiffany's.
1898: In a close vote, residents approve a merger with the City of Greater New York
       (a.k.a. "Great Mistake of 1898").
1899: Brooklyn Children's Museum opens to become world's first museum dedicated to kids.
1902: Air conditioner invented by Willis Carrier, thereby allowing future elderly Brooklynites to flee to Florida.
1913: Subway deal completed that will extend lines to outer Brooklyn and spur massive development.
1914: Topless bathing at Coney Island leads to arrest of 50 men.
1916: Nathan's sells its first nickel hot dog.
1928: Brooklyn Paramount Theatre opens as world's first cinema dedicated to talking pictures.
1930: Brooklyn residential population surpasses Manhattan's.
1933: G line begins service between Brooklyn and Queens. The first train should be pulling in shortly.
1939: Brooklynite Alex Steinweiss designs the first-ever album cover.
1947: Jackie Robinson bravely joins the Dodgers, breaking the MLB's color barrier.
1954: The BQE rips apart Brooklyn, but offers sweeping views of Manhattan to truck drivers
       (Thank you again, Mr. Moses).
1955: Dodgers win the World Series against the Yankees, setting off the biggest street party in Brooklyn's
       history.
1957: Dodgers run off to LA. Depression/nostalgia engulfs Brooklyn to this day.
1960: Airplane crashes in Park Slope, killing 90.
1964: Verrazano-Narrows Bridge crowned longest suspension bridge in the world.
1968: Brooklynite Shirley Chisholm becomes the first black woman elected to Congress.
1969: First annual West Indian Carnival.
1973: Park Slope Food Co-op founded.
1976: Rheingold and Schaefer breweries shut down in Brooklyn.
1983: Next Wave festival debuts at Brooklyn Academy of Music.
1987: MetroTech Center finishes development in downtown Brooklyn.
1988: Coney Island's Cyclone, the iconic roller coaster, named an official NYC landmark.
1991: Crown Heights riots rage for three days.
1995: Brooklyn Brewery starts producing tasty microbrews.
2001: Brooklyn Metropolitan Detention Center holds numerous immigrants indefinitely after 9/11.
2002: Nation's first urban Audubon center opens in Prospect Park.
2004: *NFT Brooklyn* published to joy of new Brooklynites looking for an ATM and liquor store in their new 'hood.
2005: "Leaving Brooklyn – Oy Vey!" sign erected on Williamsburg Bridge
2007: Legendary pizzeria DiFara's shut down temporarily by the DOH.
2009: The battle of the Bedford Avenue bike lane.
2011: New basketball arena at Atlantic Yards starts going up.

General Information · **Practical Info**

Websites

www.abrooklynlife.com · Living it up in Brooklyn.
www.bedstuyblog.com · All things Bed-Stuy.
www.bklyn-genealogy-info.com · Old School website on obscure Brooklyn.
www.brooklyn.net · America's most creative diasporic culture captured in a website.
www.brooklyn.about.com · Edited by an avid Brooklynphile.
www.brooklynbased.net · Guide to life in Brooklyn.
www.brooklyn-usa.org · Website of the Brooklyn Borough President with tons of info.
www.brooklyneagle.com · Only daily newspaper devoted to Brooklyn.
www.brooklynheightsblog.com Chronicling America's first suburbs
www.brooklynhistory.org · Website of the Brooklyn Historical Society.
www.brooklynparrots.com · Blog dedicated to Brooklyn's wild monk parrots.
www.brooklynvegan.com · Music, photos, and news from a vegan. In Brooklyn.
www.brownstoner.com · An unhealthy obsession with historic Brooklyn brownstones.
www.clintonhillblog.com · All things Clinton Hill.
www.dailyslope.com · All things Park Slope.
www.freewilliamsburg.com · Essential guide to Brooklyn's hippest 'hood.
www.newyorkshitty.com All things Greenpoint and beyond.
www.onlytheblogknowsbrooklyn.typepad.com · Park Slope and beyond.

Essential Brooklyn Books

Leaves of Grass, Walt Whitman, 1855
A Tree Grows in Brooklyn, Betty Smith, 1943
The Assistant, Bernard Malamud, 1957
Last Exit to Brooklyn, Hubert Selby, 1964
The Chosen, Chaim Potok, 1967
Boys of Summer, Roger Kahn, 1972
The Gift, Pete Hamill, 1973
The Great Bridge, David McCullough, 1983
The Neighborhoods of Brooklyn, Kenneth Jackson and John Manbeck, 1998
Motherless Brooklyn, Jonathan Lethem, 1999
Brooklyn Dreams, J. M. DeMatteis and Glenn Barr, 2003
Brooklyn Noir, Tim McLoughlin, 2004
Dew Breaker, Edwidge Danticat, 2004
The Brooklyn Follies, Paul Auster, 2005
Brooklyn Was Mine, 2008

Essential Brooklyn Songs

"Brooklyn Bridge," Frank Sinatra, 1946
"The Bridge," Sonny Rollins, 1962
"Brooklyn Roads," Neil Diamond, 1970
"No Sleep 'Till Brooklyn," The Beastie Boys, 1986
"Brooklyn Blues," Barry Manilow, 1987
"Brooklyn," Mos Def, 1999

Essential Brooklyn Movies

Arsenic and Old Lace (1944)
The Kid From Brooklyn (1946)
It Happened in Brooklyn (1947)
Bela Lugosi Meets a Brooklyn Gorilla (1952)
A View from the Bridge (1961)
The Landlord (1970)
The Gang that Couldn't Shoot Straight (1971)
The French Connection (1971)
Education of Sonny Carson (1974)
The Super Cops (1974)
The Lords of Flatbush (1975)
Dog Day Afternoon (1975)
Saturday Night Fever (1977)
The Sentinel (1977)
Nunzio (1978)
The Warriors (1979)
Turk 182! (1985)
Brighton Beach Memoirs (1986)
Moonstruck (1987)
Do the Right Thing (1989)
Last Exit to Brooklyn (1989)
Goodfellas (1990)
Straight Out Of Brooklyn (1991)
Crooklyn (1994)
Little Odessa (1994)
Smoke/Blue in the Face (1995)
Someone Else's America (1995)
Vampire in Brooklyn (1995)
The Search For One-Eyed Jimmy (1996)
Soul in the Hole (1997)
Pi (1998)
Girlfight (2000)
Requiem for a Dream (2000)
Everyday People (2004)
The Squid and the Whale (2005)
Block Party (2005)
Half Nelson (2006)
Life Support (2007)
Brooklyn's Finest (2009)

General Information • **Schools**

Map 1 • Greenpoint

Automotive High	50 Bedford Ave
PS 110 The Monitor	124 Monitor St
PS 31 Samuel F Dupont	75 Meserole Ave
PS 34 Oliver H Perry	131 Norman Ave
St Stanislaus Kostka	10 Newell St

Map 2 • Williamsburg

Bais Yakov of Khal Adas Yereim	563 Bedford Ave
Be'Ikvei Hatzoin	31 Division Ave
Beth Chana	204 Keap St
Beth Chana	620 Bedford Ave
Bnos Chayil	345 Hewes St
Bnos Yaakov Education Center	274 Keap St
Bnos Yakov School for Girls	62 Harrison Ave
El Puente Academy for Peace & Justice	183 S 3rd St
Harry Van Arsdale High	257 N 6th St
Jewish Center for Special Education	430 Kent Ave
JHS 126 John Ericsson	424 Leonard St
JHS 50 John D Wells	183 S 3rd St
Juan Morel Campos Secondary	215 Heyward St
Kedishas Naftoli	117 Keap St
Mesivta Nachlas Yacov-A Yerim	185 Wilson St
Mesivta Tifereth Zvi Spinka	199 Lee Ave
Northside Catholic Academy	10 Withers St
Nuestros Ninos Child Development	384 S 4th St
PS 16 Leonard Dunkly	157 Wilson St
PS 17 Henry D Woodworth	208 N 5th St
PS 19 Roberto Clemente	325 S 3rd St
PS 319	360 Keap St
PS 380 John Wayne	370 Marcy Ave
PS 84 Jose De Diego	250 Berry St
St Peter & Pauls	288 Berry St
St Vincent de Paul RC	180 N 7th St
Talmud Torah Dnitra	712 Wythe Ave
Talmud Torah of Kasho	324 Penn St
Talmud Torah Toldois Yakov Yos	105 Heyward St
Transfiguration	250 Hooper St
United Talmudical Academy	227 Marcy Ave
United Talmudical Academy	590 Bedford Ave
United Talmudical Academy	82 Lee Ave
United Talmudical Academy-Will	212 Williamsburg St E
Williamsburg High School of Architecture & Design	257 N 6th St
Williamsburg Prep	257 N 6th St
Yeshiva Ateres Tzvi	162 Ross St
Yeshiva Beth Joseph Zvi Dushinsky	135 Ross St
Yeshiva Beth Yitchak Dspinka	575 Bedford Ave
Yeshiva Bnai Yesucher	467 Bedford Ave
Yeshiva Bnos Ahavas	12 Franklin Ave
Yeshiva Chasdei Tzvi	219 Keap St
Yeshiva Gedolah Ohr Yisroel	281 Rutledge St
Yeshiva Jesode Hatorah	505 Bedford Ave
Yeshiva Kehilath Yaakov	206 Wilson St
Yeshiva & Mesivta Arugath	40 Lynch St
Yeshiva Ohel Shaim	128 Hewes St
Yeshiva Tzemach Tzadik Viznitz	186 Ross St

Map 3 • East Williamsburg

Beginning with Children Charter	11 Bartlett St
Boricua College	9 Graham Ave
Brooklyn Temple	3 Lewis Ave
Bushwick Leaders High	797 Bushwick Ave
Central Brooklyn SDA	130 Beaver St
Cong Ahavas Shulem Dna Tiferes Bnos	545 Broadway
Enterprise, Business and Technology High	850 Grand St
IS 347 School of Humanities	35 Starr St
IS 349 Math, Science, and Technology	35 Starr St
JHS 318 Eugenio Maria Dehostos	101 Walton St
JHS 49 William J Gaynor	223 Graham Ave
MS 577	320 Manhattan Ave
MS 582	207 Bushwick Ave
Progress High School for Professional Careers	850 Grand St
PS 120 Carlos Tapia	18 Beaver St
PS 132 Conselyea	320 Manhattan Ave
PS 145 Andrew Jackson	100 Noll St
PS 147 Issac Remsen	325 Bushwick Ave
PS 18 Edward Bush	101 Maujer St
PS 196 Ten Eyck	207 Bushwick Ave
PS 250 George H Lindsay	108 Montrose Ave
PS 257 John F Hylan	60 Cook St
PS 373 Brooklyn Transition Center	185 Ellery St
PS 59 William Floyd	211 Throop Ave
School for Legal Studies	850 Grand St
School of Legal Studies	850 Grand St
St Cecilia	1-15 Monitor St
St John the Evangelist	195 Maujer St
St Joseph and Dominic Catholic Academy	140 Montrose Ave
St Mark's Lutheran	626 Bushwick Ave
St Nicholas Elementary	287 Powers St
United Talmudical Academy	110 Throop Ave

Map 4 • Bushwick

Academy of Urban Planning	400 Irving Ave
Acorn High School for Social Justice	1396 Broadway
All City Leadership Secondary	1474 Gates Ave
Bushwick Community High	231 Palmetto St
Bushwick School for Social Justice	400 Irving Ave
Charles Churn Christian Academy	1052 Greene Ave
EBC High School for Public Service	1155 DeKalb Ave
JHS 162 The Willoughby	1390 Willoughby Ave
JHS 291 Roland Hayes	231 Palmetto St
JHS 296 The Halsey	125 Covert St
JHS 383 Phillippa Schuyler	1300 Greene Ave
New York Harbor	400 Irving Ave
PS 106 Edward Everett Hale	1314 Putnam Ave
PS 116 Elizabeth L Farrell	515 Knickerbocker Ave
PS 123 Suydam	100 Irving Ave
PS 151 Lyndon B Johnson	763 Knickerbocker Ave
PS 274 Kosciusko	800 Bushwick Ave
PS 299 Thomas Waren Field	88 Woodbine St
PS 376	194 Harman St
PS 377 Alejandrina B Degautier	200 Woodbine St
PS 45 Horace E Greene	84 Schaefer St

PS 5 Dr Ronald McNair	820 Hancock St
PS 75 Mayda Cortiella	95 Grove St
PS 86 The Irvington	220 Irving Ave
St Brigid	438 Grove St
St Elizabeth Seton	751 Knickerbocker Ave
St Frances Cabrini	181 Suydam St
St Mark's Lutheran	66 Weirfield

Map 5 • Brooklyn Heights / DUMBO / Downtown

A Fantis Parochial	195 State St
Brooklyn Friends	375 Pearl St
Brooklyn International High	49 Flatbush Ave Ext
Brooklyn Law	250 Joralemon St
Freedom Academy	116 Nassau St
George Westinghouse Career and Technical Education High	105 Tech Pl
Institute of Design & Construction	141 Willoughby St
Long Island University	1 University Plz
NYC Technical College	300 Jay St
Pacific High	112 Schermerhorn St
Packer Collegiate Institute	170 Joralemon St
Polytechnic University	6 Metrotech Ctr
PS 287 Bailey K Ashford	50 Navy St
PS 307 Daniel Hale Williams	209 York St
PS 369 Coy L Cox	383 State St
PS 67 Charles A Dorsey	51 St Edwards St
PS 8 Robert Fulton	37 Hicks St
Satellite West Middle	209 York St
Science Skills High	49 Flatbush Ave Ext
St Ann's	124 Henry St
St Ann's	129 Pierrepont St
St Charles Borromeo	23 Sidney Pl
St Francis College	180 Remsen St
St Joseph High	80 Willoughby St
The Urban Assembly School for Law & Justice	50 Navy St
The Urban Assembly School of Music & Art	49 Flatbush Ave Ext

Map 6 • Fort Greene / Clinton Hill

Benjamin Banneker Academy	71 Clinton Ave
Bethel Elementary	457 Grand Ave
Bishop Loughlin Memorial High	357 Clermont Ave
Bnei Shimon Yisroel of Sopron	18 Warsoff Pl
Bnos Square of Williamsburg	2 Franklin Ave
Brooklyn Preparatory High	300 Willoughby Ave
Brooklyn Technical High	29 Ft Greene Pl
Francis Scott Key Junior High	300 Willoughby Ave
Hanson Place Elementary	38 Lafayette Ave
Hensen Preparatory	144 St Felix St
Hychel Hatorah	70 Franklin Ave
JHS 113	300 Adelphi St
JHS 265 Susan S McKinney	101 Park Ave
Metropolitan Corporate Academy High	362 Schermerhorn St
Pratt Institute	200 Willoughby Ave

PS 11 Purvis J Behan	419 Waverly Pl
PS 157 Benjamin Franklin	850 Kent Ave
PS 20 Clinton Hill	225 Adelphi St
PS 256 Benjamin Banneker	114 Kosciusko St
PS 270 Johann Dekalb	241 Emerson Pl
PS 297 Abraham Stockton	700 Park Ave
PS 46 Edward C Blum	100 Clermont Ave
PS 54 Samuel C Barnes	195 Sandford St
PS 56 Lewis H Latimer	170 Gates Ave
PS 753 School for Career Development	510 Clermont Ave
Queen of All Saints	300 Vanderbilt Ave
Satellite Three	170 Gates Ave
St Joseph's College	245 Clinton Ave
Talmud Torah Toldos Hillel-Krasna	35 Hewes St
United Talmudical Academy	45 Williamsburg St W

Map 7 • Bedford-Stuyvesant

Bedford Academy High	1119 Bedford Ave
Bethel Christian Academy	344 Tompkins Ave
Boys & Girls High	1700 Fulton St
Bridge Street Prep	277 Stuyvesant Ave
Brooklyn Academy High	832 Marcy Ave
Brooklyn Excelsior Charter	856 Quincy St
Clara Muhammad School of Masjid Khalifah	1174 Bedford Ave
College of New Rochelle	1368 Fulton St
Concord Elementary Day	833 Dr G C Taylor Blvd
Dr CR Johnson Christian Academy	600 Lafayette Ave
Empire State College	20 New York Ave
Frederick Douglass Academy IV	1014 Lafayette Ave
JHS 258 David Ruggles	141 Macon St
JHS 33 Mark Hopkins	70 Tompkins Ave
JHS 57 Whitelaw Reid	125 Stuyvesant Ave
MS 143 Performing & Fine Arts	800 Gates Ave
MS 267 Math, Science & Tech	800 Gates Ave
Mt Pisgah Christian Academy	760 DeKalb Ave
PS 21 Crispus Attucks	180 Chauncey St
PS 23 Carter C Woodson	545 Willoughby Ave
PS 25 Eubie Blake	787 Lafayette Ave
PS 26 Jesse Owens	1014 Lafayette Ave
PS 262 El Hajj Malik Shabazz	500 Macon St
PS 3 The Bedford Village	50 Jefferson Ave
PS 304 Casimir Pulaski	280 Hart St
PS 305 Dr Peter Ray	344 Monroe St
PS 308 Clara Cardwell	616 Quincy St
PS 309 George E Wibecan	794 Monroe St
PS 35 Stephen Decatur	272 McDonough St
PS 44 Marcus Garvey	432 Monroe St
PS 81 Thaddeus Stevens	990 DeKalb Ave
PS 93 William H Prescott	31 New York Ave
School of Business, Finance and Entrepreneurship	125 Stuyvesant Ave
St John the Baptist	82 Lewis Ave
Tabernacle Elementary	264 Lexington Ave
The Urban Assembly School for the Urban Environment	70 Tompkins Ave
Williston Academy	1 Jefferson Ave

General Information • **Schools**

Map 8 • BoCoCa / Red Hook

Agnes Y Humphrey School for Leadership	27 Huntington St
Brooklyn School for Global Studies	284 Baltic St
Brooklyn Secondary School for Collaborative Studies	610 Henry St
Cobble Hill School for American Studies	347 Baltic St
Hannah Senesh	215 Pacific St
Mary McDowell Center for Learning	20 Bergen St
New Horizons	317 Hoyt St
PS 146	610 Henry St
PS 15 Patrick F Daly	71 Sullivan St
PS 261 Philp Livingston	314 Pacific St
PS 29 John M Harrigan	425 Henry St
PS 38 The Pacific	450 Pacific St
PS 58 The Carroll School	330 Smith St
School for International Research	284 Baltic St
School for International Studies	284 Baltic St
South Brooklyn Community High	173 Conover St
The Sterling	299 Pacific St

Map 9 • Park Slope / Prospect Heights / Windsor Terrace

Acorn High	561 Grand Ave
Al-Madinah	383 Third Ave
Berkeley-Carroll	181 Lincoln Pl
Brooklyn Conservatory of Music	58 Seventh Ave
Brooklyn Free School	120 16th St
Brooklyn High School of the Arts	345 Dean St
Cathedral	910 Union St
Holy Name	241 Prospect Park W
International School of Brooklyn	237 Park Pl
IS 340	227 Sterling Pl
JHS 266 Park Place Community	62 Park Pl
Magnet School of Math, Sciencey & Design Technolog	511 Seventh Ave
The Math & Science Exploratory School	345 Dean St
Montessori School of NY	105 Eighth Ave
MS 51 William Alexander	350 Fifth Ave
MS 571	80 Underhill Ave
New Voices	330 18th St
Park Slope Christian Academy	98 Fifth Ave
Poly Prep--Lower	50 Prospect Park W
PS 107 John W Kimball	1301 Eighth Ave
PS 124 Silas B Dutcher	515 Fourth Ave
PS 133 William A Butler	375 Butler St
PS 154 Magnet School for Science & Technology	1625 11th Ave
PS 22	443 St Marks Ave
PS 282 Park Slope	180 Sixth Ave
PS 295/MS 827	330 18th St
PS 321 William Penn	180 Seventh Ave
PS 372 The Children's School	512 Carroll St
PS 39 Henry Bristow	417 Sixth Ave
PS 77K Special Education School	62 Park Pl
PS 9 Teunis G Bergen	80 Underhill Ave

Rivendell	421 7th St
Secondary School for Journalism	237 Seventh Ave
Secondary School for Law (HS 462)	237 Seventh Ave
Secondary School for Research	237 Seventh Ave
Soterios Ellenas Parochial	224 18th St
St Francis Xavier	763 President St
St Saviour Elementary	701 Eighth Ave
St Saviour High	588 6th St
St Thomas Aquinas	211 8th St

Map 10 • Prospect-Lefferts Gardens / Crown Heights

Arista Prep	275 Kingston Ave
Arista Prep	755 Eastern Pkwy
Beth Rivkah	470 Lefferts Ave
Beth Rivkah High	310 Crown St
Brooklyn Academy of Science and the Environment	883 Classon Ave
Brooklyn Jesuit Prep	560 Sterling Pl
Clara Barton High	901 Classon Ave
Cush Campus	221 Kingston Ave
Darchai Menachem	823 Eastern Pkwy
Educational Inst Oholei Torah	667 Eastern Pkwy
Elijah Stroud Middle	750 Classon Ave
Epiphany Lutheran Elementary	721 Lincoln Pl
Full Gospel Christian Academy	836 Franklin Ave
Hebron SDA Bilingual	920 Park Pl
International Arts Business School	600 Kingston Ave
International High School at Prospect Heights	883 Classon Ave
Irving	402 Fenimore St
John Dinkins School of Arts	395 Maple St
John Hus Moravian	153 Ocean Ave
League School	567 Kingston Ave
Lubavitcher Yeshiva	570 Crown St
MACADEMY	1313 Union St
Machon Chana	433 Crown St
Medgar Evers College	1650 Bedford Ave
Middle College High at Medgar Evers	1186 Carroll St
MS 2	655 Parkside Ave
MS 61 Gladstone H Atwell	400 Empire Blvd
Paul Robeson High	150 Albany Ave
PS 138 Brooklyn	760 Prospect Pl
PS 161 The Crown School	330 Crown St
PS 241 Emma L Johnston	976 President St
PS 289 George V Brower	900 St Marks Ave
PS 316 Elijah Stroud	750 Classon Ave
PS 375 Jackie Robinson	46 McKeever Pl
PS 397 Foster-Laurie	490 Fenimore St
PS 92 Adrian Hegeman	601 Parkside Ave
School for Democracy and Leadership	600 Kingston Ave
School for Human Rights	600 Kingston Ave
St Francis De Sales School for the Deaf	260 Eastern Pkwy
St Francis of Assisi	400 Lincoln Rd
St Gregory the Great Elementary	991 St Johns Pl
St Mark's	1346 President St
SUNY Downstate Medical Center	450 Clarkson Ave

United Lubavitcher Yeshivoth	885 Eastern Pkwy
WEB Dubois Academic High	402 Eastern Pkwy
Yeshiva Chanoch Lenaar	876 Eastern Pkwy

Map 11 • Sunset Park / Green-Wood Heights

Al Madrasa Al Islamiya	5224 Third Ave
Al-Noor	675 Fourth Ave
Bay Ridge Christian Academy	6324 Seventh Ave
Hellenic Classical Charter	646 Fifth Ave
IS 136 Charles O Dewey	4004 Fourth Ave
JHS 220 John J Pershing	4812 Ninth Ave
JHS 88 Peter Rouget	544 Seventh Ave
Our Lady of Perpetual Help	5902 Sixth Ave
PS 1 The Bergen	309 47th St
PS 169 Sunset Park	4305 Seventh Ave
PS 172	825 Fourth Ave
PS 24	427 38th St
PS 371 Lillian L Rashkis	355 37th St
PS 506 School of Journalism and Technology	330 59th St
PS 69 Vincent D Grippo	884 63rd St
PS 94 The Henry Longfellow	5010 Sixth Ave
St Agatha's	736 48th St
St Michael	4222 Fourth Ave
Sunset Park Prep	4004 Fourth Ave
Tomer Dvora	4500 Ninth Ave
Yeshiva Machzikel Hadas	695 Sixth Ave

Map 12 • Borough Park

Bais Brocho of Karlin Stolin	4314 10th Ave
Bais Ruchel School of Boro Park	5301 14th Ave
Bais Sarah-Educ School for Girls	1363 50th St
Bais Yaakov D'Gur High	1975 51st St
Bais Yaakov D'Khal Adas Yereim	1169 43rd St
Bais Yaakov of Brooklyn	1362 49th St
Beth Jacob High	4421 15th Ave
Beth Jacob of Boro Park	1371 46th St
Bnos Zion of Bobov	5000 14th Ave
Franklin Delano Roosevelt High	5800 20th Ave
Hebrew Academy for Special Children	5902 14th Ave
Holy Spirit	1668 46th St
JHS 223 The Montauk School	4200 16th Ave
Martin De Porres High	500 19th St
Mosdos Bnos Frima	1377 42nd St
Mosdos Chasidei SQ-TYY Boro Park	1373 43rd St
PS 105 The Blythebourne	1031 59th St
PS 121 Nelson A Rockefeller	5301 20th Ave
PS 131	4305 Ft Hamilton Pkwy
PS 160 William T Sampson	5105 Ft Hamilton Pkwy
PS 164 Caesar Rodney	4211 14th Ave
PS 180 Homewood	5601 16th Ave
PS 192	4715 18th Ave
PS 230 Doris L Cohen	1 Albermarle Rd
PS 48 Mapelton	6015 18th Ave
St Catharine of Alexandria	1053 41st St
Tiferes Bais Yaakov High	4508 16th Ave
Tomer Devora High School for Girls	5801 16th Ave
United Talmudical Academy	5411 Ft Hamilton Pkwy

Viznitzer Chaider Tiferes Yisroel	1424 43rd St
Yeshiva Bais Yitzchok	1413 45th St
Yeshiva Beis Meir (Boys)	1327 38th St
Yeshiva Beth Hillel of Krasna	1364 42nd St
Yeshiva Beth Hillel of Krasna	1371 42nd St
Yeshiva Boyan	1205 44th St
Yeshiva Ch San Sofer	1876 50th St
Yeshiva Derech Chaim	1573 39th St
Yeshiva Imrei Yosef Spinka	5801 15th Ave
Yeshiva Karlin Stolin	1818 54th St
Yeshiva Kehilath Yakov	4706 10th Ave
Yeshiva Machzikei Hadas	1601 42nd St
Yeshiva Tiferes Bunim	5202 13th Ave
Yeshiva Tifereth Elimelech	1650 56th St
Yeshiva Toras Chesed	5506 16th Ave
Yeshiva Yesode Hatorah	1350 50th St
Yeshivas Novominsk-Kol Yehuda	1569 47th St
Yeshivat Ohel Torah	1760 53rd St

Map 13 • Kensington / Ditmas Park

Bais Yaakov D'Rav Meir High	85 Parkville Ave
Bais Yaakov of 18th Ave	4419 18th Ave
Bnos Yerushalayim	600 McDonald Ave
Brooklyn College	2900 Bedford Ave
Brooklyn College Academy	2900 Bedford Ave
Cortelyou Early Childhood Cent	1110 Cortelyou Rd
Cycle Educ Center	2414 Church Ave
Erasmus High	911 Flatbush Ave
Flatbush Catholic Academy	2520 Church Ave
Get Set Kindergarten	2301 Snyder Ave
Holy Innocents	249 E 17th St
Immaculate Heart of Mary	3002 Ft Hamilton Pkwy
IS 246 Walt Whitman	72 Veronica Pl
JHS 62 The Ditmas	700 Cortelyou Rd
K134	4001 18th Ave
Midwood High	2839 Bedford Ave
Our Lady of Refuge	1087 Ocean Ave
PS 130 The Parkside	70 Ocean Pkwy
PS 139 Alexine A Fenty	330 Rugby Rd
PS 179 Kensington	202 Ave C
PS 217 Colonel David Marcus	1100 Newkirk Ave
PS 245	49 E 17th St
PS 249 The Caton School	18 Marlborough Rd
PS 269 Nostrand	1957 Nostrand Ave
PS 315	2310 Glenwood Rd
PS 399 Stanley Eugene Clark	2707 Albemarle Rd
PS 6	43 Snyder Ave
School of Science and Technology	725 E 23rd St
Shaare Torah Girls Elementary	222 Ocean Pkwy
St Jerome	465 E 29th St
St Rose of Lima Elementary	259 Parkville Ave
UCP NYC Brooklyn Childrens Pro	160 Lawrence Ave
Yeshiva Ketana of Bensonhurst	953 Coney Island Ave
Yeshiva Torah Temimah	555 Ocean Pkwy
Yeshiva Torah Vodaath	425 E Ninth St
Yeshivat Shaare Torah Girls' D	500 Church Ave

Map 14 • Bay Ridge

Bay Ridge Prep High	7420 Fourth Ave
Bay Ridge Prep—Lower	8101 Ridge Blvd
Fontbonne Hall	9901 Shore Rd
Fort Hamilton High	8301 Shore Rd
High School of Telecommunications	350 67th St
Holy Cross Parochial	8502 Ridge Blvd
IS 30 Mary White Ovington	415 Ovington Ave
Lutheran Elementary	440 Ovington Ave
New Hope Christian Academy	257 Bay Ridge Ave
Our Lady of Angels	337 74th St
Poly Prep Country Day	9216 Seventh Ave
PS 102 The Bayview	211 72nd St
PS 170 Lexington	7109 Sixth Ave
PS 185 Walter Kassenbrock	8601 Ridge Blvd
PS / IS 104 The Fort Hamilton School	9115 Fifth Ave
St Anselm's	365 83rd St
Visitation Academy	8902 Ridge Blvd
Xaverian High	7100 Shore Rd

Map 15 • Dyker Heights / Bensonhurst

IS 187	1171 65th St
JHS 201 Dyker Heights	8010 12th Ave
JHS 227 Edward B Shallow	6500 16 Ave
JHS 259 William McKinley	7301 Ft Hamilton Pkwy
Leif Ericsson	1037 72nd St
New Utrecht High	1601 80th St
Our Lady of Guadalupe	1518 73rd St
PS 112 Lefferts Park	7115 15th Ave
PS 163 Bath Beach	1664 Benson Ave
PS 176 Ovington	1225 69th St
PS 186 Dr Irving A Gladstone	7601 19th Ave
PS 200 Benson	1940 Benson Ave
PS 204 Vince Lombardi	8101 15th Ave
PS 205 Clarion	6701 20 Ave
PS 229 Dyker	1400 Benson Ave
Regina Pacis	1201 66th St
St Bernadette's	1313 83rd St
St Finbar	1825 Bath Ave
St Frances Cabrini	21 Bay 11th St
St Patrick	401 97th St
Tiferes Miriam High School for Girls	6510 17th Ave

Map 16 • Midwood

Andries Hudde	2500 Nostrand Ave
Bais Yaakov Academy	1213 Elm Ave
Bet Yaakov Ateret Torah	1750 E 4th St
Bet Yakov Ateret Torah High	1649 E 13th St
Bnos Yisroel School for Girls	1401 Kings Hwy
Edward R Murrow High	1600 Ave L
IS 381	1599 E 22nd St
James Madison High	3787 Bedford Ave
Lev Bais Yaakov	1033 E 22nd St
Lubavitcher School Chabad	841 Ocean Pkwy
Masores Bais Yaakov	1395 Ocean Ave
Midwood Catholic Academy	1340 E 29th St

Mirrer Yeshiva	1795 Ocean Pkwy
Nefesh Academy	1750 E 18th St
Prospect Park Bnos Leah High	1601 Ave R
Prospect Park Yeshiva	1784 E 17th St
PS 193 Gil Hodges	2515 Ave L
PS 197	1599 E 22nd St
PS 199 Frederick Wachtel	1100 Elm Ave
PS 215 Morris H Weiss	415 Ave S
PS 238 Anne Sullivan	1633 E 8th St
PS 99 Isaac Asimov	1120 E 10th St
Shaare Torah	1680 Coney Island Ave
Shulamith School for Girls	1277 E 14th St
St Edmund Elementary	1902 Ave T
St Ephrem	7415 Ft Hamilton Pkwy
Sts Simon & Jude Elementary	294 Ave T
Three Hierarchs Parochial	1724 Ave P
Windmill Montessori	1317 Ave T
Yeshiva Ahavas Torah	2961 Nostrand Ave
Yeshiva of Brooklyn	1470 Ocean Ave
Yeshiva of Brooklyn Boy's Div	1200 Ocean Pkwy
Yeshiva of Flatbush-Joel Braverman H	1609 Ave J
Yeshiva Ohr Shraga D'Veretzky	1102 Ave L
Yeshiva Rabbi Chaim Berlin	1310 Ave I
Yeshiva Ruach Chaim	2294 Nostrand Ave
Yeshiva Vyelipol	860 E 27th St
Yeshivah of Flatbush Elementary	919 E 10th St
Yeshivat Mizrachi L'Banim	2810 Nostrand Ave

Map 1 · Greenpoint

Insta-Press	10 Bedford Ave	718-389-3223
Staples	535 Morgan Ave	718-388-3447

Map 2 · Williamsburg

Internet Garage	218 Bedford Ave	718-486-0059
The UPS Store	144 N 7th St	718-218-6440

Map 5 · Brooklyn Heights / DUMBO / Downtown

Brooklyn Progress Blue Printing	193 Joralemon St	718-875-0696
Copyrite	45 Washington St	718-243-0959
C Two Copy Center	90 Livingston St	718-797-9700
FedEx Kinko's	16 Court St	718-852-5631
Long Island Copy & Printing	394 Flatbush Ave Ext	718-501-0019
Superior Copy Center	90 Livingston St	718-797-9701
The UPS Store	93 Montague St	718-802-0900

Map 6 · Fort Greene / Clinton Hill

Save Mor Copy Center	25 Flatbush Ave	718-624-6136

Map 8 · BoCoCa / Red Hook

Copy Cottage	249 Smith St	718-237-8267
The UPS Store	165 ourt St	718-254-0392

Map 9 · Park Slope / Prospect Heights / Windsor Terrace

Graphicolor Corporation	89 Fifth Ave	718-398-8745
Mail Boxes of Park Slope	328 Flatbush Ave	718-857-5858
Office Max	625 Atlantic Ave	718-783-2614
Park Slope Typing Service & Copy Center	123 Seventh Ave	718-783-0268
Seventh Avenue Copy & Office Supply	315 Seventh Ave	718-965-2707
Staples	348 Fourth Ave	718-222-5732
The UPS Store	320 Seventh Ave	718-499-0464
The UPS Store	315 Flatbush Ave	718-701-5294

Map 11 · Sunset Park / Green-Wood Heights

One Stop Blueprinting	4202 Third Ave	718-499-6466

Map 12 · Borough Park

Copy Graph	4403 14th Ave	718-436-3800
M&S Copy Center	4401 15th Ave	718-972-4806

Map 13 · Kensington / Ditmas Park

Far Better Printing & Copy Center	43 Hillel Pl	718-859-3137
Staples	1011 Flatbush Ave	718-703-0979

Map 14 · Bay Ridge

Staples	9319 Fifth Ave	718-833-1270
The UPS Store	8225 Fifth Ave	718-680-8225
The UPS Store	9322 Third Ave	718-759-9100
The UPS Store	7103 Third Ave	718-238-1805

Map 16 · Midwood

Advance Copies	1417 Ave J	718-677-9781
Command Copy	1918 Ave M	718-339-2244
Ink Shop	1958 Coney Island Ave	718-627-1020
Mail N Pack	1412 Ave M	718-376-6245
PIP Printing	1323 E 15th St	718-627-6177
Staples	1880 Coney Island Ave	718-376-8336

Map 1 • Greenpoint

Self-service	66 Meserole Ave	Wed 6:45 PM
Self-service	1155 Manhattan Ave	Wed 6:30 PM
Self-service	557 Leonard St	Wed 6:30 PM
Self-service	79 Bridgewater St	Wed 6:30 PM
P&P Shipping & Handling	790 Manhattan Ave	Wed 5:30 PM

Map 2 • Williamsburg

Self-service	129 S 8th St	Wed 7:00 PM
Self-service	134 Broadway	Wed 7:00 PM
Self-service	185 Marcy Ave	Wed 7:00 PM
Champion Wireless	190 Bedford Ave	Wed 7:00 PM
Self-service	263 S 4th St	Wed 7:00 PM
Self-service	11 Harrison Ave	Wed 6:45 PM
FedEx Authorized Ship Center	442 Lorimer St	Wed 5:30 PM

Map 3 • East Williamsburg

Self-service	303 Johnson Ave	Wed 7:15 PM
Office 11211	331 Graham Ave	Wed 6:30 PM
Self-service	395 Graham Ave	Wed 6:30 PM
Parcel Plus	402 Graham Ave	Wed 6:00 PM

Map 4 • Bushwick

Sandbox Pack & Ship	1446 Myrtle Ave	Wed 6:30 PM

Map 5 • Brooklyn Heights / DUMBO / Downtown

Self-service Center	3 Chase Metrotech	Wed 8:15 PM
Self-service	20 Jay St	Wed 7:45 PM
Self-service	45 Main St	Wed 7:45 PM
Self-service	50 Washington St	Wed 7:45 PM
Self-service	57 Front St	Wed 7:45 PM
Self-service	16 Court St	Wed 7:30 PM
Self-service Center	4 Chase Metrotech	Wed 7:30 PM
Self-service	142 Joralemon St	Wed 7:15 PM
Self-service	225 Cadman Plaza E	Wed 7:15 PM
United Shipping Agency	16 Court St	Wed 7:00 PM
FedEx Kinko's Office & Print Center	16 Court St	Wed 7:00 PM
Self-service	63 Flushing Ave	Wed 7:00 PM
Shippers Express	41 Schermerhorn St	Wed 6:00 PM
Copy Rite	45 Washington St	Wed 5:00 PM

Map 6 • Fort Greene / Clinton Hill

Dickerson And Associates	115 S Oxford St	Wed 7:00 PM
Self-service	15 Washington Ave	Wed 7:00 PM
Packing Source	257 Nostrand Ave	Wed 5:00 PM

Map 7 • Bedford-Stuyvesant

Self-service	1368 Fulton St	Wed 4:00 PM

Map 8 • BoCoCa / Red Hook

Self-service	51 20th St	Wed 8:45 PM
FedEx Express Ship Center	51 20th St	Wed 8:45 PM
Self-service	615 Clinton St	Wed 7:15 PM
Self-service	540 Court St	Wed 6:15 PM
Copy Cottage	249 Smith St	Wed 6:00 PM
Cobble Hill Mailing	495 Henry St	Wed 6:00 PM
Smalls It / Dba Sandbox	141 Smith St	Wed 5:00 PM

Map 9 • Park Slope / Prospect Heights / Windsor Terrace

Self-service	227 4th Ave	Wed 7:15 PM
Self-service	275 9th St	Wed 7:15 PM
Self-service	625 Atlantic Ave	Wed 7:15 PM
Park Slope Copy Center	123 7th Ave	Wed 6:00 PM
Mailboxes On Fifth	172 5th Ave	Wed 6:00 PM
Mailboxes Of Park Slope	328 Flatbush Ave	Wed 6:00 PM
552 Atlantic Corp	552 Atlantic Ave	Wed 6:00 PM
Active Transport Services	285 5th Ave	Wed 4:00 PM
Self-service	557 Atlantic Ave	Wed 4:00 PM

Map 10 • Prospect-Lefferts Gardens / Crown Heights

Self-service	315 Empire Blvd	Wed 6:30 PM
M&E Enterprises	476 Albany Ave	Wed 6:30 PM
Express Mail	327 Empire Blvd	Wed 6:00 PM
Mo-betta Ventures	1647 Bedford Ave	Wed 5:30 PM
Kaydmailboxetc	521 Rogers Ave	Wed 5:00 PM
Self-service	866 Eastern Pkwy	Wed 3:30 PM

Map 11 • Sunset Park / Green-Wood Heights

Self-service	140 58th St	Wed 7:45 PM
Self-service	225 25th St	Wed 7:15 PM
Self-service	5600 First Ave	Wed 7:15 PM
Self-service	900 3rd Ave	Wed 7:00 PM
Americomp Technology	5202 8th Ave	Wed 6:00 PM
JP Cellular	5222 8th Ave	Wed 5:30 PM

Map 12 • Borough Park

Self-service	4626 18th Ave	Wed 7:30 PM
Self-service	1200 51st St	Wed 7:15 PM
Self-service	1312 44th St	Wed 7:00 PM
Self-service	4510 16th Ave	Wed 7:00 PM
Self-service	5014 16th Ave	Wed 7:00 PM
Self-service	5811 16th Ave	Wed 7:00 PM
Self-service	1450 37th St	Wed 6:45 PM
Self-service	1333 60th St	Wed 6:30 PM
Brooklyn Mailing Center	1274 49th St	Wed 6:00 PM
Mr Mailman	1303 53rd St	Wed 6:00 PM
Talk About Shipping	4403 15th Ave	Wed 4:00 PM

Map 13 • Kensington / Ditmas Park

Self-service	419 Mcdonald Ave	Wed 7:00 PM
Metropolis Multi Service	1398 Flatbush Ave	Wed 6:00 PM
Xpress Mail Svc Ctr	3001 Church Ave	Wed 5:00 PM
Supreme Shipping	921 Coney Island Ave	Wed 4:30 PM

Map 14 • Bay Ridge

NYC Postal Services	6904 Colonial Rd	Wed 7:00 PM
Self-service	8801 5th Ave	Wed 7:00 PM
Self-service	9319 5th Ave	Wed 6:45 PM
Global Express Service	7013 Ft Hamilton Pkwy	Wed 6:30 PM
Self-service	9710 3rd Ave	Wed 6:30 PM
Shiprite	7304 5th Ave	Wed 5:15 PM
Bay Ridge Mail Station	9728 Third Ave	Wed 5:00 PM

Map 15 • Dyker Heights / Bensonhurst

Self-service	6618 20th Ave	Wed 7:15 PM
Silver Rod Shipping	6402 18th Ave	Wed 7:00 PM
Self-service	1865 Benson Ave	Wed 6:45 PM
Self-service	7502 13th Ave	Wed 6:45 PM
Self-service	1475 86th St	Wed 6:30 PM
Self-service	7302 13th Ave	Wed 6:30 PM
FedEx Authorized Ship Center	7622 13th Ave	Wed 6:30 PM
Postal Plaza	2220 65th St	Wed 5:30 PM
The Fast Mail Station	7816 New Utrecht Ave	Wed 5:30 PM
The Shipping Depot	6801 20th Ave	Wed 5:00 PM

Map 16 • Midwood

Self-service	1288 Coney Island Ave	Wed 7:00 PM
Self-service	1639 E 13th St	Wed 7:00 PM
Self-service	2319 Nostrand Ave	Wed 7:00 PM
Self-service	1608 E 19th St	Wed 6:45 PM
Mailbox Plus Of Midwood	1375 Coney Island Ave	Wed 6:30 PM
Self-service	2302 Ave U	Wed 6:30 PM
Five Star Global	2010 Coney Island Ave	Wed 6:00 PM
Mail-n-pack	1412 Ave M	Wed 5:30 PM
Mail Drop Corporation	1204 Ave U	Wed 5:00 PM
Smalls It / Dba Sandbox	1704 Flatbush Ave	Wed 5:00 PM
Best Mail & Copy Center	2920 Ave R	Wed 5:00 PM
E-z Photo	1673 E 16th St	Wed 4:30 PM

Hospitals / Police / Libraries

Emergency Rooms

	Address	Phone	Map
Woodhull	760 Broadway St	718-963-8000	3
Wyckoff Heights Medical Center	374 Stockholm St	718-963-7272	4
Brooklyn Hospital Center	121 DeKalb Ave	718-250-8000	6
Long Island College	339 Hicks St	718-780-1000	8
New York Methodist	506 6th St	718-780-3000	9
Downstate Medical Center	450 Clarkson Ave	718-270-1000	10
Interfaith Medical Center	1545 Atlantic Ave	718-613-4000	10
Kings County	451 Clarkson Ave	718-245-3131	10
Lutheran Medical Center	150 55th St	718-630-7000	11
Maimonides Medical Center	4802 Tenth Ave	718-283-6000	12
Victory Memorial	699 92nd St	718-567-1234	15

Other Hospitals

	Address	Phone	Map
NY State VA Medical Center	800 Poly Pl	718-836-6600	15

Police

	Address	Phone	Map
94th Precinct	100 Meserole Ave	718-383-3879	1
90th Precinct	211 Union Ave	718-963-5311	2
Police Service Area 3	25 Central Ave	718-386-5357	3
83rd Precinct	480 Knickerbocker Ave	718-574-1605	4
84th Precinct	301 Gold St	718-875-6811	5
88th Precinct	298 Classon Ave	718-636-6511	6
79th Precinct	263 Tompkins Ave	718-636-6611	7
81st Precinct	30 Ralph Ave	718-574-0411	7
76th Precinct	191 Union St	718-834-3211	8
78th Precinct	65 Sixth Ave	718-636-6411	9
71st Precinct	421 Empire Blvd	718-735-0511	10
72nd Precinct	830 Fourth Ave	718-965-6311	11
66th Precinct	5822 16th Ave	718-851-5611	12
67th Precinct	2820 Snyder Ave	718-287-3211	13
70th Precinct	154 Lawrence Ave	718-851-5511	13
68th Precinct	333 65th St	718-439-4211	14
62nd Precinct	1925 Bath Ave	718-236-2611	15

Public Libraries

	Address/Phone	Phone	Map		Address	Phone	Map
Brooklyn Public	107 Norman Ave	718-349-8504	1	Brooklyn Public	Grand Army Plz	718-230-2100	9
Brooklyn Public	240 Division Ave	718-302-3485	2	Library (Central Branch)			
Brooklyn Public	81 Devoe St	718-486-3365	2	Brooklyn Public	725 St Marks Ave	718-773-7208	10
Brooklyn Public	340 Bushwick Ave	718-602-1348	3	Brooklyn Public	560 New York Ave	718-773-1180	10
Brooklyn Public	790 Bushwick Ave	718-455-3898	4	Brooklyn Public	5108 Fourth Ave	718-567-2806	11
Brooklyn Public	360 Irving Ave	718-628-8378	4	Brooklyn Public	1265 43rd St	718-437-4085	12
Brooklyn Public	8 Thomas S Boyland St	718-573-5224	4	Brooklyn Public	1702 60th St	718-256-2117	12
Brooklyn Public	280 Cadman Plz W	718-623-7100	5	Brooklyn Public	2035 Nostrand Ave	718-421-1159	13
Brooklyn Public	93 St Edwards St	718-935-0244	6	Brooklyn Public	160 E 5th St	718-686-9707	13
Brooklyn Public	25 Fourth Ave	718-638-1531	6	Brooklyn Public	1305 Cortelyou Rd	718-693-7763	13
Brooklyn Public	380 Washington Ave	718-398-8713	6	Brooklyn Public	22 Linden Blvd	718-856-0813	13
Brooklyn Public	617 DeKalb Ave	718-935-0032	7	Brooklyn Public	410 Ditmas Ave	718-435-9431	13
Brooklyn Public	496 Franklin Ave	718-623-0012	7	Brooklyn Public	7223 Ridge Blvd	718-748-5709	14
Brooklyn Public	361 Lewis Ave	718-573-5606	7	Brooklyn Public	9424 Fourth Ave	718-748-6919	14
Macon Branch				Brooklyn Public	1742 86th St	718-236-4086	15
Brooklyn Public	396 Clinton St	718-596-6972	8	Brooklyn Public	6802 Ft Hamilton Pkwy	718-748-8001	15
Brooklyn Public	7 Wolcott St	718-935-0203	8	Brooklyn Public	8202 13th Ave	718-748-6261	15
Brooklyn Public	431 Sixth Ave	718-832-1853	9	Brooklyn Public	975 E 16th St	718-252-0967	16

Other Libraries

	Address	Phone	Map
Brooklyn Bar Association Foundation	123 Remsen St	718-624-0875	5
Brooklyn Law Library	250 Joralemon St	718-780-7973	5
New York State Supreme Court	360 Adams St	347-296-1144	5
Brooklyn Hospital Medical	121 DeKalb Ave	718-250-6944	6

General Information • **Hotels**

Although the borough is not really a hotbed for tourism yet, these listings should prove useful to adventurous out-of-town guests, or those seeking less adventurous intra-borough "romantic getaways." In the case of the latter, see the hotels with hourly rates. Prices are ballpark estimates and subject to change—go to one of the many middle-man websites (Hotels.com, Expedia, Hotwire, etc.) to find the best bargains.

Map 1 • Greenpoint

	Address	Phone	Rate
YMCA	99 Meserole Ave	718-389-3700	43

Map 2 • Williamsburg

Glenwood Hostel	339 Broadway	718-387-7858	30

Map 3 • East Williamsburg

Bushwick Hotel	171 Bushwick Ave	718-386-1801	140
New York Loft Hostel	249 Varet St	718-366-1351	35

Map 4 • Bushwick

Hotel Neptune	1461 Broadway	718-455-1500	75
Kings Hotel	820 39th St	718-851-8188	140
Kings Hotel Apartments	1078 Bushwick Ave	718-452-9743	130
Red Carpet Inn	980 Wyckoff Ave	718-417-4111	120

Map 5 • Brooklyn Heights / DUMBO / Downtown

3BB	136 Lawrence St	347-762-2632	100
Hotel Princess	211 Schermerhorn St	718-468-3565	85
Marriott New York at the Brooklyn Bridge	333 Adams St	718-246-7000	300
Nu Hotel	85 Smith St	347-694-5822	250

Map 6 • Fort Greene / Clinton Hill

Prince Lefferts Hotel	127 Lefferts Pl	718-783-2984	85
Regina's New York Bed & Breakfast	16 Ft Greene Pl	718-834-9253	120
Washington Hotel	400 Washington Ave	718-783-9545	95

Map 8 • BoCoCa / Red Hook

Brooklyn Motor Inn	140 Hamilton Ave	718-875-2500	110
Union Street Bed & Breakfast	405 Union St	718-852-8406	125

Map 9 • Park Slope / Prospect Heights / Windsor Terrace

Holiday Inn Express Brooklyn	625 Union St	718-797-1133	170
Hotel Le Bleu	370 4th Ave	718-625-1500	300
The Sofia Inn	288 Park Pl	917-865-7428	135

Map 10 • Prospect-Lefferts Gardens / Crown Heights

Lefferts Manor Bed and Breakfast	80 Rutland Rd	347-351-9065	119

Map 11 • Sunset Park / Green-Wood Heights

Days Inn Brooklyn	437 39th St	718-853-4141	109

Map 12 • Borough Park

Avenue Plaza Hotel	4624 13th Ave	718-552-3200	179
Mosaic Suites	4320 16th Ave	718-972-4377	55
Park House Hotel	1206 48th St	718-871-8100	149

Map 13 • Kensington / Ditmas Park

Bibi's Garden B&B	762 Westminster Rd	718-434-3119	120
Dekoven Suites	30 Dekoven Ct	718-421-1052	130
Honey's B&B	770 Westminster Rd	718-434-7628	95
The Strange Dog Inn	51 Dekoven Ct	718-338-7051	195

Map 14 • Bay Ridge

Best Western Gregory Hotel	8315 Fourth Ave	718-238-3737	150
Prince Hotel	315 93rd St	718-748-8995	75

Map 16 • Midwood

Midwood Suites	1078 E 15th St	718-253-9535	99

They may not make the itinerary of the casual tourist, but Brooklyn is still home to some stupendous destinations. You often simply look up and realize that you are standing at the oldest, biggest, or first... something. Amazing and unique sights around every corner define a native's Brooklyn. And many of the families that built these landmarks still live amongst them. Take that, Manhattan!

Best Views

One of the best things about Brooklyn is how underrated it is. Try the **Beard Street Pier (Map 8)** in way-out Red Hook for a stunning view of the Statue of Liberty and Lower Manhattan, sans crowds no matter what the season. For an incredible vista, visit the Shore Parkway Greenway, a waterfront bike and pedestrian trail that you can enter from Owls Head Park (Map 14) in Bay Ridge. The **Empire-Fulton Ferry State Park (Map 5)**, located on the water in DUMBO, leads a bevy of scenic vistas near downtown Brooklyn, and it has a few patches of green grass to boot. On the **Brooklyn Heights Promenade (Map 5)** there may be a few more people, though for a sunset or sunny afternoon it's the best panorama around. The pedestrian pathway across the **Manhattan Bridge (Map 5)** is another destination often overshadowed by its more famous neighbor. The views of the river and the shimmering Financial District are just as good as those from the **Brooklyn Bridge (Map 5)**, and you can also see the **Jetsons Building (Map 5)** on the Brooklyn side, variously lit depending on the whims of its owners. The **Williamsburg Bridge (Map 2)** also offers exciting views of the city (as well as hipsters in oversized sunglasses). Heading toward Queens on the BQE you'll have to cross the **Kosciusko Bridge (Foldout A5)**, named for a Polish general who fought in the Revolutionary War. While keeping your eyes on the road, take a quick glimpse towards Midtown from one of the borough's highest points.

Architecture

Brooklyn has its own "Arc de Triomphe" at **Grand Army Plaza (Map 9)**, formally named the Soldiers' and Sailors' Arch. It, too, clogs traffic around its gigantic rotary, and marks the way to both the **Brooklyn Museum (Map 10)** and the **Brooklyn Botanic Gardens (Map 9)**, two venerable architectural marvels. Both have a very antique air about them, though the museum steps have been renovated in

a somewhat futuristic fashion. The arch also houses the must-see **New York Puppet Library (Map 9)**, open only on Saturdays in the summer. Even Paris can't top that. Prospect Park West runs along the most expensive side of the park where turn-of-the-century homes that might redefine some people's concept of Brooklyn still stand. In north Brooklyn, the **Williamsburg Savings Bank (Map 6)** with its gigantic golden dome is similarly opulent.

Historical

In Bed-Stuy, the **Akwaaba Mansion (Map 7)** is an example of the area's early glory, and many of the surrounding brownstones follow in its stylistic footsteps. Back in Walt Whitman's old neighborhood in Fort Greene is the Pratt Institute where university buildings include a former shoe factory, several original sealed subway tunnels, and a working **Power Plant (Map 6)**. Litchfield Villa (p.143) is an Italian-style castle just across 5th Street in Prospect Park. Some historic farmhouses worth visiting include the Lefferts House (p.143) in the "Children's Corner" of Prospect Park and the **Lott House (Eastern Brooklyn)** on E 36th Street in Marine Park. Both were built in the 18th century and now look slightly odd in their respective neighborhoods, having remained wholly untouched for years. Way before real estate developers began pillaging Brooklyn, the Vikings may have done some speculation of their own as commemorated by the **Leif Ericsson Runestone (Map 14)**. And speaking of dead people, **Green-Wood Cemetery (Map 11)** in Sunset Park has more famous corpses than you can shake a stick at, and is also beautiful in a somber sort of way.

Out of the Ordinary

Broken Angel (Map 6) is a funky, free-form private residence that will soon be transformed into expensive condos (like everything else in Brooklyn). **Junior's Restaurant (Map 5)** is a mecca for those wishing to visit rap star Notorious B.I.G.'s old stomping ground. The cheesecake is world-famous as well, so no matter what motivates you, you'll be satisfied. If you find yourself suddenly in need of more underground mix tapes or perhaps some fresh new kicks, then it's off to the **Fulton Street Mall (Map 5)** for these and other urban necessities. The **Brooklyn Brewery (Map 2)** is also a great place to sample some of the best Brooklyn has to offer, in the form of its delicious lagers and ales.

Map 1 · Greenpoint

Greenpoint Historic Distric	137 Oak St	Charming rowhouses that were built for workers of early merchants.
Newtown Creek Nature Walk	100 Paidge Ave	Great views of the sewage plant!
Newtown Creek Wastewater Treatment Plant	Greenpoint Ave & Provost St	Take a moment to contemplate all of the famous and beautiful peoples' crap floating around in here.
Saint Anthony of Padua Church	862 Manhattan Ave · 718-383-3339	Beautiful church sticking out like a healthy thumb on congested avenue.

Map 2 • Williamsburg

Bedford L Train Station	Bedford St & N 6th St	Hipster epicenter, including bike racks and occasional friendly riots.
Brooklyn Brewery	79 N 11th St • 718-486-7422	Connect with your beer by witnessing its birth; free samples also encourage closeness. Open Friday nights only. Tours on Saturdays.
City Reliquary	370 Metropolitan Ave	Artifacts from New York's vast and rich history.
East River State Park	90 Kent Ave • 347-297-9470	Swath of waterfront greenspace, Williamsburg style.
McCarren Park	N 12th St & Bedford Ave	Hipsters, Poles, and athletes unite!
McCarren Pool	Lorimer St & Bayard St	Really cool abandoned pool that we hope continues to be used as a venue for concerts and film screenings.
Steiner Studios	15 Washington Ave • 718-858-1600	Film studio in the Brooklyn Navy Yard. Spike Lee's Inside Man was recently shot here.
Williamsburg Bridge	S 5th St & Driggs St	Bridge of the chosen people—Jews and well-off hipsters.

Map 3 • East Williamsburg

Boerum Street Graffiti Mural	153 Boerum St	Cool, easy to miss street art.
Pfizer Pharmaceutical	630 Flushing Ave • 718-780-8800	Now-derelict plant mirrors now-derelict economy.
Williamsburg Houses	172 Maujer St	A public housing project proclaimed a landmark in 2003.

Map 4 • Bushwick

St Barbara's Roman Catholic Church	138 Bleecker St • 718-452-3660	A little piece of Europe in the middle of Bushwick.

Map 5 • Brooklyn Heights / DUMBO / Downtown

Brooklyn Borough Hall	209 Joralemon St • 718-802-3700	Built in the 1840s, this Greek Revival landmark was once employed as the official City Hall of Brooklyn.
Brooklyn Bridge	Adams St & East River	If you haven't walked over it at least twice yet, you're not cool.
Brooklyn Bridge Park	Park Plymouth St	City park w/ stellar downtown views & cool playground.
Brooklyn Heights Promenade	Pierrepont St & Columbia Heights	The best place to really see Manhattan. It's the view that's in all the movies.
Brooklyn Historical Society	128 Pierrepont St • 718-222-4111	Want to really learn about Brooklyn? Go here.
Brooklyn Ice Cream Factory	1 Water St • 718-246-3963	Expensive, old-fashioned ice cream beneath the bridge.
Brooklyn Tabernacle	17 Smith St • 718-290-2000	Home of the award-winning Brooklyn Tabernacle Choir.
Jetsons Building	110 York St	View this sculptural roof from the Manhattan Bridge at night when it's lit with colored lights.
Junior's Restaurant	386 Flatbush Avenue Ext • 718-852-5257	For the only cheesecake worth its curds and whey. (Free pickles, great if you're preggers.)
Manhattan Bridge	Flatbush Avenue Ext & Nassau St	Connecting Brooklyn to that other borough.
New York Transit Museum	Boerum Pl & Schermerhorn St • 718-694-1600	Everything one can say about the MTA.
Vinegar Hill	Water St & Hudson Ave	NYC's coolest micro-neighborhood. Promise.

Map 6 • Fort Greene / Clinton Hill

Broken Angel	4 Downing St	Crazy architectural home soon to be condos. Home of Dave Chappelle's Block Party.
Brooklyn Academy of Music	30 Lafayette Ave • 718-636-4100	America's oldest continuously operating performing arts center. Never dull.
Brooklyn Masonic Temple	317 Clermont Ave • 718-638-1256	Its vestrymen have included Robert E. Lee and Thomas J. (Stonewall) Jackson.
Brooklyn Navy Yard	Flushing Ave & Clinton Ave • 718-907-5900	Nation's first navy yard employed 70,000 people during WWII. Today, it houses a diverse range of businesses.
Fort Greene Park	Willoughby Ave & Washington Park • 718-222-1461	Liquor store proximity is a plus on a warm afternoon when you visit this welcome chunk of green.
Fulton Street Mall	Fulton St b/w Flatbush Ave & Borough Hall Plz	The shopping experience, Brooklyn style. Hot sneakers can be had for a song.
Presbyterian Church Lafayette Avenue	85 S Oxford St • 718-625-7515	Nationally known church with performing arts; former Underground Railroad stop

187

Long Island Rail Road Station	Flatbush Ave & Hanson Pl • 718-217-5477	A low red-brick building hosting more than 20 million passengers annually. A total craphole.
Pratt Institute Steam Turbine Power Plant	200 Willoughby Ave • 718-636-3600	This authentic steam generator gets fired up a few times a year to impress the parents. Cool.
Steiner Studios	15 Washington Ave	Film studio in the Brooklyn Navy Yard. Spike Lee's *Inside Man* was recently shot here.
Williamsburg Savings Bank Building	1 Hanson Pl	Still the tallest building in the borough and when you're lost, a sight for sore eyes.

Map 7 • Bedford-Stuyvesant

Akwaaba Mansion	347 MacDonough St • 718-455-5958	Restored 1860s villa that now operates as a beautiful B&B.
Magnolia Tree Earth Center Grandiflora	679 Lafayette Ave • 718-387-2116	One of two landmarked trees in all of NYC. Visit in spring when it blossoms.
Von King Park	Lafayette Ave & Marcy Ave	One of the first parks in Brooklyn's history. BYO dog.

Map 8 • BoCoCa / Red Hook

Beard Street Pier	Van Brunt St & Reed St	Historic 19th Century warehouses, now a cluster of shops and offices.
Brooklyn Clay Retort and Fire Brick Building	76 Van Dyke St	Red Hook's first official Landmark building dates to the mid-19th century.
Cobble Hill Park	Clinton St & Verandah Pl	One of the cutest parks in all of New York.
Cool House	26 Reed St	One of the coolest single-family dwellings in the city.
Gowanus Canal	Smith St & 9th St	Brooklyn's answer to the Seine.
Phone Booth	Huntington St & Hamilton Ave	Where hookers, pimps, and dealers call mom for money.
Red Hook Ball Fields	Clinton St & Bay St	Watch futbol and eat Central American street food every Saturday from spring through fall.
Red Hook Grain Terminal	Columbia St & Halleck St	Visit just to wonder what it's doing there.
Warren Place	Warren Pl	Public housing from the 1870s.

Map 9 • Park Slope / Prospect Heights / Windsor Terrace

Bailey Fountain	Grand Army Plaza	With sculpted figures of Neptune, Triton and attendants (some said to represent Wisdom and Felicity), the power eminating from this fountain could supply the Justice League.
Brooklyn Conservatory of Music	58 Seventh Ave • 718-622-3300	This Victorian Gothic brownstone hosts performances by its students and guest artists.
Brooklyn Museum	200 Eastern Pkwy • 718-638-5000	Recently completed renovations lend a futuristic air, but the collections are a Brooklyn jewel.
Brooklyn Public Library	10 Grand Army Plz • 718-230-2100	The building looks like a book!
Grand Army Plaza	Flatbush Ave & Plaza St	Site of John H. Duncan's Soldiers' and Sailors' Memorial Arch.
New York Puppet Library	Grand Army Plz • 617- 623-203	The Memorial Arch at Grand Army Plaza has a funky theater at the top. A must see (summer Saturdays only).
Park Slope Food Co-op	782 Union St • 718-622-0560	These farm-fresh veggies will do for those in search of their peck of dirt. Rinse. Members Only...

Map 10 • Prospect-Lefferts Gardens / Crown Heights

Brooklyn Botanic Garden	1000 Washington Ave • 718-623-7200	A beautiful and peaceful spot inside and out. Cherry blossoms in spring are awe inspiring.
Brooklyn Children's Museum	145 Brooklyn Ave • 718-735-4400	Take your own kids or someone else's so you can get in on the fun without looking silly.
The Carousel	Ocean Ave & Flatbush Ave & Empire Blvd • 718-282-7789	Carved in 1912 and restored in 1990.
Prospect Park Zoo	450 Flatbush Ave • 718-399-7339	Home to approximately 400 animals.

Map 11 • Sunset Park / Green-Wood Heights

Green-Wood Cemetery	500 25th St • 718-768-7300	Lots of winding paths and greenery good for contemplation.

General Information · **Landmarks**

Map 12 · Borough Park

Bobover Hasidic World Headquarters	4909 15th Ave · 718-853-7900	So you think you can daven?
Congregation Anshe Lubawitz (Temple Beth El)	4024 12th Ave · 718-436-2200	Graceful, neoclassical synagogue is the area's first - built in 1906.
Kensington Stables	51 Caton Ave · 718-972-4588	Riding horses is one of life's small pleasures. Combine that with subway proximity and you're in business.
Shmura Matzoh Factory	1285 36th St · 718-438-2006	The real deal. Only open in the pre-passover season.

Map 13 · Kensington / Ditmas Park

Brooklyn Historic Railway Association	599 E 7th St · 718-941-3160	Explore the world's oldest subway tunnel.
Erasmus Hall Academy	911 Flatbush Ave · 718-282-7804	Boasts famous graduates such as Alexander Hamilton, Neil Diamond, and Barbara Streisand.
Flatbush Dutch Reform Church	890 Flatbush Ave · 347-482-7386	Originally constructed in 1654 by order of Bloomberg's predecessor, Peter Stuyvesant.

Map 14 · Bay Ridge

69th Street Pier / 9/11 Memorial	Shore Rd & Bay Ridge Ave	Once the embarkation point for the Bay Ridge St. George ferry, it offers a panoramic harbor view.
The Barkaloo Cemetery	Narrows Ave & Mackay Pl	The smallest cemetery founded in 1725 by Dutch immigrant William Harmans Barkaloo.
Dyker Heights Christmas Lights	244 84th St	Out-of-state visitors schlep to see these incredible lights.
Fontbonne Hall	9901 Shore Rd · 718-748-2244	Now a Catholic school, this 1890s private residence once belonged to actress Lillian Russell.
Fort Hamilton	Fort Hamilton Pkwy & 101st St · 718-630-4848	Established in the 1820s as a garrison for protecting the harbor and city against attack.
The Gingerbread House	8220 Narrows Ave	The best example of Arts and Crafts architecture in the city.
James F Farrell House	125 95th St	This 1849 Greek Revival house evokes the neighborhood's days as a wealthy seaside retreat.
Leif Ericson Runestone	Fourth Ave & 67th St	Commemorating the viking explorer's discovery of America…way before that other guy.
St John's Episcopal Church	9818 Ft Hamilton Pkwy · 718-745-2377	Established in 1834, the present structure dates to 1890; its vestrymen have included Robert E. Lee and Thomas J. (Stonewall) Jackson.
Verrazano-Narrows Bridge	92nd St & Gatling Pl	The longest span in North America really puts things into perspective. Awesome views below.

Map 16 · Midwood

Flipper the Dolphin	Avenue S & E 14th St	Meet Flipper the Dolphin, the statue.
JC Studios	1268 E 14th St · 718-780-6400	Formerly NBC studios where *The Cosby Show* was filmed; is now the production site of *As the World Turns*.
Wyckoff House	1669 E 22nd St	What things used to look like. Not open to the public.

Coney Island / Brighton Beach

Abe Stark Ice Skating Rink	Coney Island Boardwalk & W 19th St · 718-946-6536	Like most of the 'hood, in need of a little TLC. Still, way fun and admission's cheap.
Coney Island Boardwalk	1208 Surf Ave · 718-372-5159	Just like the old days. But for how long?
MCU Park	1904 Surf Ave · 718-449-8497	Baseball without steroids? Who knew?
New York Aquarium	Surf Ave & W 8th St · 718-265-3474	Sprightly seahorses and others herald the variety of the seas.
Parachute Jump	Surf Ave & W 19 St	BK's Eiffel Tower. Glows nightly thanks to a lighting installation commissioned in 2006.
Sideshows by the Seashore / Coney Island Museum	1208 Surf Ave · 718-372-5159	All manner of curiosities, both old-timey and modern. NFT pick.

189

Storage / Truck Rental

Storage

Storage	Address	Phone	Map
Storage Post	46-05 Metropolitan Ave	718-366-7464	3
Storage Deluxe	1220 Broadway	718-573-4555	4
American Self Storage	202 Tillary St	718-260-8601	5
American Self Storage	45 Clinton St	718-246-5600	5
Extra Space Storage	160 John St	718-797-4040	5
Public Storage	269 Gold St	877-788-2028	5
Shurgard Storage	30 Prince St	718-852-7100	5
Extra Space Storage	41 Flatbush Ave	718-596-4060	6
iStoreGreen	12 Hall St	718-855-4477	6
Lockaway Self Storage	1 Carlton Ave	718-522-5050	6
Moishe's Mini Storage	22 Grand Ave	718-237-9735	6
Public Storage	72 Emerson Pl	718-638-1287	6
Storage Deluxe	945 Atlantic Ave	718-399-6037	6
Storage Mart	50 Wallabout St	718-522-9055	6
Affordable Self Storage	1680 Atlantic Ave	718-363-2825	7
Moving Officials	63 9th St	718-832-5793	8
Pack-it-Away Storage	808 Pacific St	718-622-4300	9
Storage Mart	718 Atlantic Ave	718-399-6037	9
U-Haul	394 Fourth Ave	718-237-2893	9
Public Storage	1062 St Johns Pl	718-771-0853	10
Safeguard Self Storage	115 Empire	718-282-1388	10
Harborside Self Storage	56 48th St	718-965-0474	11
Stop & Stor	534 63rd St	718-833-8600	11
Storage Mart	980 Fourth Ave	718-499-3999	11
Storage USA	201 64th St	718-748-4499	11
Extra Space Storage	2207 Albemarle Rd	718-287-0496	13
Stop & Stor	40 Erasmus St	718-284-8000	13
U-Haul New Utrecht	6615 New Utrecht Ave	718-232-1400	15
Mobile Self Storage	210 42nd St	718-439-1088	n/a
Affordable Self Storage	2553 Atlantic Ave	718-363-2825	n/a
Public Storage	1250 Rockaway Ave	718-922-7099	n/a
Safeguard Self Storage	2941 Atlantic Ave	718-383-8200	n/a
Shurgard Storage	1534 Utica Ave	718-434-3000	n/a
Stop & Stor	12501 Flatlands Ave	718-272-8800	n/a
Stop & Stor	4710 Glenwood Rd	718-421-8000	n/a
Stop & Stor	1700 Shore Pkwy	718-714-4000	n/a
Storage Deluxe	2887 Atlantic Ave	718-235-2999	n/a
Storage Deluxe	2990 Cropsey Ave	718-373-0517	n/a
USA Mini Storage			

Truck Rental

Truck Rental		Address	Phone	Map
U-Haul	S&C Truck & Auto Center	176 McGuiness Blvd	718-349-7168	1
Penske	PSTP	28 N 3rd St	718-797-4098	2
U-Haul	F&B Truck Repair	986 Metropolitan Ave	718-782-9805	3
U-Haul	Koordy Corp	1127 Flushing Ave	718-381-1763	3
Budget	JMC Automotive	376 Classon Ave	718-857-1555	6
U-Haul	Lockaway Self Storage	1 Carlton Ave	718-797-5098	6
U-Haul	Jules Management	257 Nostrand Ave	718-638-7161	7
U-Haul	Petroleum DeKalb	10 Malcolm X Blvd	718-573-5120	7
Budget	Park Slope Rental Corp	519 Smith St	718-596-0280	8
U-Haul	9th Street Self-Storage	88 9th St	718-788-3370	8
U-Haul	U-Haul Center	394 Fourth Ave	718-237-2893	9
U-Haul	Mike's Travel & Tours	465 Fenimore St	718-756-7743	10
Budget	LAD Service	5410 Third Ave	718-836-0079	11
Budget	Perfect Car Rental	6302 17th Ave	718-837-8174	12
U-Haul	Affordable Rentals	29 Church Ave	718-972-6865	12
U-Haul	Metro Fleet Systems	705 McDonald Ave	718-431-0659	13
U-Haul	U-Haul New Utrecht	6615 New Utrecht Ave	718-232-1400	15

Gyms

	Address	Phone	Map
Exodus Fitness	510 Metropolitan Ave	718-599-1073	2
Equinox	194 Joralemon St	718-522-7533	5
Harbor Fitness	191 15th St	718-965-6200	9

Locksmiths

	Phone
All Brooklyn Locksmiths	718-826-2800
Aladdin Locksmiths	718-693-8100
Champion Locksmiths	718-906-9665
All Security	866-752-2081

Pharmacies

	Address	Phone	Map
Duane Reade	386 Fulton St	718-330-0363	5
Neergaard	454 Fifth Ave	718-768-0600	9
Pathmark Pharmacy	625 Atlantic Ave	718-399-6239	9
*Prescription counter closes at 9			
Pathmark	1245 61st St	718-853-8633	12
Duane Reade	436 86th St	718-833-7758	14
CVS	2925 Kings Hwy	718-677-3871	16
Walgreens	946 Kings Hwy	718-645-0417	16
*Prescription counter closes at 10 pm			
CVS	2472 Flatbush Ave	718-253-0200	p134
CVS	4901 Kings Hwy	718-252-3791	p134
Rite Aid	185 Kings Hwy	718-331-2019	p134
Rite Aid	2324 Flatbush Ave	718-951-6869	p134

Plumbers

	Phone
A-1 Water Main & Sewer Contractors	718-272-4784
Alex Figiolia	718-643-0900
Allcounty Plumbing & Heating	718-284-6200
Capital	718-492-8057
Downtown Plumbing and Sewer	718-858-7070
Fast Repair	718-645-0089
RR Plumbing Roto-Rooter	718-763-6464
Sewers	718-234-8411
Sewers	718-495-3600
Vigilante	718-522-6111

Restaurants

	Address	Phone	Map
Bridgeview Diner	9011 Third Ave	718-680-9818	14
Farmer in the Deli	357 Myrtle Ave	718-875-9067	6
George's	753 Coney Island Ave	718-282-0152	13
God Bless Deli	818 Manhattan Ave	718-349-0605	1
Grand Morelos	727 Grand St	718-218-9441	3
Kellogg's Diner	518 Metropolitan Ave	718-782-4502	2
Kestane Kebab	110 Nassau Ave	718-349-8601	1
La Gran Via Bakery	4516 Fifth Ave	718-853-8021	11
Nyonya	5323 Eight Ave	718-633-0808	11
Piaxtla es Mexico Deli	505 51st St	718-633-4816	11
Seventh Avenue Donuts	324 Seventh Ave	718-768-0748	9
Turkish Café Restaurant	1618 E 16th St	718-375-9237	16
Del'Rio Diner	166 Kings Hwy	718-331-3107	p134
El Greco Diner	1821 Emmons Ave	718-934-1288	p134

Supermarkets

	Address	Phone	Map
Golden Farm	239 Church Ave	718-789-3007	9
Key Food	369 Flatbush Ave	718-789-3007	9
Pathmark	137 12th St	718-788-5100	9
Pathmark	625 Atlantic Ave	718-399-6161	9
Peas & Pickles	55 Washington St	718-488-8336	5
Peas & Pickles	79 Henry St	718-596-8219	5
Shop Rite	1080 McDonald Ave	718-252-5770	16

Overview

Platoons of artists are moving to Brooklyn from Manhattan, so it's no surprise that many galleries have followed suit. Working-class artists are producing some great work that subverts the radar of Manhattan's upscale gallery tastemakers. Most art galleries in Brooklyn are located in Williamsburg and DUMBO, although spaces are opening up in Greenpoint, Fort Greene, Carroll Gardens, and Red Hook. The DUMBO Arts Festival and the Gowanus Open Studios Tour are solid introductions to the scene. **The Brooklyn Arts Council (Map 5)** (www.brooklynartscouncil.org) is a local organization that supports artists in addition to having its own art gallery, film festival, seminars, education programs, and other events.

DUMBO

Home to a good number of local artists, DUMBO takes center stage during the Art Under the Bridge Festival each October. Galleries and studios throw open their doors with hundreds of artists displaying their work. Permanent galleries with regular exhibitions include the **DUMBO Arts Center (Map 5)**, the group of second-floor galleries at **111 Front Street (Map 5)**, and the always-interesting **Jan Larsen Gallery (Map 5)** at 63 Pearl Street.

Williamsburg and Greenpoint

Be it an apartment, T-shirt, or gallery, all of Williamsburg is a canvas. **Jack the Pelican (Map 2)** and **McCaig-Welles Gallery (Map 2)** have consistently stellar shows. **Cave (Map 2)** features Asian artists and dance exhibitions. **Brooklyn Fire Proof (Map 2)**, in the no-man's land between Williamsburg and Greenpoint, has a large raw space featuring sculptures, installations, and paintings. The morbidly curious may enjoy a trip to the **Dabora Gallery (Map 1)** in Greenpoint for a brushstroke with the gothic.

Other Areas

Carroll Gardens and Red Hook are home to numerous studios. Many are clustered around the Gowanus Canal, Brooklyn's working-class response to Venice. This has inspired the Gowanus Open Studios Tour held every October, when local artists admit you into their spaces to view their work. There are several galleries with permanent exhibitions on Atlantic and Fulton Avenues east of Smith Street. The **Bruno Marina Gallery (Map 8)** often hosts worthwhile exhibitions that focus on serenity and naturalism. In Clinton Hill, home to many artists, especially on Lexington Avenue between Grand and Classon, **Danny Simmons' Corridor Gallery (Map 6)** is open on weekends and showcases local Brooklyn artists

Map 1 · Greenpoint

Axis Gallery	50 Dobbin St	212-741-2582
Dabora Gallery	1080 Manhattan Ave	917-656-2106
Galeria Janet	205 Norman Ave	718-383-9380

Map 2 · Williamsburg

AG Gallery	107 N 3rd St	718-599-3044
Art 101	101 Grand St	718-302-2242
Black & White	483 Driggs Ave	718-599-8775
Capla Kesting Fine Art	121 Roebling St	917-650-3760
Cave	58 Grand St	718-388-6780
Causey Contemporary	293 Grand St	718-218-8939
Cinders	103 Havemeyer St	718-388-2311
Dollhaus	37 Broadway	718-486-0330
Figureworks	168 N 6th St	718-486-7021
Fleetwing Gallery	111 Grand St	716-388-0044
The Front Room Gallery	147 Roebling St	718-782-2556
Holland Tunnel	61 S 3rd St	718-384-5738
Jack the Pelican	487 Driggs Ave	718-782-0183
Like the Spice Gallery	224 Roebling St	718-388-5388
Momenta Art	359 Bedford Ave	718-218-8058
Parker's Box	193 Grand St	718-388-2882
Pierogi Brooklyn	177 N 9th St	718-599-2144
Williamsburg Art & Historical Society	135 Broadway	718-486-7372

Map 3 • East Williamsburg

3rd Ward	195 Morgan Ave	718-715-4961
Ad Hoc Art	49 Bogart St	718-366-2466
Chez Bushwick	304 Boerum St	718-418-4405
Factory Fresh	1053 Flushing Ave	917-682-6753
Grace Space	840 Broadway	646-578-3402
House of Yes	342 Maujer St	
NurtureArt Gallery	910 Grand St	718-782-7755

Map 4 • Bushwick

Norte Maar	83 Wyckoff Ave	646-361-8512

Map 5 • Brooklyn Heights / DUMBO / Downtown

5+5 Gallery	111 Front St	718-624-6048
BAC Gallery	111 Front St	718-625-0080
DUMBO Arts Center	30 Washington St	718-694-0831
Gloria Kennedy Gallery	111 Front St	718-858-5254
Henry Gregg Gallery	111 Front St	718-408-1090
JLA Studios	63 Pearl St	718-797-2557
Jubilee	117 Henry St	718-596-1499
Nelson Hancock Gallery	111 Front St	718-408-1190
powerHouse Arena	37 Main St	718-666-3049
The Rotunda Gallery	33 Clinton St	718-875-4047
Salena Gallery – LIU	1 University Plz	718-488-1051
Spring	126 Front St	718-222-1054
Wessel + O'Connor Fine Art	111 Front St	718-596-1700

Map 6 • Fort Greene / Clinton Hill

Corridor Gallery	334 Grand Ave	718-230-5002
EX	872 Kent Ave	718-783-0060
Sarafina	411 Myrtle Ave	718-643-1382
Schafler Gallery – Pratt	200 Willoughby Ave	718-636-3517

Map 7 • Bedford-Stuyvesant

A Space Gallery	1138 Broadway	917-776-0772
Brooklynite Gallery	334 Malcolm X Blvd	347-405-5976

Map 8 • BoCoCa / Red Hook

Artez'N	444 Atlantic Ave	718-596-2649
Brooklyn Waterfront Artists Coalition	499 Van Brunt St	718-596-2507
Bruno Marina Gallery	372 Atlantic Ave	718-797-2077
Kentler International Drawing Space	353 Van Brunt St	718-875-2098
Metal & Thread	398 Van Brunt St	718-414-9651
Metaphor Contemporary Art	382 Atlantic Ave	718-254-9126
MF Gallery	213 Bond St	917-446-8681
Micro Museum	123 Smith St	718-797-3116
Rocketship	208 Smith St	718-797-1348
Space 414	414 Van Brunt St	718-408-1643

Map 9 • Park Slope / Prospect Heights / Windsor Terrace

440 Gallery	440 Sixth Ave	718-499-3844
Brooklyn Artist Gym	168 7th St	718-858-9069
JK Flynn	471 Sixth Ave	718-369-8934
Object-Image Gallery	91 Fifth Ave	718-623-2434

Map 11 • Sunset Park / Green-Wood Heights

Tabla Rasa Gallery	224 48th St	718-833-9100

Arts & Entertainment · **Bookstores**

Though there are still far fewer bookstores in Brooklyn than there are writers, each of the borough's major neighborhoods has a few decent options. Perhaps the top place is Williamsburg's elegant **Spoonbill & Sugartown (Map 2)**. In Cobble Hill/Carroll Gardens, check out the excellent independent **Book Court (Map 8)**, the fire-hazard of the **Community Book Store (Map 9)**, and the funky **Freebird Books (Map 9)**, which has the perfect combo of used titles and great coffee. Park Slope is home to **Community Book Store (Map 9)**, a cozy neighborhood meeting place complete with a café and garden. Also check out the very respectable used and new selection at the new storefront **Babbo's Books (Map 9)**, late-night selections at **Unnameable Books (Map 9)**, and local author readings downstairs at the **Barnes & Noble (Map 9)**.

In the fall of 2009 Fort Greene finally got its first full-service bookstore, **Greenlight Books (Map 6)**; it was worth the wait. Head to Borough Park and Brighton Beach for dizzying selections of Jewish and Russian bookstores, respectively. For more specific needs, however, you'll need to head into that other borough…

Map 1 · Greenpoint

Ex Libris Polish Book Gallery	140 Nassau Ave	718-349-0468	Polish.
Open Air Modern	606 Manhattan Ave	718-383-6465	Old and rare books and furniture.
Polish American Bookstore	648 Manhattan Ave	718-349-3756	Polish.
Polish Bookstore & Publishing	161 Java St	718-349-2738	Polish.
Polonia Book Store	882 Manhattan Ave	718-389-1684	Polish.
Word	126 Franklin St	718-383-0096	Literary fiction, non-fiction, and kids books.

Map 2 · Williamsburg

Spoonbill & Sugartown	Mini Mall, 218 Bedford Ave	718-387-7322	Art, architecture, design, philosophy, and literature. New and used.

Map 3 · East Williamsburg

Libreria Cristiana Bethel	666 Broadway	718-388-3195	Religious.

Map 5 · Brooklyn Heights / DUMBO / Downtown

A&B Books	146 Lawrence St	718-596-0872	African-American books.
A&B Books	223 Duffield St	718-783-7808	General African-American books.
Barnes & Noble	106 Court St	718-246-4996	Chain.
Heights Books	109 Montague St	718-624-4876	Rare, out of print, used.
Long Island University Book Store	1 University Plz	718-858-3888	General.
powerHouse Arena	37 Main St	718-666-3049	One of our favorite gallery/bookstores.
St Mark's Comics	148 Montague St	718-935-0911	Comics.
Trazar's Variety Book Store	40 Hoyt St	718-797-2478	African-American books.
Zakka	155 Plymouth St	718-801-8037	Graphic design books.

Map 6 · Fort Greene / Clinton Hill

Dare Books	33 Lafayette Ave	718-625-4651	General.
Greenlight Bookstore	686 Fulton St	718-246-0200	Ft. Greene's newest and immediately best bookstore.
Pratt Institute Bookstore	550 Myrtle Ave	718-789-1105	Art supplies, books, ephemera.

Map 7 · Bedford-Stuyvesant

Brownstone Books	409 Lewis Ave	718-953-7328	Excellent neighborhood bookshop..

Map 8 · BoCoCa / Red Hook

Anwaar Bookstore	428 Atlantic Ave	718-875-3791	Arabic books.
Book Court	163 Court St	718-875-3677	General.
Community Book Store	212 Court St	718-834-9494	General.
Dar Us Salam	486 Atlantic Ave	718-625-5925	Islamic books.
Freebird Books	123 Columbia St	718-643-8484	Used.
Pranga Book Store	354 Court St	718-624-2927	General new and used.

Map 9 • Park Slope / Prospect Heights / Windsor Terrace

Babbo's Books	242 Prospect Park W	718-788-3475	Used & new.
Barnes & Noble	267 Seventh Ave	718-832-9066	Chain.
Community Book Store	143 Seventh Ave	718-783-3075	Used & new.
Park Slope Books	200 Seventh Ave	718-499-3064	Mostly used.
Unnameable Books	600 Vanderbilt Ave	718-789-1534	General new and used.

Map 10 • Prospect-Lefferts Gardens / Crown Heights

Goodwill Gospel Store	759 Flatbush Ave	718-287-9001	Christian.
Maverick Comics	210 Parkside Ave	718-284-5185	Comics.
Yoruba Book Center	610 New York Ave	718-774-5800	Yoruba religious bookstore.

Map 11 • Sunset Park / Green-Wood Heights

Libreria Jovenes Cristianos	5703 Fifth Ave	718-439-7873	Christian.

Map 12 • Borough Park

Ateres Sofrim	5302 16th Ave	718-633-4721	Judaica.
Bulletproof Comics	4507 Ft Hamilton Pkwy	718-854-3367	Comics. If you're into that sort of thing.
Eichler's	5004 13th Ave	718-633-1505	Borough Park Judaica superstore.
Hecht Hebrew Book & Religious	265 Coney Island Ave	718-258-9696	Judaica.
Pinters Hebrew Book Store	4408 14th Ave	718-871-2260	Hebrew Bookstore.

Map 13 • Kensington / Ditmas Park

Brooklyn College Bookstore	2900 Bedford Ave	718-434-0333	Selection of bestsellers and children's books.
Morija Book Store	1387 Flatbush Ave	718-282-9997	Religious.
Rincher's Bookstore	2804 Church Ave	718-282-4033	General.
Shakespeare & Co	150 Campus Rd	718-434-5326	Brooklyn outpost of Manhattan mini-chain.

Map 14 • Bay Ridge

The Bookmark Shoppe	8415 Third Ave	718-833-5115	Mostly bestsellers and children's.
Galaxy Comics	6823 Fifth Ave	718-921-1236	Comics.
Islamic Books & Tapes	6805 Fifth Ave	718-567-8540	Islamic.

Map 15 • Dyker Heights / Bensonhurst

International Bookstore	1914 86th St	718-236-1090	Russian.

Map 16 • Midwood

A Torah Treasures Books & Gifts	3005 Ave L	718-758-1221	Judaica.
Bulletproof Comics	2178 Nostrand Ave	718-434-1800	Comics.
Harnik's Happy House	1403 Ave J	718-951-9805	General.
Here's A Book Store	1964 Coney Island Ave	718-645-6675	Quaint and impressive, rare finds, new and used, knowledgeable staff.
Mekor Hasfarim	1973 Coney Island Ave	718-627-4385	Judaica.
Rusbook Co. Russian Bookseller	1742 E 13th St	718-336-7680	Russian.

Arts & Entertainment · **Movie Theaters**

Brooklyn used to be teeming with hundreds of grand movie theaters. Unfortunately, almost all of the neighborhood movie palaces have been lost to the bulldozer or recycled into 99-cent stores. Despite its huge population, today Brooklyn offers very few movie theaters and even fewer decent ones. Nonetheless, for those who resist the urge to hop a subway to Manhattan, there are some worthwhile options. Movie buffs who are especially interested in independent and experimental films will be happy to know that Brooklyn has the most vibrant scene in the city.

There are a number of soulless multiplexes showing typical Hollywood fare, complete with stale popcorn and annoying commercials. Check the newspaper or the Web for the latest listings in various locations around Brooklyn. A better alternative is the handful of neighborhood cinemas still in operation. What they may lack in sound quality or screen size, they make up for in grit and charm. **Cobble Hill Cinemas (Map 8)** shows first-run and independent films and offers cheap tickets on Tuesdays and Thursdays. Even though it's unrenovated, the small and intimate **Pavilion Brooklyn Heights (Map 5)** remains a favorite, due to its charming miniscule lobby and fabulous location on Henry Street. The **Kent Triplex Theater (Map 16)** in Midwood could use a major renovation, but it shows Russian films and offers reduced-rate tickets on Wednesdays. The Brooklyn Public Library has the best deal in the borough with regular free screenings.

Brooklyn's gem for the true cinemaphile is the **BAM Rose Cinemas (Map 6)**. It boasts a gorgeously appointed space with tasty popcorn, pleasant service, and an exceptional choice of art house and foreign films. The theaters are rarely overcrowded and it is always clean and inviting, which is unique to the New York movie going experience. Manhattanites have even been known to make the colossal effort to leave their sacred island every so often to attend movies there! Specifically worth checking out is BAMcinématek, which hosts retrospectives, special screenings, and appearances by the finest directors and actors.

Some of the hippest cinema in Brooklyn happens a bit under the radar. At the top of the list is **Rooftop Films** (www.rooftopfilms.com; 718-417-7362) which mixes independent cinema with fresh air on various roofs around Brooklyn during the warmer months. **Café Steinhof (Map 9)** shows all types of film favorites with its Austrian grub on Sundays. Two major annual film festivals are now hosted each year in Brooklyn—the Sundance Film Festival at BAM the end of January, and the Brooklyn International Film Festival in June. With cutting-edge events like this taking place, Brooklyn can once again be proud of its contribution to the New York film scene.

Movie Theaters	Address	Phone		Map
BAM Rose Cinemas	BAM, 30 Lafayette Ave	718-636-4100	Great seating and mix of first runs and revivals.	6
Cobble Hill Cinemas	265 Court St	718-596-9113	Great indie destination, though theaters are small.	8
Kent Triplex	1170 Coney Island Ave	718-338-3371	Moron blockbuster destination.	16
Pavilion Brooklyn Heights	70 Henry St	718-596-7070	Intimate, classy, and just about perfect.	5
Pavilion Movie Theatres	188 Prospect Park W	718-369-0838	Nice mix of stuff right across from Propsect Park.	9
Regal/UA Court Street	108 Court St	718-246-7995	Audience-participation-friendly megaplex.	5
Rooftop Films	various locations	718-417-7362	Summer rooftop series—check website for locations!	n/a

Museums

Brooklyn is not generally known for its museums, but culture buffs still have plenty to love. The main attraction is the **Brooklyn Museum (Map 10)** which became famous (or infamous) by igniting former Mayor Giuliani's ire with its controversial *Sensation* exhibit. In addition to viewing an extensive permanent collection, crowds can dance and socialize at their ever-popular "First Saturdays," and admire the cutting-edge architecture (a transparent, space-age exterior fronting an old-world, Romanesque facade). History aficionados will enjoy the **Brooklyn Historical Society (Map 5),** housed in a four-story Queen Anne-style building and the fascinating vintage-subway-car-depot that is the **New York Transit Museum (Map 5)**, both of which are located downtown. Williamsburg's funky and fascinating **City Reliquary Museum (Map 2)** is a must see for New Yorkphiles. And kids and adults alike shouldn't miss the touchy-feely exhibits at the **Brooklyn Children's Museum (Map 10)**, which is regarded as the best of its kind in New York.

Museums	Address	Phone	Map
Brooklyn Children's Museum	145 Brooklyn Ave	718-735-4400	10
Brooklyn Historical Society	128 Pierrepont St	718-222-4111	5
Brooklyn Museum	200 Eastern Pkwy	718-638-5000	9
City Reliquary	370 Metropolitan Ave	718-782-4842	2
Coney Island Museum	1208 Surf Ave	718-372-5159	p136
Doll & Toy Museum of NYC	157 Montague St	718-243-0820	5
Harbor Defense Museum	230 Sheridan Loop	718-630-4349	15
Kurdish Library and Museum	345 Park Pl	718-783-7930	9
Museum of Contemporary African Diasporan Arts	80 Hanson Pl	718-230-0492	6
New York Aquarium	Surf Ave & West 8th	718-265-3474	p136
New York Transit Museum	Boerum Pl & Schermerhorn St	718-694-1600	5
The Living Torah Museum	1601 41st St	718-686-8174	12
The Old Stone House	336 3rd St	718-768-3195	9
Simmons Collection African Arts Museum	1063 Fulton St	718-230-0933	7
Waterfront Museum	290 Conover St	718-624-4719	8
Wyckoff-Bennett Homestead	5816 Clarendon Rd	718-629-5400	p134

Theaters

Broadway and Lincoln Center may have the big bucks and the well-known stars, but New York's abundance of talented artists is spread throughout the five boroughs. Brooklyn is the home of many firmly rooted theater, dance, and music companies and, with the increasing number of Manhattan groups getting priced out of their venues, is welcoming many new and adventurous artists who have chosen to hop across the East River.

The Brooklyn Academy of Music (just call it BAM) serves as the centerpiece for performing arts in Kings County. Consisting of the gorgeous, if slightly in need of some restoration, Beaux-Arts **Harvey Lichtenstein Theater (Map 6)**, the **Howard Gilman Opera House (Map 6)**, Rose Cinemas, and BAMcafé, it's a popular stopping point for an assortment of international, national, and local theater, dance, and classical music companies. BAM supplies a healthy mix of the traditional, contemporary, and experimental and serves as home to the illustrious and very hip Brooklyn Philharmonic. See the full schedule at www.bam.org

For classical recitals in a casual setting, you can't get less formal than **Bargemusic (Map 5)**, moored at the Fulton Ferry landing. Concerts (some free) are presented year round, but with a romantic view of the Manhattan skyline it's especially popular on date nights during the warmer months. www.bargemusic.org

For opera lovers on a budget who don't want to stand in the nosebleed section of the Metropolitan Opera House, where you can't tell a mezzo from a countertenor, the Regina Opera Company gives you all the classics in their cozy space **Regina Hall (Map 15)**. Production values are modest, but do you really need live horses to do *La Boheme*?

The **Galapagos Arts Space (Map 5)** sneers at the thought of applying for grants while the folks at **St. Ann's Warehouse (Map 5)** happily accept private and public funding. Both spaces encourage artists to experiment into new territory that sometimes results in non-traditional theater pieces. St. Ann's has seen two of its shows move to Broadway. Galapagos regularly hosts a new breed of retro-yeah-feminist-approved burlesque shows, where mixed-gender audiences cheer on female striptease dancers whose routines are so funny and bizarre you'll probably forget to become aroused. The **Brooklyn Lyceum (Map 9)** has a regular hodgepodge of vaudeville and theater shorts. **Charlie Pineapple Theater Company (Map 2)** fits no more than two dozen patrons into its intimate space, but the young company has been tempting lovers of good drama with well-received productions of edgy plays such as *True West* and *One Flew Over the Cuckoo's Nest*. www.charliepineapple.com

Is your iPod loaded up with Rodgers and Hammerstein? Can't get enough of those Neil Simon comedies and Arthur Miller dramas? **The Heights Players (Map 5)** have been entertaining Brooklynites with popular favorites and recent Broadway and Off-Broadway hits since the days when Tennessee Williams was a fresh new voice. The slightly younger **Gallery Players (Map 9)** lean more toward off-beat works by the likes of Terrence McNally and Stephen Sondheim, often mounting the first New York revivals of recently closed plays and musicals. www.heightsplayers.org, www.galleryplayers.com

Many of these companies offer subscriptions to their seasons of plays, but you never know when a play will pop up at some place that is suddenly being called a theater. For extensive listings of plays all over New York, visit www.broadwayworld.com and www.theatermania.com

Theaters	Address	Phone	Map
651 Arts	651 Fulton St	718-636-4181	6
Bargemusic	Fulton Ferry Landing	718-624-2083	5
The Billie Holiday Theater	1368 Fulton St	718-636-0918	7
BRIC Studio	647 Fulton St	718-855-7882	5
Brick Theatre	575 Metropolitan Ave	917-907-6189	2
Brooklyn Arts Council	55 Washington St	718-625-0080	5
Brooklyn Arts Exchange	421 Fifth Ave	718-832-0018	9
Brooklyn Conservatory of Music	58 Seventh Ave	718-622-3300	9
Brooklyn Family Theatre	1012 Eighth Ave	718-670-7205	9
Brooklyn Lyceum	227 Fourth Ave	718-857-4816	9
Charlie Pineapple Theater Company	208 N 8th St	718-907-0577	2
Galapagos Art Space	16 Main St	718-222-8500	5
Gallery Players Theater	199 14th St	718-595-0547	9
Gershwin Theater	2900 Bedford Ave	718-961-5666	13
Harvey Lichtenstein Theater	651 Fulton St	718-636-4100	6
The Heights Players	26 Willow Pl	718-237-2752	5
Howard Gilman Opera House	30 Lafayette Ave	718-636-4100	6
Indie Screen	285 Kent Ave	347-512-6422	2
Jalopy	315 Columbia St	718-395-3214	8
Paul Robeson Theatre	54 Greene Ave	718-783-9794	6
Public Assembly	70 N 6th St	718-782-5188	2
Puppetworks	338 Sixth Ave	718-965-3391	9
Regina Hall	65th St & 12th Ave	718-232-3555	15
reRun Gastropub Theater	147 Front St	718-797-2322	5
St Ann's Warehouse	38 Water St	718-254-8779	5
Walt Whitman Theatre, Brooklyn Center for the Performing Arts	2900 Campus Rd	718-951-4500	13

In terms of nightlife, it's no longer about whether Brooklyn can match up to Manhattan. Those days are long past, dear friends—the question now is: why bother to go into Manhattan at all? The live music scene in Brooklyn is better, the drinks are cheaper, and you have to deal with far fewer tourists, fratboys, and suits (although you will have to deal with far more hipsters, so maybe that one's a push). There are now even more bowling alleys in Brooklyn than Manhattan—crazy, right? Well, below are some of our favorite sports to listen, drink, groove, or simply hang. Enjoy!

Live Music

Brooklyn is enough of a tastemaker to now demand the attention of touring acts. The largest venues, **Warsaw (Map 1)**, **Music Hall of Williamsburg (Map 2)**, **The Bell House (Map 9)**, **Knitting Factory (Map 2)**, and **Southpaw (Map 9)**, book rock, hip-hop, and experimental music (respectively) for panting droves of audiophiles. Williamsburg abounds with tons of smaller venues; **Glasslands Gallery (Map 2)** is a current favorite. For a more intimate feel, and an emphasis on folk music, check out **Pete's Candy Store (Map 2)** or **Jalopy (Map 8)**. **Barbes (Map 9)** is the spot for world music, including great African gigs every Wednesday night. Jazz is also alive and well at places like **Zebulon (Map 2)**, **Barbes (Map 9)**, **Issue Project Room (Map 9)**, and **The Jazz Spot (Map 7)**.

Hipster Bars

If you're not sure whether you've stumbled into a hipster enclave, look for board games and quiz-night emcees and a swarm of oddly dressed folks trying their damnedest not to enjoy themselves. Of course, hipsters aren't all bad. At least they know how to pick bars. They've made several their own, including **Buttermilk (Map 9)** in Park Slope, **Enid's (Map 1)** in Greenpoint, and **Union Pool (Map 2)** in Williamsburg.

Atmosphere

This is a subjective category to be sure, but there are just certain bars that you go to for more than simply the beer selection or the drink specials. You go there because the ambience is interesting and inviting. **Iona (Map 2)** in Williamsburg, with its backyard patio and fire pits, is a case in point, as is secret-entrance **Larry Lawrence (Map 2)**. Since 1890, **Sunny's (Map 8)** has been the bar in Red Hook. It once took in patrons on a pay-what-you-wish basis, but Red Hook's rise has given them reason to actually charge for the alcohol served in this charming hideaway. And if you just want to go somewhere to relive the glory days of your teen years (but with legal drinking), rush over to **Barcade (Map 2)**, which is filled with '80s video games including NFT fave Q*bert.

Jukebox

If the DJ won't take requests and the bartender is only interested enough to put an iPod on shuffle, then you've got to go for the jukebox. For pure eclecticism, you can't beat **Daddy's (Map 2)** in Williamsburg. Indie rock fans should visit **Commonwealth (Map 9)** or **Great Lakes (Map 9)** in Park Slope. For classic rock, new wave, and everything in-between, check out **Boat (Map 8)** in Carroll Gardens. **The Levee (Map 2)** and **Moonshine (Map 8)** also have stellar jukeboxes.

The Great Outdoors

One of our favorite trends is the proliferation of outdoor drinking that's been happening in Brooklyn. Perhaps the most well-known spot is the **Gowanus Yacht Club (Map 8)** in Carroll Gardens. **Franklin Park (Map 10)** gives Crown Heights a breath of fresh air, while the back patio at **Sweet Revenge (Map 6)** on the Clinton Hill/Bed-Stuy border features tons of tables, greenery, and a grill for patron's use, as does **Moonshine (Map 8)** in Carroll Gardens West. In Prospect Heights, check out **Soda (Map 9)** for a cool backyard. In Williamsburg, hit the rooftop at **Berry Park (Map 2)** or the backyard at **Nita Nita (Map 2)**. And you can hear the rumble of the Williamsburg Bridge's cars and subways from the patio at **East River Bar (Map 2)**, just so you're reminded that even though you're outside, you're still in the middle of Gotham.

Dive Bars

Brooklyn has a few hundred years of drinking under its belt, so many establishments' heydays happened in the last millennium. Still, these places are newly embraced for their easy-going vibe and cheep beer. The ultimate Brooklyn dive is the **Turkey's Nest (Map 2)**, because it's not a hipster joint pretending to be seedy; it is a proudly certified craphole. If you want something a little more tame, try **Greenpoint Tavern (Map 2)** for long-time locals and newbie hipsters all drinking cold Bud in Styrofoam cups. **Tommy's Tavern (Map 1)** or **Palace Café (Map 1)** in Greenpoint are also great armpits of a bar, and on the weekends Tommy's has live music in the back room that is surprisingly good. While in Park Slope, you can always drink for cheap at **O'Connor's (Map 9)**. In Bed-Stuy, say hello to the locals at **Liquid Love (Map 8)**. For those in need of a brewski in Midwood, the perfectly dingy atmosphere of **Nitecaps (Map 16)** will treat you right. If you're ever in Bay Ridge, your best bet is **JJ Bubbles (Map 14)**. And by "best" we mean utter and total dive. Finally, it's worth the trek to Greenwood Heights to experience the awesomeness dive-o-rama of **Smolen (Map 11)**.

Best All Around

Certain bars, for whatever reason, simply rule. It might be because they attract a certain type of patron, or play a certain type of music, or sit in a certain neighborhood. However, the real reason people revisit these places over and over is for the emotional connection. Below are examples of places that have such a pull on their customers. If you like a strong drink with no attitude and a touch of history, saddle up to the ancient bar at **The Brooklyn Inn (Map 8)**. This is an excellent watering hole for locals to chat and drink up among friends. Plus, they get major bonus points for being one of the few TV-free bars left in the city. For Manhattan-quality cocktails at Brooklyn prices, check out **Brooklyn Social (Map 8)** in Carroll Gardens. Their old-fashioned mixology makes it worth dealing with the crowds. We highly recommend making the trek out to Red Hook for **Bait & Tackle (Map 8)**. Perfect on a lazy Sunday afternoon or a lively Friday night, this place has everything going for it—pinball, funky décor, laid-back bartenders, stiff drinks, and the perfect soundtrack. **Spuyten Duyvil (Map 2)** in Williamsburg is usually bursting with patrons due to its beer cultish following, but it's worth weaving through the hordes to sample over 80 international beers that will blow your mind. Luckily, the warm, knowledgeable staff will help you decipher the menu. **The Beast (Map 9)** in Prospect Heights is also just about perfect, since they serve up excellent food to go along with a friendly, laid-back vibe at the front bar. For the perfect modern day Brooklyn bar, you can't do better than **Sycamore (Map 13)**. Friendly bartenders, a nice back patio, and a chill vibe add up to one of the best places to down a drink with friends. Plus, what other bar has a flower shop in the front room? Try finding that in Manhattan. Finally, an honorary mention goes to **Freddy's Backroom and Bar (Map 9)**. This dive-o-rama was booted of their awesome old location by the gigantic Antlantic Yards project, but unlike most New York stories, this one has a happy ending. Freddy's found a good new location about 2 miles away complete with a back room for live music. Stop by for a shot and a beer to celebrate an institution that not only survived, but reinvented itself so it's better than ever.

To eat in Brooklyn—the stuff that dreams are made of…

Welcome to Italy

You got ya two kinds of Italian places in Brooklyn—the old ones and the new ones. And, with a few notable exceptions, the new ones are waaay better than the old ones. A few exceptions—**Ferdinando's (Map 8)** for killer Sicilian (no pun intended), **Queen (Map 5)** for classic white-linen Italian, and **Joe's of Avenue U (Eastern Brooklyn)** for buffet-style. But for daily life in the 21st Century, almost every nabe in BK has got it goin' on—so check out **Acqua Santa (Map 2)** in Williamsburg, **Locanda Vini & Olii (Map 6)** in Clinton Hill, **Al Di La (Map 9)** in Park Slope, **Frankie's 457 (Map 8)** in Carroll Gardens, **The Good Fork (Map 8)** in Red Hook, **Bocca Lupo (Map 8)** in Cobble Hill, **Scopello (Map 6)** in Fort Greene, and **The Tuscany Grill (Map 14)** in Bay Ridge. Trust us—any one of these "new" joints will make you feel quite close to the old country.

Liberté, égalité, fraternité!

In case you thought that the other great cuisine of the world was underrepresented, think again. There is pretty much at least one, if not more than one, French response to the Italian options above—so be sure and check out **Belleville (Map 9)** in Park Slope, **Quercy (Map 8)** and **Bar Tabac (Map 8)** in Cobble Hill, **Chez Oskar (Map 6)** and **Chez Lola (Map 6)** in Fort Greene, **Petit Oven (Map 14)** in Bay Ridge, **Pomme de Terre (Map 13)** in Ditmas Park, and **Fada (Map 2)** and **Juliette (Map 2)** in Williamsburg.

The Rest of the World

The entire world's ethnic make-up is represented in Brooklyn, somewhere or other. Fortunately this translates into an abundance of food choices—from the great Mexican at **Alma (Map 8)** in Carroll Gardens West to the extremely simple and unpretentious Middle Eastern **Bedouin Tent (Map 8)**. And then, everything else…Michelin-starred **Ki Sushi (Map 8)**, **Madiba** (South African, **Map 6**), **Lomzynianka** (Polish, **Map 1**), **Convivium Osteria** (Portuguese, **Map 8**), **Joya** (Thai, **Map 8**), **Nyonya** (Malaysian, **Map 11**), **Kush** (African, **Map 6**), **Pacificana** (Dim Sum Chinese, **Map 11**), **Sheep Station** (Australian, **Map 8**), **Tacos Matamoros (Map 11)**, etc…

The Unquestionably Hip

While we know that what is "hip" tends to change with the wind, there are some places that we'd like to call out as useful for when your Manhattan friends deign to come to Brooklyn and think they're going to eat at some sort of craphole diner. The following places should shut their damned hole(s): in Williamsburg, **Zenkichi (Map 2)**, **Diner (Map 2)**, and **Dressler (Map 2)**. In Bushwick, **Northeast Kingdom (Map 4)**. In Vinegar Hill, **the Vinegar Hill House (Map 5)**. In Brooklyn Heights, **Jack the Horse (Map 5)**. In BoCoCa, **Char No. 4 (Map 7)**, and **Buttermilk Channel (Map 7)**. In Fort Greene, **The General Greene (Map 6)** and **No. 7 (Map 6)**. In Clinton Hill, **Locanda Vini & Olii (Map 6)**. And in Park Slope, **Flatbush Farm (Map 9)** and, of course, **Blue Ribbon (Map 9)**. That should shut them up.

The Pizza War

You just can't beat Brooklyn for pizza, although trying to come to some sort of consensus as to which is the "best" is beyond impossible. Newcomers to check out are **Motorino (Map 3)** in East Williamsburg, voted #1 by Frank Bruni in the New York Times and hip **Roberta's (Map 3)** on the Bushwick border. The classics in each neighborhood include **Grimaldi's (Map 5)** in Brooklyn Heights (always top-rated by Zagat), the utterly fresh+brilliant **Franny's (Map 9)** in Park Slope/Prospect Heights, **Totonnos (p. 136)** in Coney Island (the thinnest thin-crust of them all), **DiFaras (Map 16)** in Midwood (see Dominic DeMarco take the pizzas out of the oven with his bare hands), **Lucali (Map 8)** in Carroll Gardens, and the furthest out there of them all, **L&B Spumoni Gardens (Eastern Brooklyn)** in Bensonhurst (get the Sicilian).

Where Everyone Knows Your Name

This is by no means an exhaustive list, but there just happen to be a few places in each nabe that are simply cool, friendly places to go to. **The Hope & Anchor (Map 8)** is close to the top of this list (that's three Red Hook mentions so far for those of you counting at home), followed closely by **Tom's (Map 9)** in Prospect Heights, **DuMont (Map 2)** in Williamsburg, **Northeast Kingdom (Map 4)** in Bushwick, and **Sherwood Café (Map 8)** in Carroll Gardens. Insert your own here:_____.

Our Favorite Restaurants

Again, just a few picks to stir things up: **Applewood (Map 9)**—slow food comes to Brooklyn; **Blue Ribbon (Map 9)**—surely you didn't think we'd forget; **Stone Park Café (Map 9)**—any place with marrow is a friend of ours; **Bar Tabac (Map 8)**—solid French food that never lets you down; **Convivium Osteria (Map 9)**—one of the best interiors (especially the basement) this side of the Atlantic; **Henry's End (Map 5)**—elk chops + Samuel Smith's Nut Brown Ale = Bliss; **Fette Sau (Map 2)**—its killer bare-bones BBQ is worth the wait, newcomer **Vinegar Hill House (Map 5)**—possibly the best cast-iron chicken on the planet; and, of course, **Peter Luger (Map 2)**—the best steak this world has ever seen. And the best spinach. And the best potatoes. And…you get the point.

Brooklyn has been called the world's largest small town, and we feel this most strongly when strolling down charming streets lined with fruit stands, cheese shops, charcuteries, bargain basements, bookstores, clothing boutiques, and other essentials. You can pretty much find everything you need without ever leaving the better borough. Most of the good stuff is concentrated in Williamsburg, BoCoCa, and Park Slope, but every neighborhood has something to offer.

Food

For anything and everything Italian, get thee to Bensonhurst or to Carroll Gardens. In Bensonhurst, **Villabate Pasticceria & Bakery (Map 15)** will make you quiver with delight, while **Frank and Sal Prime Meats (Map 15)** can supply you with mozzarella and sopressata for life. In Carroll Gardens, it's **Mazzola (Map 8)** for lard bread, **Caputo's (Map 8)** for imported goods and home-made mozzarella, and **G Esposito & Sons (Map 8)** for killer sopressata. For all of your cheese needs, the **Bedford Cheese Shop (Map 2)** in Williamsburg is your best bet, though **Stinky (Map 8)** in BoCoCa is a contender. Check out the specialty dry goods at **Sahadi Importing Company (Map 8)** in Cobble Hill. In BoCoCa, **D'Amico Foods (Map 8)** is definitely a top NYC destination for fresh-ground coffee, and butcher **Staubitz (Map 8)** delivers up one of the city's best meat selection. In Fort Greene, both **Greene Grape Provisions (Map 6)** and **Choice Greene (Map 6)** have opened up, each with excellent meat/fish/cheese counters and fresh produce (and a fabulous sushi chef at Choice Greene, to boot). In Park Slope, choices abound with **Bklyn Larder (Map 9)**, **Cobblestone Foods (Map 9)**, and **Grab (Map 9)**. For god's gift to man (re: chocolate), **Jacques Torres Chocolate (Map 5)** in DUMBO can't be beat. And **Marlow & Daughters (Map 2)** in Williamsburg has a fabulous selection of meats. With all of the above, who needs restaurants?

Vino

To go along with all that food you've just picked up, how about a nice bottle of wine? In Greenpoint, **Dandelion Wine (Map 1)** can help. In Williamsburg, hit **Uva Wines (Map 2)** or **Blue Angel Wines (Map 3)**. Fort Greene's **Gnarly Vines (Map 6)**, **Greene Grape (Map 6)**, **Olivino (Map 6)**, and **Thirst (Map 6)** all have their loyal clientele. In BoCoCa, **Smith & Vine (Map 8)** will never lead you wrong.

Clothing

For unique boutiques, take a stroll along Smith and Court Streets in Carroll Gardens or Fifth Avenue in Park Slope. **Beacon's Closet (Map 2)** is a great vintage shop in Williamsburg. We also love **Pop's Popular Clothing (Map 1)** in Greenpoint. For all your underwear needs, check out the bargains at **Underworld Plaza (Map 12)** in Borough Park. Hats can be found at **Malchijah Hats (Map 6)** in Fort Greene, and, of course, **Kova Quality Hatters**

(Map 12) in Borough Park. For those with suburban nostalgia, the soul-sucking **Atlantic Terminal Mall (Map 6)** provides a home to Victoria's Secret, Old Navy, Daffy's, and other chains we secretly love. And, of course, we can't forget the **Century 21 (Map 14)** in Bay Ridge—not as good as its Manhattan counterpart, but still a madhouse any day of the week. For higher-end clothing, hit the retail strip of Smith Street in Carroll Gardens; lots of little boutiques such as **Dear Fieldbinder (Map 6)** to spend your parents' credit card money in.

Home

Brooklyn has an array of big-time chains such as **Target (Map 6)**, and **Costco (Map 11)** that have a little bit of everything. Some good spots for home furnishings include **Design Within Reach (Map 5)** and **West Elm (Map 5)**. For something posher and hipper, check out Smith Street's **Environment 337 (Map 8)**. For jewelry, **Metal and Thread (Map 8)**, **Swallow (Map 8)**, **Cog & Pearl (Map 9)**, and **Clay Pot (Map 9)** are excellent gift-giving destinations— they all also carry a lot of fun, random eclectic items. For vintage, mid-century, and modern pieces, try Williamsburg's **Two Jakes (Map 2)**, Fort Greene's **Yu Interiors (Map 6)** or Park Slope's **Trailer Park (Map 9)**. Turns out all the rumors about **IKEA (Map 8)** in Red Hook were true. Now open for better or worse.

Miscellaneous

Check out **Earwax Records (Map 2)**, **Academy Records (Map 2)**, or **Sound Fix Records (Map 2)** in Williamsburg for great record shopping, **American Beer Distributors (Map 8)** on Court Street for hundreds of imported brews, and the McSweeney's shop/tutoring center, **Brooklyn Superhero Supply (Map 9)**, on Fifth Avenue in the Slope. Bookworms can happily wile away the hours amidst the stacks at Williamsburg's **Spoonbill & Sugartown (Map 2)**, or Fort Greene's great new shop, **Greenlight (Map 6)**. **Spuyten Duyvil Grocery (Map 2)** has the best Belgian beer selection outside of Belgium, while **Bierkraft (Map 9)** covers at least three obsessions— cheese, chocolate, and beer—while **Blue Marble (Map 8)** has a great slant: Organic ice cream. Come summertime, handmade jewelry, clothes and bags, used books, and irresistibly hip baby clothes are sold for a song at the many crafts fairs that land in artsy Williamsburg—the Renegade Arts Fair (www.renegadecraft.com) in McCarren Park is always a good bet. Another outdoor option is the fantastic **Brooklyn Flea (Map 6)** (www.brooklynflea.com) every Saturday in Fort Greene and Sunday in Williamsburg. During the colder months it moves inside to the **Williamsburg Savings Bank Building (Map 6)**. We also love trolling neighborhoods like Park Slope and Williamsburg for stoop sales—you'll find incredible bargains, unique finds, and you may just make a new friend.

Street	Page	Grid
36th St		
(200-699)	11	A1/A2
(1100-1598)	12	A1/A2
E 36th St		
(1000-1749)	*	F4
(1750-2199)	*	G5
W 36th St	*	H2
37th St		
(201-899)	11	A1/A2
(960-1599)	12	A1/A2
E 37th St		
(69-200)	10	B2
(241-999)	*	E4
(1013-1799)	*	E4
(1800-2199)	*	G5
W 37th St	*	H2
38th St		
(300-449)	11	A1
(1000-1599)	12	A1/A2
E 38th St		
(69-204)	10	B2
(205-894)	*	E4
(895-1649)	*	F4
(1650-1849)	*	F5
(1850-2299)	*	G5
39th St		
(1-899)	11	A1/A2
(930-1698)	12	A1/A2
E 39th St		
(1-116)	10	B2
(113-957)	*	E4
(1029-1312)	*	F4
40th St		
(100-948)	11	A1/A2
(959-1699)	12	A1/A2
E 40th St		
(1-929)	*	E4
(930-1299)	*	F4
(1301-1449)	*	F5
41st St		
(100-949)	11	A1/B1/B2
(950-1699)	12	B1/B2
E 41st St	*	F5
42nd St		
(1-899)	11	B1/B2
(970-1798)	12	B1/B2
E 42nd St		
(25-969)	*	E4
(950-1198)	*	F5
43rd St		
(1-899)	11	B1/B2
(1000-1799)	12	B1/B2
E 43rd St		
(1-72)	*	D4
(73-592)	*	E4
(593-834)	*	E5
(867-1699)	*	F5
44th St		
(40-949)	11	B1/B2
(950-1799)	12	B1/B2
45th St		
(200-899)	11	B1/B2
(1000-1799)	12	B1/B2
E 45th St		
(73-171)	*	D4
(227-315)	*	D5
(331-1162)	*	E5
(1159-1749)	*	F5
46th St		
(200-899)	11	B1/B2
(1000-1799)	12	B1/B2
E 46th St		
(67-310)	*	D5
(340-1098)	*	E5
(1162-1799)	*	F5
47th St		
(100-949)	11	B1/B2
(950-1941)	12	B1/B2
E 47th St	*	E5
48th St		
(52-899)	11	B1/B2
(1000-1899)	12	B1/B2
E 48th St		
(24-304)	*	D5
(339-1034)	*	E5
(1166-1899)	*	F5
49th St		
(100-899)	11	B1/B2
(1000-1899)	12	B1/B2
E 49th St		
(73-305)	*	D5
(336-1010)	*	E5
(1161-1899)	*	F5
50th St		
(100-949)	11	B1/B2
(950-1998)	12	B1/B2
51st St		
(1-899)	11	B1/B2
(950-2099)	12	B1/B2
E 51st St		
(2-294)	*	D5
(321-966)	*	E5
(1151-1872)	*	F5
(1927-2049)	*	G5
52nd St		
(1-899)	11	B1/B2
(1000-1999)	12	B1/B2
E 52nd St		
(2-228)	*	D5
(253-1016)	*	E5
(1100-1899)	*	F5
(1951-2099)	*	G5
E 53rd Pl	*	G5
53rd St		
(1-956)	11	B1/B2
(1001-1999)	12	B1/B2
E 53rd St		
(2-215)	*	D5
(216-244)	11	B1
(245-1023)	*	E5
(1071-1859)	*	F5
(2000-2099)	*	G5
54th St		
(100-899)	11	B1/B2
(971-1999)	12	B1/B2
E 54th St		
(1-154)	*	D5
(166-999)	*	E5
(1025-1815)	*	F5
(2000-2099)	*	G5
55th St		
(100-899)	11	B1/B2
(900-2099)	12	B1/B2
E 55th St		
(1-104)	*	D5
(140-1000)	*	E5
(1001-1950)	*	F5
56th Dr	*	G5
56th St		
(80-899)	11	B1/B2
(900-2099)	12	B1/B2
E 56th St		
(2-79)	*	D5
(109-850)	*	E5
(851-1999)	*	F5
E 57th Pl	*	G5
57th St		
(1-899)	11	B1/B2
(1000-1799)	12	B1/B2
(2000-2198)	*	F3
E 57th St		
(1-53)	*	D5
(54-699)	*	E5
(800-1999)	*	F5
(2000-2099)	*	F3
58th St		
(100-899)	11	B1/B2
(1000-1899)	12	B1/B2
(2050-2167)	*	F3
E 58th St		
(1-884)	*	E5
(801-2099)	*	F5
E 59th Pl	*	G5
59th St		
(200-899)	11	B1/B2
(950-1999)	12	B1/B2
(2050-2299)	*	F3
E 59th St		
(1-699)	*	E5
(800-2099)	*	F5
E 60th Pl	*	G5
60th St		
(200-938)	11	B1/B2
(2050-2363)	*	F3
(939-2384)	12	B1/B2
E 60th St	*	F5
61st St		
(200-935)	11	B1/B2
(936-1999)	12	B1/B2
(2050-2399)	*	F3
E 61st St	*	F5
62nd St		
(200-933)	11	B1/B2
(934-2049)	12	B1/B2
(2050-2349)	*	F3
(2350-2414)	*	G3
63rd St		
(200-929)	11	B1/B2
(930-1999)	12	B1/B2
(2050-2299)	*	F3
(2250-2499)	*	G3
E 63rd St		
(1400-2199)	*	F5
(2300-2799)	*	G5
64th St		
(200-499)	11	B1
(600-849)	14	A2
(850-2014)	15	A1/A2
(2023-2199)	*	F3
(2200-2299)	*	F5
(2250-2499)	*	G3
E 64th St		
(1295-2249)	*	F5
(2400-2549)	*	G6
(2550-2799)	*	F5
65th St		
(200-849)	14	A1/A2
(850-2049)	15	A1/A2
(2101-2199)	*	F3
(2200-2550)	*	G3

Street Index

Street Index

Street Index

Street	Page	Grid
Bragg St		
(2000-2149)	*	G4
(2150-2499)	*	G5
(2700-2901)	*	H5
Branton St	*	E5
Brevoort Pl	7	B1
Bridge Plz	5	A2/B2
Bridge St	5	A1/B2
Bridge Plaza Ct	5	A2
Bridgewater St		
(3-77)	*	A4
(78-91)	*	H5
Brigham St		
(2100-2499)	*	G5
(2773-2899)	*	H5
W Brighton Ave	*	H3
Brighton Ct	*	H3
Brighton 10th Ct	*	H4
Brighton 10th Ln	*	H4
Brighton 10th Path	*	H4
Brighton 10th St	*	H4
Brighton 10th Ter	*	H4
Brighton 11th St	*	H4
Brighton 12th St	*	H4
Brighton 13th St	*	H4
Brighton 14th St	*	H4
Brighton 15th St	*	H4
Brighton 1st Ct	*	H3
Brighton 1st Ln	*	H3
Brighton 1st Path	*	H3
Brighton 1st Pl	*	H3
Brighton 1st Rd	*	H3
Brighton 1st St	*	H3
Brighton 1st Ter	*	H3
Brighton 1st Walk	*	H3
Brighton 2 Path	*	H3
Brighton 2nd Ln	*	H3
Brighton 2nd Pl	*	H3
Brighton 2nd St	*	H3
Brighton 2nd Walk	*	H3
Brighton 3 Pl	*	H3
Brighton 3rd Ct	*	H3
Brighton 3rd Ln	*	H3
Brighton 3rd Rd	*	H3
Brighton 3rd St	*	H3
Brighton 3rd Walk	*	H3
Brighton 4 Pl	*	H3
Brighton 4th Ct	*	H3
Brighton 4th Ln	*	H3
Brighton 4th Rd	*	H3
Brighton 4th St	*	H3
Brighton 4th Ter	*	H3
Brighton 4th Walk	*	H3
Brighton 5th Ct	*	H3
Brighton 5th Ln	*	H3
Brighton 5th Pl	*	H3
Brighton 5th St		
(1-3038)	*	H3
(3039-3199)	*	H4
Brighton 5th Walk	*	H3
Brighton 6th Ct	*	H4
Brighton 6th St		
(1-2909)	*	H3
(2910-3199)	*	H4
Brighton 7th Ct	*	H4
Brighton 7th Ln	*	H4
Brighton 7th St	*	H4
Brighton 7th Walk	*	H4
Brighton 8th Ct	*	H4
Brighton 8th Ln	*	H4
Brighton 8th Pl	*	H4
Brighton 8th St	*	H4
Brighton Beach Ave		
(100-449)	*	H3
(450-1199)	*	H4
Brightwater Ave	*	H4
Brightwater Ct		
(2-449)	*	H3
(450-799)	*	H4
Bristol St		
(1-609)	*	D5
(675-757)	*	E6
Broadway		
(10-497)	2	B1/B2
(498-1026)	3	B1/B2
(1027-1134)	7	A2
(719-1849)	4	B1/B2
(1850-2119)	*	C6
Brooklyn Ave		
(1-65)	7	B1
(66-887)	10	A2/B2
(888-1634)	*	E4
(1635-1899)	*	F4
Brooklyn Rd	*	E4
Broome St	1	B2
Brown St		
(1816-2487)	*	G4
(2600-2845)	*	H4
Bryant St	8	B2
Buffalo Ave		
(1-77)	*	C5
(132-398)	*	D5
Bulwer Pl	*	C6
Burnett St		
(1600-1649)	*	C6
(1650-1899)	*	G4
(2200-2499)	*	G5
Bush St	8	B1/B2
Bushwick Ave		
(2-799)	3	A1/B1/B2
(792-1519)	4	B1/B2
(1520-1780)	*	C6
Bushwick Ct	3	B1
Bushwick Pl	3	A1/B1
Butler Pl	9	A2
Butler St		
(1-272)	8	A2
(273-435)	9	A1
Cadman Plz E	5	A1/B1
Cadman Plz W	5	A1/B1
Calder Pl	9	B1
Calhoun St	3	A1
Calyer St	1	A2/B1/B2
Cambridge Pl	6	B2
Cameron Ct	15	A2
Campus Pl	*	C7
Campus Rd	13	B2
Canal St		
(3-50)	*	H3
(3500-3699)	*	H2
Canarsie Ln	*	E5
Canarsie Rd		
(1501-1562)	*	E6
(1563-2199)	*	F6
Canda Ave	*	H4
Canton Ct	*	H5
Carlton Ave		
(1-459)	6	A1/B1
(460-659)	9	A1/A2
Carroll St		
(1-454)	8	A1/A2
(455-898)	9	A1/A2
(875-1538)	10	A1/A2
(1515-1746)	*	D5
Cary Ct	16	A1
Cass Pl	*	H4
Cathedral Pl	5	B2
Catherine St	3	A1
Caton Ave		
(2-149)	12	A1
(150-2236)	13	A1/A2
Caton Pl	13	A1
Cedar St		
(1-62)	3	B2
(63-106)	4	A1
(1600-1799)	16	A2
Celeste Ct	*	G5
Center Market St	*	E5
Central Ave		
(1-164)	3	B2
(161-798)	4	A1/B1/B2
Centre St	8	B1/B2
Channel Ave	*	G5
Chapel St	5	B2
Charles Pl	3	B2
Charles St	3	B2
Chase Ct	*	E5
Chauncey Ave	5	A2
Chauncey St		
(37-229)	7	B2
(264-512)	*	C5
(510-799)	4	B2
Cheever Pl	8	A1
Cherry St		
(2-76)	*	A4
(1-187)	*	A5
Chester Ave	12	A1
Chester Ct	10	B1
Chester St		
(2-526)	*	D5
(527-622)	*	D6
(689-752)	*	E6
Chestnut Ave	16	A1/A2
Chestnut St		
(1-456)	*	C7
(457-576)	*	D7
Christopher Ave	*	D6
Church Ave		
(2-110)	12	A1
(111-3049)	13	A1/A2
(3050-4449)	*	E4
(4450-9449)	*	E5
(9450-9799)	*	D5
Church Ln	*	E6
Clara St	12	A1
Clarendon Rd		
(2163-3049)	13	B2
(3050-4349)	*	E4
(4350-5999)	*	E5
Clark St	5	B1
Clarkson Ave		
(1-559)	10	B1/B2
(560-697)	*	D4
(698-1160)	*	D5
Classon Ave		
(2-532)	6	A1/A2/B2
(533-612)	7	B1
(613-925)	10	A1
Claver Pl	7	B1
Clay St	1	A1
Clermont Ave	6	A1/B1/B2

Street Index

Street Index